AF833166

The State of the Alliance
1986–1987

About the North Atlantic Assembly

Founded in 1955, the NORTH ATLANTIC ASSEMBLY is the interparliamentary organization of the Atlantic Alliance. Composed of 186 legislators from the 16 member nations of the Alliance, the Assembly provides a unique forum where politicians can meet and discuss issues of common concern. In this way the Assembly has continually promoted the principle of transatlantic understanding within the framework of a free, democratic Alliance.

As the NATO Heads of State mentioned in Article 13 of the 1974 "Declaration on Atlantic Relations," one of the primary means by which Alliance cohesion can be furthered is by encouraging the free exchange of views among the elected representatives of the peoples of the Alliance. Within this context the Assembly's task is to:

1. strengthen the contacts between the national parliaments to promote Alliance cohesion;
2. serve as an important source of accurate information on Alliance issues for legislators;
3. encourage a mutually beneficial information exchange between NATO leaders and legislators;
4. provide a communication link between NATO, Alliance parliaments, and the general and specialized public.

The majority of Assembly activities are carried out within the framework of six committees dealing with civilian, economic, military, political, scientific and technical affairs, and nuclear strategy and arms control. The committees meet twice annually, during the spring and autumn sessions, to discuss and vote on draft reports and policy recommendations. The policy recommendations are subsequently submitted to the Assembly's plenary. If approved, they are then passed on to the NATO Secretary General, who in consultation with the NATO Council formulates a reply.

Under the auspices of the committees there are seven subcommittees that conduct fact-finding missions to gather information for the draft reports. The subcommittees are: The Free Flow of Information and People, Public Information, Conventional Defence, Defence Co-operation, Eastern Europe, Terrorism, and Advanced Technology and Technology Transfer.

About the Book and Authors

Leaders of NATO countries are continually faced with the need for highly accurate information on complex issues such as arms control, nuclear strategy, electronic warfare, ABM compliance, SDI, terrorism, economic cooperation, East-West relations, and diverging public opinion. To provide ongoing analysis of these issues, the North Atlantic Assembly conducts extensive research, fact-finding missions, and interviews with high-level government experts. Committees then analyze the data and meet annually to present the results. The studies in this volume, which were presented to the 1986 annual session of NATO legislators, focus on the state of the Alliance. This collection provides a comprehensive evaluation of political developments within the Alliance, probes fundamental controversies underlying Alliance security, and sheds light on the aggregate of concerns surrounding the direction of arms control negotiations and the state of NATO's nuclear strategy. The book includes an appendix containing the policy recommendations that the Assembly has adopted and forwarded to the secretary general of NATO and heads of Alliance governments.

John Cartwright is a member of the Social Democratic Party of the United Kingdom; Dr. David Clark, the British Labour Party; Bruce George, the British Labour Party; Lothar Ibrügger, Federal Republic of Germany, the Social Democratic Party; Dr. Jules de Waart, the Dutch Labour Party; and Dr. Ludolf-Georg von Wartenberg, the Christian Democratic Party.

Published in cooperation with
the North Atlantic Assembly

The State of the Alliance 1986–1987

North Atlantic Assembly Reports

John Cartwright, David Clark, Bruce George,
Lothar Ibrügger, Jules de Waart,
and Ludolf-Georg von Wartenberg

Routledge
Taylor & Francis Group
LONDON AND NEW YORK

First published 1987 by Westview Press, Inc.

Published 2019 by Routledge
52 Vanderbilt Avenue, New York, NY 10017
2 Park Square, Milton Park, Abingdon, Oxon OX14 4RN

Routledge is an imprint of the Taylor & Francis Group, an informa business

Copyright © 1987 Taylor & Francis

All rights reserved. No part of this book may be reprinted or reproduced or utilised in any form or by any electronic, mechanical, or other means, now known or hereafter invented, including photocopying and recording, or in any information storage or retrieval system, without permission in writing from the publishers.

Notice:
Product or corporate names may be trademarks or registered trademarks, and are used only for identification and explanation without intent to infringe.

Library of Congress Catalog Card Number: 86-51673

ISBN 13: 978-0-367-29632-2 (hbk)

Contents

Tables

Foreword

Since its founding in 1955 as an informal group of Alliance politicians, the North Atlantic Assembly has become an influential body composed of 186 legislators meeting biannually to debate Alliance issues. The Assembly's rapid development over the past thirty-two years is a testament to the serious commitment of its members to promoting a common feeling of Alliance cohesion among the sixteen legislative Assemblies which have ratified the North Atlantic Treaty.

The vitality of the Assembly is also evidence that the widely stated axiom of the 1950s, that Alliance political unity at the governmental level would remain precarious and perhaps illusory unless underpinned by unity at the level of popular representative institutions, is as relevant today as it was then.

The Assembly supports Alliance unity in a unique manner by providing a forum where Alliance legislators representing every political persuasion can constructively work on consensus building.

When former Secretary of State John Foster Dulles prophesied in 1954 that "an advisory Atlantic Assembly representing the NATO area as a whole would have genuine value particularly as a means of fostering better public understanding of the common problems of the Atlantic nations and of focusing the outstanding skills and talents of parliamentarians upon these problems" one may have wondered to what future such an organization could aspire.

Over the years, however, any lingering doubts about the value of the Assembly as a contributor to Alliance solidarity have vanished. The Assembly today is, in the words of President Reagan, "the only interparliamentary consultative body in which elected representatives of the United States, Canada, and their Western European allies meet regularly to address issues of world peace, collective deterrence and defense, and international co-operation".

Throughout its history the Alliance has always had to surmount the myriad of challenges that inevitably arise in an Alliance of democracies. The member governments are now faced with an extensive list of urgent challenges that include arms control, terrorism, economic, technological and defence co-operation, and waning public support for the Alliance on both sides of the Atlantic. The North Atlantic Assembly is playing an important role in helping NATO members meet these challenges through its research, debates, and concrete policy recommendations which are passed on to Alliance officials at the highest level. In this way the Assembly is working to maintain a healthy, viable and unified Alliance capable of defending the free democratic institutions we all cherish so dearly.

Ton Frinking
President
North Atlantic Assembly

Introduction

This volume is a collection of the General Reports presented to the North Atlantic Assembly's five permanent committees during the 32nd Annual Session held in Istanbul from 13 to 18 November 1986.

They represent an ongoing analysis of the prominent issues confronting the Alliance. The contents of the reports are modified and updated yearly to reflect the ever-changing complexities facing Alliance leaders. The primary purpose of the reports is to provide Alliance politicians with the timely highly accurate information they need to debate Alliance issues in their respective legislatures.

The reports are authored by Alliance politicians representing a variety of different nations and political views. With all but two exceptions* the reports have been adopted by the Assembly Committee to which each was presented. The final product is the fruit of extensive research, fact-finding missions, high level meetings with government experts and Committee debate.

In Chapter 1 the General Rapporteur of the Civilian Affairs Committee, Dr. David Clark, examines the key problems in NATO's approach to public relations. The chapter also looks in detail at the areas of weakness in obtaining public support for the Alliance. Dr. Clark concludes that measures should be taken to inform more effectively the public at large and in particular women, the Churches and opposition parties. He recommends a thorough reform of the NATO information structure as a valuable first step in this direction. The author also identifies a dangerous divergence of transatlantic perceptions in public opinion on both sides of the Atlantic. He argues that European "anti-Americanism" is due largely to Europe's dependence on the United States while America's "anti-Europeanism" stems from an impatience with Europe that tends to reinforce a unilateralist approach to foreign policy.

Dr. von Wartenberg, the General Rapporteur of the Economic Committee, focuses in Chapter 2 on the principal areas of concern for the economies of Alliance member

---

* The Report entitled "NATO's Public Relations Problems" was "taken note of" rather than "adopted" by the Civilian Affairs Committee due to the inability of the members to agree on its content. Chapter 6 is an interim report and therefore was not considered for adoption.

nations. While noting that the fall in the price of oil, the depreciation of the US dollar and the further decline of interest rates improve near-term prospects for sustained non-inflationary growth in most Alliance countries, the author emphasizes that high unemployment in Europe, escalating national debt in the United States, and rising current account deficits in many Alliance countries portend increasing transatlantic frictions for the future. The author points out that if no measures are taken to resolve these more urgent economic problems they could have a serious impact on Alliance cohesion. The chapter concludes by calling for the increased co-ordination of the world's leading industrialized nations' economic policies and encourages steps toward improving the international trading system both bilaterally and within the framework of the eighth round of multilateral trade negotiations.

The General Report for the Military Committee, authored by Dr. Jules de Waart, probes the fundamental controversies underlying Alliance security. The report begins by presenting an overview of recent Alliance security developments and looks in detail at the NATO-Warsaw Pact military balance. The author then centres his attention on a whole range of arms control issues including the future of the SALT II and ABM Treaties, the MBFR negotiations, the Midgetman debate, chemical weapons and the arguments surrounding negotiations for a comprehensive test ban. In the final section of the report, Dr. de Waart examines the debate on the development of anti-tactical ballistic missiles (ATBMs) to counter Soviet shorter-range missiles. The author offers some comments on the nature of this new threat and examines some of the options being proposed by analysts on each side of the debate.

Mr. Bruce George, the General Rapporteur of the Political Committee, provides in Chapter 4 an in-depth analysis of the pertinent political developments taking place within the Alliance. He begins by re-examining the political environment that gave birth to the Alliance and highlights the common elements existing today that compel Alliance nations to maintain a system of collective defence. Mr. George devotes the rest of the report to assessing intra-Alliance and East-West relations. Of particular interest is the section on the defence policies of the major opposition parties and the challenge this may pose to NATO in the near future. Other challenges to intra-Alliance relations discussed in the report include

US budgetary problems and their implications for US expenditures for the Alliance, burden sharing and chemical weapons modernization. On East-West relations, the author offers a brief analysis of US-Soviet relations in the immediate aftermath of Reykjavik and potential implications for the Alliance.

In Chapter 5, Mr. Lothar Ibrügger, the General Rapporteur for the Scientific and Technical Committee, examines the issues surrounding strategic defence technologies. The author covers in significant detail the current state of both US and Soviet strategic defence technologies and then presents a comprehensive analysis of strategic defence and ABM Treaty compliance. Mr. Ibrügger concludes the chapter with a section on Alliance participation in the SDI in which he discusses, among other things, the potential for technological "spin-offs" and the inherent complexities in SDI participation. He argues, however, that the technological and economic advantages and disadvantages of participating in the SDI are not yet clear.

In the final chapter Mr. John Cartwright, the Rapporteur for the Special Committee on Nuclear Strategy and Arms Control, casts a penetrating light on the aggregate of concerns surrounding the direction of the arms control negotiations and the state of NATO's nuclear strategy. He begins the study with an analysis of the evolving US and Soviet positions since May 1986 at the Geneva arms talks, and looks at the allied reaction to these developments particularly regarding Intermediate Range Nuclear Forces (INF). The author also examines the possible implications of strategic defences for the future of NATO's nuclear strategy and the ABM Treaty regime. Finally Mr. Cartwright evaluates current Alliance nuclear strategy including that of the UK and France, and after presenting some alternative defence concepts, provides a political assessment of the prospects, opportunities and dangers for NATO in the future development of nuclear strategy.

Finally a special mention of appreciation is due to my predecessor Mr. Philippe Deshormes whose years of dedication to the Assembly have made an inestimable contribution to the work of this organization. A word of thanks should also go to Mr. Radboud van den Akker, Mr. James Cross, Mr. Richard Grant, Mr. David Hobbs,

Mr. Martin McCusker, Mr. Guillaume Parmentier and the rest of the staff at the North Atlantic Assembly International Secretariat for making this publication possible.

Peter Corterier
Secretary General
North Atlantic Assembly

1

NATO's Public Relations Problems

David Clark

INTRODUCTION

No less an authority than General Rogers, SACEUR (Supreme Allied Commander Europe), asserted in September 1986 that he "had never known as much antipathy within the Alliance as had been generated by President Reagan's appeal for allied help in dealing with Col. Gaddafi and by the US Administration's desire not to be bound by the provisions of the SALT II nuclear arms control agreement".[1] Ex US Assistant Secretary of State for European Affairs Lawrence Eagleburger stated in Congress in June 1986 that "US relations with Europe are deteriorating and that the NATO alliance could be virtually meaningless by the end of the century".[2] The aim of this report will be to try and examine whether these pessimistic predictions are correct or exaggerated, and to suggest ways of improving the situation because, as Mr. Eagleburger added: "It would be a historic tragedy to let this process continue without doing everything we can to reverse it."

There is no doubt that NATO's policies have become a matter of controversy in every Alliance country, dividing the politicians and the public. Furthermore, the respective images of Europe and of the United States have been deteriorating recently, not only because of exceptional circumstances like the April 1986 US attack against Libya, but also because of more deep-seated reasons. How serious the situation has become is a question which this report will try to answer.

Furthermore, the Soviet Union is trying to drive a wedge between the Allies. Mr. Gorbachev makes intelligent use of his public relations skills. He is undoubtedly better than his predecessors at presenting the Soviet Union as a "normal" country, and at giving an impression of openness to Western opinion. Even the handling of the Chernobyl accident, or of the incident of the nuclear submarine which recently sank in the Atlantic Ocean, have been noticeable for the relative openness of Soviet reactions. This is not the wonderful revolution in Soviet ways which many newpapers have portrayed: it is clear that Mr. Gorbachev has to a large extent been playing to the gallery of Western opinions. In the present improved climate of East-West relations, the Soviet leadership once more relies on public pressures upon Allied governments - and especially upon the influence of European public opinion on the United States - to place the Soviet Union in a position of strength in the arms control negotiations, which may define the terms of the superpower relationship for the remainder of the century.

The initial outcome of the Reykjavik summit re-emphasizes the point of view stated above. The Soviet Union took the initiative in Europe in public relations terms, even to the extent of sending one of its senior officials to brief the European governments. Its message to the general public in Western Europe was the incompatibility of interests between the US Administration's preoccupation with the Strategic Defense Initiative and the European concern for a reduction in nuclear weapons in Europe.

This Soviet public campaign underlines the continued importance for NATO and for Alliance member-countries of rebuilding public support for NATO and for defence policy. The Civilian Affairs Committee, by stressing the deficiencies in public understanding of the Alliance and thereby emphasizing the defects in some Alliance mechanisms and policies, and by proposing remedies to those, has been playing a not insignificant role in this field. This was demonstrated by NATO's reactions to Civilian Affairs Committee recommendations and in particular by Lord Carrington's comments. The Committee will continue to act as a spur to NATO and to member governments, because its role is to remind bureaucracies that the Alliance will only survive if a public consensus on its existence and policies is maintained.

In March 1986, the Spanish people voted overwhelmingly in favour of continued Spanish membership of the Alliance. This result will be analysed in the first chapter, which will try to assess what lessons NATO should draw from this experience. The report will then proceed to highlight some specific deficiencies in public support for NATO. The third chapter will examine transatlantic perceptions, and the conclusion will outline the Civilian Affairs Committee's case for a reform of NATO information.

THE SPANISH REFERENDUM: LESSONS FOR NATO

The Good News

From a public perspective, the 12 March referendum in Spain has been the most important NATO event of the past few months. This has been a welcome development, because this first opportunity for a people to answer directly the question of its country's participation in the Alliance drew a positive answer. It was therefore perfectly legitimate for Lord Carrington to express his delight on hearing the result.

The result of the Spanish referendum was very positive for NATO, because the question of Spain's membership in NATO will not be raised again. The Spanish people were given the opportunity to choose, and it followed the government's advice, and supported NATO membership. There will therefore never be a majority in Parliament for withdrawal from NATO, and nobody will call for another referendum. Spanish participation will also strengthen the case of those who believe NATO to be primarily a political - as opposed to a military - organization, since Spain will not be integrated in the military command. Furthermore, Felipe Gonzalez's insistence - in his "dialogue" concerning the conditions for NATO membership - on European defence co-operation, coupled with the fact that Spain is in the chair of the Independent European Programme Group for 1986 and 1987, will strengthen the support now being built within and without NATO in favour of a powerful "second pillar" of the Alliance in Europe. The referendum campaign in Spain has shown that a public which was very difficult to convince of the need for NATO membership supported the European approach of its government. One of the most telling arguments of the campaign was that of Alfonso Guerra, the Vice-President of the Government. He stressed that leaving NATO would increase Spanish dependence upon the United States, because Spain would be weaker relatively if she had to deal with the United States alone on the matter of the bases than if, participating in NATO, she could rely upon the support of her European neighbours. Voting for NATO, in Spain, meant also voting for Europe.

A Victory for Mr. Felipe Gonzalez

In spite of the results, there were nevertheless worrying underlying concerns for NATO. The referendum was fought on domestic political grounds. NATO was continuously mentioned by supporters of the "No" vote, because "OTAN" has a pejorative connotation in Spain, whereas the Government campaign was built upon the theme: "In Spain's interest, vote yes", making no allusion to NATO and few to the Alliance, the emphasis being on Spanish participation in Europe. Indeed, Gallup-Espana - the only polling organization to have forecast correctly the referendum result - showed that in early 1986, the Spanish public when asked: "Do you approve of Spain's continued membership of NATO ?", answered 27% yes, 47% no, and 26% don't know, whereas the answers were respectively 41%, 29% and 30% when the question was: "Do you approve the Government's external security policy, which means maintaining Spain within NATO ?" Another example of the fact that NATO was little mentioned by proponents of the "Yes" vote would be the Spanish Prime Minister's address to the closing rally of the "Yes" campaign, which was widely reported in the press and on television. In this address, Mr. Gonzalez did not mention "NATO", mentioned the "Atlantic Alliance" only twice, but used the word "peace" forty times.

During the last week of the campaign, Mr. Felipe Gonzalez, who is an immensely popular leader, gave a very large number of interviews in which he conveyed the message: "If you want to punish me, do it on the occasion of the elections, not by voting no in the referendum." In other words, the President of the Government was implying that he might take a failure in the referendum as vote of no confidence in himself. The main opposition party, the Coalicion Popular, in spite of the fact that it supports full integration in NATO, advised its supporters to abstain from voting. Its intention was to make the referendum into a motion of no confidence in the Prime Minister. The fact is that

Felipe Gonzalez gambled and won. The result of the referendum, albeit reassuring for NATO, cannot be interpreted in any other way than as a Gonzalez victory. Indeed, a close analysis of the campaign and the vote confirms the findings of the Civilian Affairs Committee on the principal weaknesses in NATO's appeal to the public. Spain's example provides a magnified version of NATO's problems in the other fifteen member countries. This analysis is corroborated by the results of the general election of 22 June 1986, which returned an overwhelming Socialist majority.

Spanish Characteristics

There are specific reasons why the case of Spain is more extreme than that of most other Alliance partners. Spain has not participated in an international European conflict since the Napoleonic wars, and an attitude of isolationism is therefore deeply entrenched in public consciousness. Spain's last international war was against the United States, over Cuba. Neutralism has only recently begun to weaken, because there is a considerable degree of support for participation in European institutions, which are equated in the public mood with the maintenance of democratic institutions and access to a status of modernity. Spain was not occupied by Germany and she was therefore not liberated from fascist rule with the help of US troops. On the contrary, in 1953 Spain signed a defence treaty with the United States, which then aided Franco's regime by establishing US bases in Spain, comprising some 25,000 men. Therefore, NATO is not perceived in Spain as a democratic organization, but as a body linked to the United States, which maintained Franco in power for so long. This feeling is amplified by the special relationship which exists between Spain and Latin America, which is above all a sentimental and cultural one, but which also has a material dimension. The policies and language of the United States in Central America, especially under the Reagan Administration, have been highly detrimental to the image of the United States in Spain, especially, although not only, on the left. The problem of Gibraltar has also been harmful to NATO's interests. All these factors do explain why Spain's membership in NATO created such formidable domestic difficulties. However, Spain is not the only country to encounter such problems: NATO's public image suffers from similar defects elsewhere, albeit to a lesser degree.

The Image of the United States

The question put to the Spanish people was ostensibly that of Spanish membership of the Alliance according to the terms set by the Spanish government: non-participation in the integrated military structure, progressive reduction of the US military presence in Spain, non-nuclearization of Spain. The opponents of NATO membership, however, based their campaign upon opposition to the United States. On posters in the streets, the word "NATO" was painted with stars and stripes. The "No" campaign misleadingly linked withdrawal from NATO with the expulsion of American bases. The slogan was "NATO: No, Bases: Out", playing upon the very real unpopularity of US bases. According to Gallup-Espana, the mention of the Spanish government condition for NATO membership that the US military presence in Spain be progressively reduced added 10% to intentions in favour of a "Yes" vote. Majorities of proponents and opponents of NATO membership alike favoured the disappearance of US bases, when asked to choose between disappearance, reduction or maintenance of the bases.[3]

The image of the US is a problem, to varying degrees, all over Europe. Even in the United Kingdom, a country which takes pride in its "special relationship" with the United States and where many people have links of kinship with North America, a recent Sunday Times - MORI opinion poll[4] shows that the power of the United States is viewed with concern. As in Spain, a majority of people resent US influence on the economy and on defence policy, and have little confidence in President Reagan's judgement. Indeed, one in three British voters now regard the USSR and the US as equal dangers to world peace. The 1984 and 1985 Civilian Affairs Committee reports showed similar trends in the Federal Republic of Germany, in the Netherlands, in Denmark and in Greece. France, with its independent strategy, is the only country where the image of the United States has actually improved recently. Clearly, the image of the United States is a function of the degree of dependence of European nations upon the United States.

Weaknesses in the Support for NATO

In Spain, as well as in other Alliance countries, there are deficiencies in support for NATO among women and minorities, or special groups. What is true of Spain is also true elsewhere, to a different degree. The Spanish government found it particularly difficult to convince women of the need to stay in NATO. In all opinion polls, the percentage of men intending to vote "Yes" was higher than that of women. Perhaps even more significantly, the number of women answering "Don't know" was always higher than the number of men, by around 10%. It seems, however, that, according to a post-electoral study by the Centre for Sociological Research in Madrid, women actually voted for NATO membership in comparable numbers to men. This shows that a government's lead on foreign policy is likely to be heeded by the groups with the least precise points of view. "Don't know" answers easily become "Yes" votes in a vote of confidence. This report will later examine the general consequences for NATO of this regrettable situation.

The Age and Education Factors

In Spain, during the referendum campaign, age was a major factor in voting attitudes. According to two opinion polls published during the week before the referendum, there was a direct correlation between age and the "Yes" vote. Only among older people was there a majority of respondents intending to vote "Yes". A Gallup poll showed the following results:

Table 1.1 VOTERS' ATTITUDES IN THE REFERENDUM ACCORDING TO AGE[5]

AGE GROUP	18-24	25-34	35-44	45-54	55-64	65 +
YES	23	31	30	41	38	43
NO	56	48	38	28	27	18
BLANK VOTES	11	7	10	11	11	3

These results show that NATO had a majority only in the over-forty-five age group, and support for NATO was minimal amongst the younger generation. Another opinion poll, in El Pais, confirms these findings:

Table 1.2 VOTING INTENTIONS[6]

	Age 18 to 34	Age 35 to 54	Age 55+
YES	21.0	25.0	34.2
NO	50.2	34.1	20.2
ABSTENTIONS	16.3	15.2	17.2

Here, the age groups are defined differently, and the results are therefore less subtle, but the conclusion is the same. Young people are more sensitive to idealistic propaganda, such as that which the neutralist proponents of the "No" vote spread around Spain, and defence matters may well be more readily understandable when seen in the light of experience. However, it is difficult for NATO to take comfort in these explanations in the face of figures showing that in Spain young people are half as likely to support NATO membership as people over the age of 65. Even the fact that the over-25s had overwhelmingly voted "Yes" in the referendum should be no cause for excessive delight. The Prime Minister's advice was followed, but the pre-referendum polls show that outright support for NATO is low among young people.

It is even more unpleasant to have to report that in Spain, after a nationwide campaign, with all the major parties in Parliament in favour of NATO membership, there is an exact correlation between the propensity to vote "Yes" and the lack of education, and that the more educated the voter, the more likely he was to vote "No".

Table 1.3 LEVEL OF EDUCATION[7]

	No education	Primary education	Secondary education	Higher education	Total
YES	31.4	26.1	22.8	20.6	26.2
NO	23.5	33.8	47.0	50.4	36.2
ABST.	16.2	14.8	17.5	16.8	15.2

The 1984 General Report of the Civilian Affairs Committee mentioned similar trends in other member countries, but Spain is a country where a popular government had been campaigning for some months on behalf of NATO membership. It is also true that the eventual results were quite different from those forecast by Alef, but the trend, if not the actual figures, would be hard to deny. Clearly, a situation where educated people are less likely to approve of the Alliance than uneducated persons cannot be allowed to continue if the Alliance is to survive.

The Left

Quite clearly, there is little need to elaborate upon the fact that it is difficult for NATO to make its policies convincing to the left and left-wing voters. In this respect, the identification of NATO with the United States was particularly damaging. A clear sign of NATO's poor image on the left was the fact that the UGT trade union, traditionally close to the Spanish Socialist Party PSOE, favoured actively the "No" vote. Indeed, the "No" campaign, which was extremely well organized, had an official budget of 36 million pesetas (around 250,000 dollars) and was able to mobilize a very considerable number of people, most of whom were natural supporters of the left, in the European country where most people will position themselves on the left on a left-right scale.[8] This is obviously a weakness of NATO throughout its European member-countries. Indeed, there may be an incidental positive consequence to the referendum in that Socialist PSOE activists may, after their party has won a resounding victory over NATO membership, see NATO in a more favourable light.

The fact is, however, that the activists of the PSOE did not participate in the referendum campaign as actively as they do during election campaigns. The PSOE is Western Europe's largest Socialist Party, and all observers have described the referendum campaign as a fight between two somewhat reluctantly-held positions in favour of "Yes" and of abstention, and a "campaign in the streets", enthusiastic and popular, in favour of "No". An English journalist aptly described the fight between "No" and "Yes" as "activists versus the machine".[9] This was mainly because the PSOE found it difficult to muster its members, perhaps because it had been advocating withdrawal from NATO before it came to power. The fact that 44% of left-wing supporters had indeed voted "yes" on 12 March, whereas abstentions had been relatively high on the right and centre, has to be analysed more as a function of the parties' positions than as a consequence of deep-seated sympathy for NATO on the part of left-wing supporters.

The Regions

An element which Spain may share with other member countries is the weakness of NATO in regions with specific historical traditions. On 12 March, in the Basque country, in Catalonia, and in Navarra, there were more "No" than "Yes" votes, whereas Spain as a whole voted 52.6% in favour of NATO membership, with 39.8% "No" out of a turn-out of 56 %. This may reflect the danger there is for NATO to rely only upon governments to convey information about the Alliance. As long as opposition parties - including regional parties - will not be associated with NATO information, the Atlantic Alliance runs the risk of being identified with the government in power and with the establishment. This is certainly a danger in Britain, especially in Northern England, and in Scotland and Wales.

DEFICIENCIES IN PUBLIC SUPPORT FOR NATO

The Civilian Affairs Committee has already

established that NATO's information fails to reach groups which are not traditional recipients of defence information. It is worth stressing, in particular, the examples of women, of Churches, and of the Left.

Women

For centuries, men were the warriors. By implication, this meant that women took no interest in military matters. Although women are now an active force in politics, and although many women have prominent positions in the peace movement and more generally in professions of influence such as teaching or journalism, defence establishments - including NATO - have not yet modified their traditional approach. The purpose of this section is to show that the specificity of feminine attitudes on defence issues amply justifies a reversal of this anachronistic attitude.

Fear of War

Women fear war in larger numbers than do men. There are many reasons for this Pact. In most countries, women do not participate in the armed forces, and they may have a particular way of solving problems: "they tend to work at peaceful negotiations".[10] Whatever the reasons may be, however, the facts are there. A January 1983 US Gallup Report showed that 52% of women feared a nuclear conflict would take place within the next ten years, while only 45% of men shared this fear. The Washington Post National Weekly, on 12 December 1983, after television showed The Day After, found a considerable difference between men's and women's attitudes: 41% of women - versus 24% of men - thought "a nuclear conflict was very or somewhat likely in the next few years". 75% of men - versus 55% of women - found this prospect "very or somewhat unlikely". More recently, another Washington Post National Weekly poll provided clear evidence of a greater fear among women than men of the consequences of nuclear war; while 41% of men would want to survive a nuclear war, only 22% of women (against 72%) share their view. In June 1986, the Women's Institutes voted for a delay in the development of new nuclear weapons.[11]

Diffidence Towards Weaponry

As a consequence of women's greater fear of war, they tend to be more suspicious than men of answering the Soviet threat by an increase in weaponry. Again according to the Washington Post poll, in 1983, 47% of women - as against 37% of men - thought "President Reagan's plans to build more nuclear weapons" were "going too far". An even more striking gender gap exists as far as the SDI is concerned. In September 1985, 51% of US men, against 43%, favoured the development of the SDI, whereas 63% of US women opposed it, while only 30% approved of it. Visibly, US women think that the SDI runs the risk of adding a new dimension to the arms race.[12]

All surveys show that women favour arms control negotiations in larger numbers than do men, and that they are more suspicious of new deployments of nuclear weapons, but it must be said that gender differences on these matters are relatively limited. It is significant, however, that in Norway women are more likely than men to support a Nordic nuclear free zone, according to an excellent study.[13] It should also be noted that, according to another survey conducted on the eve of the Geneva summit meeting between President Reagan and General Secretary Gorbachev, women felt more strongly than men (55% to 42%) that the President should do "whatever is necessary in negotiating to reduce the likelihood of nuclear war".[14]

As a result, women in general support reduced military spending or at least oppose expanding defence budgets. In a survey of British attitudes on defence questions,[15] women were shown to be substantially less disposed than men (9% to 19%) to increase expenditure on nuclear weapons. Fewer women than men (17% to 36%) approved of the British government's decision to modernize the British nuclear fleet by purchasing the Trident system. Similar results were found in Germany.[16]

The Need for Information

The most striking characteristic of women as a group, however, is their clear lack of information on Alliance issues. This is because girls' education induces some of them to believe - quite wrongly - that these matters are best left to men. "Don't know" and "No answer" responses are invariably higher, indicating lack of familiarity with defence issues. The same is true of women's knowledge of international politics in general. While 48% of Italian men expressed great or moderate interest in international politics, only 23% of women indicated this level of interest. By the same token, 75% of women, as opposed to only 51% of men, expressed little or no interest.[17] Levels of uncertainty among women are comparable to those of "older people, the less educated and those from the lower social classes".[18] Gallup reports on British opinion show significantly higher "don't know" responses among women than among men on questions pertaining to NATO and nuclear weapons questions.

This is, therefore, an area where a systematic information effort could make a considerable degree of difference. The Rapporteur indeed feels that more should be known about women's attitudes, where only scattered information is available. He would strongly recommend that NATO finance some research on women's attitudes to defence issues, with a view to enlightening the Secretary General, and also member nations' authorities, on the scope of the problem, so that precise information campaigns can be devised in NATO countries.

The value of information campaigns is all the more obvious if the case of Norway is taken into account, where women as a whole seem better informed. In a Louis Harris survey of eight industrial countries, the "don't know" answers are lowest among Norwegian women. Women's opposition to NATO membership has also fallen to the same level as that of men. From 1977 to 1981, the increase in concern for foreign policy has been noticeable among women.

Norway has created a remarkable - and unique - NATO information structure, where the opposition is represented, and which focuses on the peace-keeping role of the Alliance. There is certainly a link between this information structure and the fact that women are better informed. This provides an added reason for NATO to look closely into women's attitudes.

The Churches and the Nuclear Debate

There have always been Christian teachings on, or at least some theological approaches to, issues of war and peace. Christianity was largely built upon the need to find alternatives to violence as a means of solving social - and in particular international - differences. However, the history of Christendom is replete with wars, some of which were waged in the name of God. There is a conflict in Christian thinking between two standards, which can be exemplified on the one hand by the tenet "Turn the other cheek", and on the other by the excessive interpretations of the "just war" concept, which induced clerics to bless armies going off to fight "holy wars". Christians have somehow had to strike a compromise between these extreme views.

Morality and Politics

The advent of weapons of mass destruction - historically opposed by most Churches - has increased the import of such a dilemma, and among those arms, none has emphasized this increase as much as nuclear weapons. In a nuclear world, war is not only capable of killing innocent victims, but indeed of destroying mankind itself. Naturally, Christian Churches and Christian believers in general, could not overlook this tremendous change in strategic history. Matters of life and death are legitimate areas of concern for Christian Churches. What makes their involvement more problematic, however, is that whilst the authority of their judgments on moral issues is considerable. Churches have no particular eminence on political issues. Nuclear weapons have the characteristic of encroaching upon both the moral dimension and the political dimension, the survival of the human species depending upon the rationality of political leaders' decisions and behaviour. The division between what pertains to moral issues and what is political is therefore uncertain: it is relatively easy to separate technical matters and moral questions, but they can all be said to be political, at least in their consequences.

From a public perspective, therefore, Churches' pronouncements on nuclear weapons as a whole have the authority which attaches only to their judgments on the moral dilemmas of deterrence. This has given the Churches - sometimes against their will - a very important role in the political debate on nuclear deterrence, which has been taking place in the West in the past few years. This report will summarize the most important elements of this involvement by the Churches.

Protestant Churches

Protestant Churches have often served to mobilize public opposition to Cruise missiles and Pershing-II deployment: the INF modernisation debate provided a catalyst for increased religious activism on security questions, and, although Protestant Churches were by no means united on the issue, activism was restricted to the opponents of deployment. Perhaps the clearest manifestation of the European Protestant Churches' ability to mobilize opinion found its expression in the so-called "Hollanditis" phenomenon, which the 1985 Report of the Civilian Affairs Committee described in political terms.

In the Netherlands, Protestant Churches have tended to hold a diffident view of power, and to take a neutralist position on international matters. Most recently, the movement against INF missile deployment was largely organized through religious groups centralized in the Interchurch Peace Council (IKV).

As the Netherlands government of Prime Minister Ruud Lubbers came round to the decision to install NATO cruise missiles, Dutch Churches, both singly and collectively through the Interchurch Peace Council, played a key role in moulding and directing public opinion on this issue. The Netherlands anti-cruise missile movement was unique in its intensity, and, indeed, the case of the Netherlands provides a unique example of how religious organizations could mobilize mass public opinion and extra-parliamentary pressure on defence questions.

Numerous observers have attested to the Churches' unequalled domination of the Dutch cruise missile controversy. When, in March 1984, the Dutch Council of Churches condemned the installation of missiles on Dutch territory as being "against the divine mission of safeguarding creation", peace movement activists claimed this assertion was valid for over nine million Dutch Protestants and Catholics. While the veracity of this assertion is questionable, the fact that it could even have been made suggests that the Churches had great influence on this question. In a society imbued with Christian ethics, such pronouncements cannot be overlooked by politicians and decision makers.

1977 saw the rise of an organization which was destined to play the leading role in mobilizing Dutch public opinion against nuclear weapons. The IKV was instrumental in moving the debate over the neutron bomb from Parliament to the street. An ecumenical organization comprising Holland's nine principal Protestant denominations, as well as the Catholic Church, the IKV would ultimately gain a reputation as a pressure group to be reckoned with in Dutch politics. Part of the "second wave" of nuclear protest after the early 1960s, it drew its strength from a highly efficient grassroots organization of approximately 400 local groups which sprang up during 1977.

In 1979, the IKV began its anti-nuclear campaign with the opening salvo: "Eliminate nuclear weapons from the world and begin with the Netherlands." The IKV's leadership had concluded that the arms race had not been mitigated by detente and in fact had itself become the main threat to detente. The starting point was therefore to be an unconditional rejection of deterrence. The ultimate aim was reciprocal disarmament, but the Netherlands had to make a unilateral gesture to set an example. Although the actual military implications of the IKV's decision were insignificant, the political ramifications were immense. This strategy based itself on the premise that confidence between blocs would increase through an exchange of unilateral measures which invite the adversary to follow the example. This was based in turn on the belief that the goodwill of individuals could influence states. In addition, the IKV called for the active democratization of foreign policy with pressure on parties and government by groups not normally involved in the policy-making process.

It is unquestionable that the IKV was the major force in the Dutch peace movement. This was due in no small measure to the charisma of the IKV Secretary Mient Jan Faber, with whose goals many Dutchmen came to identify. Yet it must be remembered that, although religious in origin, the IKV aimed to achieve blatantly political goals. Some sceptics have gone so far as to charge that the IKV was in fact a political vehicle designed to legitimize the pacifist aims of its founders, giving them an aura of respectability by associating them with the political centre. Aware of its influence and realizing that its progress could isolate the Netherlands politically, the IKV sought to influence opposition movements in other countries, substituting people-to-people action for government-to-government contacts.

While the general theme of nuclear disarmament provided the IKV's point of departure, the Dutch government's acceptance of the NATO dual-track decision and the likely installation of Cruise missiles in the Netherlands soon became the centre of the peace movement's attention. From 1979, the IKV had warned that both options of the dual-track decision could only have one outcome: missile deployment. Here was an issue around which the anti-nuclear movement could rally; refusing the installation of Cruise missiles represented that first positive gesture which would rekindle goodwill between the blocs and facilitate eventual disarmament.

Although the IKV did provide the focus for concentrated Church action on the nuclear issue, the conduct of individual Protestant denominations and the Catholic Church showed differences of approach to this issue. Protestants on the whole seemed to have thrown themselves into the effort with more vigour than the Catholic hierarchy. As early as 1980, for instance, the Synod of the Netherlands Reformed Church issued a Pastoral Letter which categorically rejected nuclear deterrence and wholeheartledly supported the IKV proposals. The decision was arrived at after thousands of parish meetings which showed the breadth of sympathy for the IKV within the Church. As with Protestant Churches in the Federal Republic of Germany, those in the Netherlands seemed to be the repository of a rather avant-garde brand of political thinking. The most radical of the religious opponents to nuclear arms were certainly to be found within the Protestant denominations.

The Federal Republic of Germany provides a similar, though perhaps less impressive, example of the mobilizing power of Churches over the INF missile question. German elites, then as now, saw the political situation in Europe as very stable, with little chance of a Soviet bloc invasion. Attitudes were therefore susceptible to influence by the important consciousness coalition which developed within the Protestant Churches. Greens, Protestants and left-oriented groups united to form a widely based protest movement. Such a coalition was, in this case, merely being resurrected from an earlier existence, during the late 1950s and early 1960s, when the issue was the peaceful use of nuclear power. Then, as in the 1980s, the extra-parliamentary opposition showed the capacity of representatives of marginality in the Federal Republic of Germany to transmit their concerns and their aspirations, if not to realize them. However, the movement was ultimately doomed to failure since so many of its components, consistent with their anti-establishment approach, based themselves on individualism (as exemplified by the Fundi [Fundamentalist] wing of the Greens) and thus found themselves afflicted by organizational weakness, which ultimately led to political impotence. Still, for a very important period, Protestant Churches, exemplified by that of Pastor Martin Niemaller, were places where the pacifist current could ferment and mature.

American Protestant Churches, as a whole, can be said to have played less of a role in publicizing the nuclear question than their European counterparts. For while Protestant Churches had certainly been first to discuss nuclear war, even as early as 1946, their discussion of the question was limited in scope and detail, and their approach fragmented. Today, most mainstream Protestant Churches have released statements condemning nuclear war, but these are generally qualified with the proviso that adequate defence is necessary and, moreover, do not deal with such fundamental issues as the morality of deterrence and the just use of nuclear weapons.

This is not the case, however, with the United Methodist Church which, in April 1986, published a brief Pastoral Letter asserting that "nuclear deterrence is fatally flawed in principle". It saw a complete contradiction between the tradition of the just war and nuclear deterrence, on the grounds that nuclear warfare is bound to be indiscriminate. The bishops assert that "nuclear deterrence has become a dogmatic licence for perpetual hostility between the superpowers and for the rigid resistence to significant measures of disarmament". This represents the most negative official Protestant view to date of nuclear deterrence in the United States.

The Catholic Church

The Catholic Church has traditionally avoided spectacular incursions into the strategic debate, although a "long moral tradition .... condemns the threat to destroy innocents as well as their actual destruction",[19] and Vatican II Council promulgated the "Gaudium et Spes" Encyclical in which limits were set to the act of war. The balance of terror is not considered a sound basis for peace by the Catholic Church, which condemns the non-interrupted arms race, while recognizing the right to legitimate self-defence.[20] Moreover, the Church has repeatedly made public its opposition to warlike activities. Paul VI's statement at the United

Nations on 4 October 1965: "Plus jamais la guerre! Plus jamais la guerre!" ("No more war ever! No more war ever!") has remained in collective memory, and John Paul II has pursued a diplomatic and public campaign to increase awareness of the dangers of a nuclear war.[21] However, the period of controversy on the INF modernization has given rise to a much more confused debate among Roman Catholics.

Many clerics and bishops went far beyond the Church's official positions and, like Christian peace movement supporters, condemned deterrence in itself: for some, non-violence is the only method of defence which is compatible with the Scriptures. For others, nuclear weapons are so harmful that their possession is unjustifiable, even if they are strictly meant to deter an attack.[22] The rise of a unilateralist tendency within the Catholic Church has created dissensions between the Vatican, some Catholic hierarchies, and the Catholics close to the peace movement. It is precisely in order to quell such controversies that a doctrinal clarification was felt to be necessary by so many national Churches.

The Netherlands provides an example of the confusing effects on the Church of involvement by Catholics in the activities of the peace movement. Within the Church, Pax Christi played the most visible role in opposing Cruise missile deployment in particular and nuclear arms in general. This elite group, whose membership is rather small, played the role of consciousness-raiser and trend-setter. But even Pax Christi did not advise Catholic bishops to accept the IKV unilateralist proposals until well after small Protestant Churches had indicated their support. The bishops, in their 1983 Pastoral Letter, while condemning the use of nuclear weapons and reiterating their opposition to Cruise missile deployment, nevertheless stopped short of supporting the IKV platform. However, Pax Christi continued to play a relatively active role in the nuclear debate. In October 1983, Pax Christi President Bishop Ernst addressed the mass demonstration in Amsterdam against installation of Cruise missiles. But while Catholic bishops agreed on the overwhelming need for disarmament, they were divided on whether this aim was better served through deployment or non-deployment.[23] And, in the end, the Catholic Church remained silent when the government finally decided to deploy Cruise missiles in November 1985.

It may be speculated that, ultimately, the reticence of the Catholic Church became contagious. For a substantial countercurrent to the IKV line began to develop in both Catholic and Protestant Churches. This would ultimately seriously weaken the IKV's influence in the anti-Cruise campaign. Reacting to the March 1984 condemnation of Cruise missile installation by the Dutch Council of Churches, many Dutch Christians wrote to newspapers indignant at being branded "bad Christians" for their support of pro-NATO arguments. It should be remembered that the Council of Churches' recommendations are no longer as scrupulously observed as they once were. A March 1984 poll indicates that half of all Dutch Protestants disagreed with the Council's position. Many were upset that the Council's Cruise missile condemnation made no reference to Soviet SS 20s pointed at Western Europe.

This substantial body of pro-NATO sentiment coalesced into ICTO, the Interchurch Committee for Bilateral Disarmament, which supported deterrence as a guarantor of peace. ICTO criticised the IKV's unilateralist approach to disarmament and supported NATO's current nuclear policy. Its leadership included a substantial majority of Catholics, including Bishop Bar of Rotterdam, Chaplain to the Dutch Armed Forces. Opinion within the Churches was polarizing. By November 1985, when the government made its decision to deploy missiles, the IKV significantly did not call for civil disobedience. The "Volkspetitionnement", circulated by the KKN - a broadly based coalition of progressive political parties, the main trade union and various peace groups, to assert popular moral pressure on the government to reverse its decision attracted somewhat less support than anticipated, especially among Protestants, gaining four million signatures[24]. This was a disappointment to the IKV leadership, which had hoped to gain the support of fully half the Dutch population.

Even in the Netherlands - the most obvious case of religious participation in an anti-nuclear movement - Churches, with their ability to reach vast numbers of believers, acted both to mobilize opinion and to restrain extreme points of view.

It is in order to prevent the occurrence of a similar situation in Germany that the Catholic bishops set up a working group which worked discreetly and produced a document on 15 April 1983 under the title of "Justice Creates Peace". Although it has received far less publicity than the letters of the US or French bishops, it is quite as important. Unlike the US Catholic hierarchy, the German bishops chose to remain on purely ethical ground and to avoid making suggestions or criticisms in the realm of "technical" policy, where it is left to persons to exert their responsibility.

The German bishops start out by stating that "peace imposed by a totalitarian or imperialist state is nothing but established disorder (...) Only a just peace is worthy of the name peace (...) The Church of Christ and its bishops are invited, in the present situation, to proclaim the word of the Prophet: 'Justice Creates Peace', and to show the consequences which it has today for our behaviour and for our action".[25]

The importance of human rights, which include freedom, but also the rights of the poorest, is therefore underlined. Peace is therefore inseparable from these rights. This explains why the bishops favour the maintenance of a "right to collective legitimate defence", and why, although "the Church is always attached to the need to protect the innocent against acts of violence and oppression", a unilateral renunciation of the right to resist would "favour exactly what it is meant to prevent: that innocents be oppressed, that they fall victim to suffering or violence". However, like the Vatican, the German bishops link this moral toleration of deterrence to the strictest conditions: the only acceptable aim is the prevention of war, and three criteria are necessary to ensure that deterrence fits in with this objective: 1. No military means should render war more feasible or more likely. 2. The kind and number of military means must be strictly limited to those required for deterrence to remain effective. 3. All military means must be compatible with the objectives of arms limitation and reduction and a bilateral and effective disarmament.[26] Moreover, the principle of the necessary immunity of civilians is re-stated. In other words: "In the long term, nuclear deterrence is not a reliable instrument to prevent war." The result of this very balanced position has been that the debate on nuclear weapons among German Catholics has been kept within a very rational framework, where technical differences were recognized as being legitimate, but where moral and doctrinal standards are strictly spelled out.

Although the Pastoral Letter of the US bishops has been widely reported as representing a fundamental challenge to NATO nuclear strategy, and as a radical break with past Church teachings on war, the document does not bear out such an excessive interpretation. The general spiritual argument of the Pastoral Letter in its final form is no different from that of the German bishops - or indeed from any other episcopal conference. The singularity of the US document is that it treats nuclear matters on two very different levels. It contains on the first hand, moral and religious considerations which have high authority, and, on the other hand, "concrete matters concerning the arms race, warlike operations at the present time, arms systems and negotiations strategies". The bishops state at the start of their letter that their opinion on the latter does not bear the same authority as their pronouncements on universal moral principles and on the official teaching of the Church. They accept that "people of goodwill may interpret differently, for example, our position concerning the 'no-first-use' of nuclear weapons". Unfortunately, the media have - predictably enough - only drawn the public's attention to this more concrete aspect of the bishops' document at the expense of the subtler sides, which are quite close to the traditional Western position on arms control. The document recommends "support for immediate bilateral and verifiable agreements in order to halt the testing, production and deployment of new systems of nuclear arms". The words "immediate" and "halt" have been overblown by most commentators. Similarly, the bishops state their support for John Paul II's relative acceptance of the concept of deterrence at the United Nations in June 1982, but they give a restrictive interpretation of the Pope's words. The restriction has been more noted than the support. Their strong criticism of Soviet totalitarianism and imperialism has generally been overlooked, and their support for an increase in conventional weapons glossed over.

It has therefore been disregarded that their position is not at substantial variance with the traditional NATO approach of multilateral and verifiable nuclear disarmament. It is of course quite contradictory to NATO doctrine, in that it advocates no first use of nuclear weapons, but it is worth noting that is does so in the context of a multilateral disarmament approach. It is fair to add, however, that the US bishops would have avoided such misinterpretations if they had not mixed in the same document judgments and positions which they themselves defined as being of unequal religious authority.

The role of the Belgian Catholic Church in the anti-nuclear debate offers an interesting contrast to that played by the Dutch Churches. Belgium lacks a substantial

Protestant presence, which put a more radical tinge on the Dutch nuclear debate. While Pax Christi Flanders was instrumental in publicizing the Cruise missile question, its position on missile deployment was more moderate than that of Pax Christi Netherlands. This tempered the more extreme elements of the Belgian anti-nuclear movement. Ultimately, the Belgian Church as a whole was far less visible in the Cruise missile deployment debate than the Dutch Church and, even when involved, played a more conservative role than its Dutch counterpart.

The Catholic Church's active role in the nuclear debate was limited largely to Dutch-speaking Flanders, the northern half of Belgium, where a clear majority of the six million inhabitants belong to the Church. In French-speaking Wallonia, the longtime stronghold of Socialism, the Church's influence is far less pervasive; coincidentally, Walloons as a group expressed far less opposition to - not to speak of interest in - the Cruise missile question. It should be added that Flanders, because of language, is acutely sensitive to Dutch political developments. The Dutch media, because of the proximity of the two countries, play a role here. Consequently, the radical opposition to deployment in Holland found a receptive audience just to the South. On the other hand, Wallonia falls under French influence through printed and electronic media. President Mitterrand's Socialist government's support of Cruise missile deployment was reflected in the somewhat guarded statements of Walloon politicians, who have always kept one eye on French political developments. As a group, Walloons expressed more concern over the economic crisis which has become endemic in their region in the past 15 years than over the installation of 48 Cruise missiles in Belgium. In the four mass anti-Cruise missile demonstrations in Brussels in 1981, 1983 and 1985, 80% of the participants were Flemish.

In Flanders, the Catholic Church has always played an integral part in the Flemish nationalist/pacifist movement. The resurgence of Flemish nationalism between the World Wars was intimately associated with pacifism engendered by the terrible destruction suffered by Flanders during the First World War. Throughout the devastating conflict, it was Flemish peasant Catholics who fought and died in the trenches, led by a bourgeois Francophone officer corps. The language barrier was acutely felt by Flemish nationalists, who after the war came to resent bitterly what they perceived as the sacrifice of their homeland to save Francophone Belgium. The Church, omnipresent in Flanders, became increasingly associated on the grassroots parish level with pacifist elements, including a number of conscientious objectors. Catholic youth groups became the "foyers" of this Flemish nationalism/pacifism, which would gain momentum throughout the 1930s. After the war, Catholic youth and popular movements became associated with calls for increased Flemish cultural activity.

In the Cruise debate, however, Church activism has not necessarily signified radicalism. It is true that Flanders' susceptibility to currents of Dutch political thought has helped to make Flemish opposition to deployment rather more strident than in most other NATO countries. However, while the Belgian Church co-operates to a certain extent with various Dutch religious peace organizations, it has clearly exercized a restraining influence on the more radical elements of the Belgian peace movement. The Belgian bishops' Pastoral Letter of July 1983 was far less extreme in tone that the Dutch bishops' letter. Taking "Gaudium et Spes" as their starting point, the bishops, while condemning deterrence as an end in itself, did not take an outright stand against Cruise missile deployment. They allowed the faithful to make their own decisions based on the dictates of conscience. It should be noted that, as an almost exclusively Catholic country, Belgium lacks the rather more avant-garde sensibilities provided in the Netherlands by the Protestant Churches. Without this influence, the Catholic Church was necessarily more conservative in its pronouncements on the nuclear question. Also, while the sentiment against Cruise missile was particularly strong among Catholic youth and trade union groups, these did not benefit from any overreaching organizational structure, such as the IKV of the Dutch Council of Churches, which might have propagated their views. These groups, then, could only hope to influence the Church hierarchy through Pax Christi Flanders, which itself lacked the radical tone of its Dutch counterpart.

Even within Pax Christi Flanders itself, opinion was divided. One faction took up the unilateralist proposals of the Dutch IKV. Another faction held deterrence still to be a valid defensive strategy and sought to reduce tensions by arms control negotiations. Pax Christi Flanders lacked the clear anti-Cruise voice of Pax Christi Netherlands. Still, by its substantial presence within larger umbrella peace groups, the Flemish Action Committee against Nuclear Weapons (VAKA) and the Centre for Peace Discussion, Pax Christi Flanders was able to soften the more strident positions within the Belgian peace movement. VAKA's president, a former Jesuit priest, was particularly sensitive to Pax Christi's proposals. Indeed, after the Belgian government's ultimate decision of 15 March 1985 to deploy the missiles, VAKA adopted Pax Christi's strategy of continuing the anti-missile campaign.

Besides being part of a Church which was more conservative-minded than that of the Netherlands, Pax Christi was particularly limited by the Belgian Church's close association with the governing Flemish Christian Social Party (CVP). While CVP Prime Minister Wilfried Martens was acutely aware of the major dissent within his party on the deployment question, he shrewdly pursued a policy of continually delaying actual missile deployment in expectation of positive results from the Geneva arms talks. In fact, the Martens government had made the actual military decision to deploy long before. The "wait and see" tactics, while putting off a potentially divisive decision until the last possible moment, restrained the peace movement with the hope of a negotiated settlement of the missile question. With the CVP holding the leading position of influence on government policies, especially through the CVP's trade union wing which has close ties with Pax Christi, it was never considered a viable option by Pax Christi Flanders to urge Catholics against Cruise to support the Flemish Socialist Party, which had taken an unambiguous anti-missile position.

Lacking avant-garde Protestantism as a political influence, the Belgian Catholic Church clearly was left to play a more reserved role in the Cruise and nuclear deterrence questions than the Dutch Catholic Church. While the Dutch Church's relative radicalism did insinuate itself somewhat into the Flemish political conscience, French-speaking Wallonia, lacking a Catholic presence as active as the Flemish, remained relatively uninvolved in the Cruise question. Catholic activism against nuclear weapons was substantial, but in the end, it restrained, rather than strengthened, the Belgian peace movement.

The document adopted on 8 November 1983 by the French bishops has often been presented as a total endorsement of French nuclear deterrence, and as being in stark contrast to the position taken by the US bishops. This interpretation is not quite correct. The French bishops place the problem of nuclear deterrence in its historical concrete form: "In the present geopolitical context, does a country threatened in its livelihood, its freedom or its identity morally have the right to ward off this radical threat by a counter-threat, even if it is a nuclear one?" This historical reasoning implies that peremptory judgments based upon deductive thought, which would not take technical aspects of the problem into account, would be fatally flawed. On the other hand, however, it would be equally wrong to examine from a theological viewpoint the technical modalities of nuclear deterrence; the French bishops refused the approach chosen by their US counterparts. In order to place the matter in its true context, the French bishops condemn what they call "nuclear blackmail" exerted by "some countries which want to benefit from all the advantages of war without paying the price of war; by simply airing the threat, they exert permanent blackmail." They name the Soviet Union in this context, citing its grip on Eastern Europe and its "constant pressure on Western democracies to neutralize them". They add that "it would be unjust to put everyone in the same category and to close one's eyes to the domineering and aggressive character of the Marxist-Leninist ideology." The French bishops therefore think that "unilateral disarmament can provoke neighbours' aggressivity by increasing the temptation to grab too easy a prey". Nuclear deterrence is therefore "morally acceptable", and is conditioned by four provisos,[27] which give a "provisional" character to this acceptability: deterrence is a lesser evil. Moral acceptability is, "not to say the least, a high ethical qualification".[28] In other words, the theological points made by the French bishops are no different from those made by their counterparts in Germany, in the United States, or in the Netherlands, even though there are nuances to distinguish between the positions of these national Churches. Their common stance is based upon John Paul II's message to the United Nations of 11 June 1982. The language of the French bishops is certainly less reticent about the morality of nuclear deterrence than that of the US bishops, but this is largely due to the difference of approach between the two Pastoral Letters. The French bishops have refused to take part in the technical/political debate, and have made the point that nuclear deterrence, albeit a "solution of distress", is compatible with Christian principles if it is meant to help a nation to resist blackmail, in the same way as defence is legitimate for individual Christians.

Peace and Justice: NATO's Role

All Pastoral Letters recognize the fact that there can be no real peace without respect for human rights. Peace and justice are inseparable. This Christian approach is very close to the purely defensive message which has traditionally been NATO's. Acting in self-defence cannot be condemned. Questions arise when the means of destruction are mainly aimed at civilians, as is the case with nuclear weapons, but nuclear deterrence has been declared contrary to evangelic teachings by no Catholic Church, and only by very few Protestant Churches.

Although the main theological points made by these Christian authorities were in line with the tenets of NATO strategy as defined in the 1967 Harmel Report (deterrence and dialogue), NATO has remained on the defensive during the course of the debate. It is true that the NATO Visits Programme has paid a considerable degree of attention to clergymen and Christian groups, but there has been no co-ordinated effort to convey to the public the real significance of the Catholic Pastoral Letters, which the media often misrepresented. Indeed, with the exception of France and to a lesser extent Germany, the debate on nuclear deterrence among Christians has been presented as the expression of public dissatisfaction with deterrence. It would have been more accurate, and also more constructive, to describe it as the result of increasing uneasiness about nuclear deterrence, which is part and parcel of a decreasing confidence in the ability of the Alliance to ensure proper defence for the citizens of its member-countries. The 1985 General Report of the Civilian Affairs Committee showed how confidence in NATO's ability to defend Europe had decreased in the last few years. The debate among Christians has been a reflection of the general public's hesitation about the validity of NATO nuclear strategy, but laying greater stress on the moral issues at stake. In this sense, it has contributed in shaping the terms of the general debate, although some misrepresentations, sometimes due to the ambiguity of the texts themselves, have obscured the facts and confused the issues. NATO and some Alliance governments bear some responsibility for this, because they have not contributed to clarifying the debate. Some of the scathing criticisms against the US bishops by members of the Reagan Administration are a case in point. It would have been more effective to concentrate on distinguishing the parts of the Pastoral Letter which have theological authority from those which are the reflection of a mere political/technical judgment.

The European Left

Traditionally, the left in Europe has been deeply divided on participation in NATO. Communists and a small section of the non-Communist extreme left opposed NATO membership, but Communist parties were only strong in Southern Europe. The non-Communist left, in Northern Europe in particular, was warmly committed to NATO, which some of its leaders had indeed initiated. In Germany, although the SPD had started out as neutralist after the war, it had changed completely in the early 1950s and had become a strong supporter of Atlanticism. In many countries, the left-of-centre parties were for a long time the backbone of the transatlantic connection.

The Image of Reaganism

The war in Vietnam altered the image of the United States among the European left, and although it did not produce a rejection of NATO participation, it certainly left some traces in public consciousness, especially among Social Democrats and Labour supporters. These feelings, which could have faded with time, have in fact been reinforced since President Reagan came to the White House. The main message which he put forward - even before being elected - that of a "new American revolution" based upon a return to traditional values of self-help and free enterprise, was bound to fall on unsympathetic ears among European Social Democrats, especially since Mr. Reagan and his supporters vilified the welfare state, which was held to be responsible for the decadence of the West. Furthermore, the Reagan Administration itself has felt uneasy with the European left: President Reagan refused to meet the Socialist mayor of Madrid, Tierno Galvan, on his visit to Spain, and Mr. Willy Brandt, Chairman of the SPD, during a visit to the Federal Republic. More recently, the Administration's comments about the British Labour Party's defence policy, and in particular Mr. Caspar Weinburger's TV broadcast attacking this policy, have constituted another example of insensitive handling by the Administration of matters pertaining to the Socialist movement. More generally, the

Reagan Administration's policies on Central America have been very unpopular with the left.

It is also true that the economic crisis, and especially unemployment, have radicalized public feelings. Increasing economic inequalities within member countries and among the countries themselves have influenced public perceptions. Supporters of the left have been particularly affected by this dire economic climate, which has had an effect on the image of the United States, because it is viewed both as a rich country and as the bastion of capitalism, and also because President Reagan, like Mrs. Thatcher and some other Conservative leaders, is seen by left-wing supporters as utilizing the economic crisis in order to further ideological ends.

In other words, the left and left-of-centre supporters - especially in Northern Europe - have recently become estranged from the United States. Although the problem can be said to be long-standing because the position of dependence of Europe towards the United States since the Second World War has traditionally produced feelings of resentment, the present situation is more worrisome in that the division of opinion is based largely on party lines, with the right supporting US policies more or less systematically and the left opposing them. In France, where the Socialists have traditionally been more Atlanticist than the Gaullist right, the recent division of parties over the Strategic Defense Initiative has probably looked like a right/left split. In actual fact, apart from the Communist Party, which is hostile to it, the other parties of the present opposition and of the present majority have given a cautious welcome to the SDI. This attitude reflects their concern that the defence of Europe might be called into question, and the impression that the European countries, particularly France, will derive only small economic benefits, for various reasons, from President Reagan's project. This makes the present setting particularly dangerous, because the lines of division on sympathy with or diffidence towards the United States are rooted in political beliefs, and may therefore be more difficult to alter if party positions do not evolve or if the United States does not improve its image among the European left.

"Escapism"

Unfortunately, the misunderstandings between the United States and left-wing parties have not been receding recently. It is true that the parties in Southern Europe - whose socialism is based on Marxism - in the past ten to twenty years have grown very disillusioned with the Soviet Union and Soviet-inspired Socialism. In some measure, this has contributed to improving the image of the United States, although this has been more true of the American people and American culture than of the use of US international power. In Scandinavia and Britain, where Socialism has been inspired by religious and humanitarian ideas rather than by Marxism, the situation has evolved in the opposite direction. The Protestant tradition, with its moralistic component, has heavily influenced Northern European social democracy. As a consequence, the latter has always held a deep-seated diffidence towards power, and in particular international power. In recent years, this feeling was aggravated by the fear of nuclear weapons. According to many, it is the possession of nuclear weapons which would attract a nuclear response. In order to escape from the consequences of nuclear conflict, therefore, it is deemed necessary to do away with nuclear weapons. The logic of "escapism" replaces the logic of deterrence. This almost neutralist feeling is pervasive in Northern Europe, especially in Scandinavia, in the Netherlands and in Northern England.

The Labour Party in the United Kingdom

In the United Kingdom, this almost neutralist feeling has spread recently, especially in those parts of the country which have suffered economically over the past few years, and which have felt left out of the benefits of EEC membership. Northern England, Scotland and Wales have become inward-looking, because of their dramatic economic situation. There is a widespread tendency to question the advisability of an international role, and the Labour Party, while taking these feelings into account, has tried to convert them into a defence policy which is compatible with NATO membership. Although the most publicized aspect of the Labour Party's defence policy has been its nuclear-free stance, it is worth noting that Labour plans to increase conventional spending to the level of present overall military spending, in line with General Rogers' admonitions. Indeed, the Labour Party Conference voted five to one in favour of continued British membership of NATO. In other words, the Labour leadership has turned a neutralist-inclined public feeling into a pro-NATO defence policy.

The SPD

In the Federal Republic of Germany, the Social Democratic Party (SPD) has recently produced a "Peace and Security Policy" proposal which also advocated a revision of NATO strategy, whilst supporting West German membership of the political and military structures. Like the Labour Party, the SPD is deeply suspicious of nuclear weapons, but Germany's specific geographical position is recognized, and a bilateral withdrawal of nuclear and short-range nuclear weapons is demanded by the SPD, in order to create a nuclear-free zone in Central Europe. The US doctrine of Airland Battle and the consequent NATO Follow-on Forces Attack (FOFA) are condemned because the SPD judges them as being based on an offensive concept. Moreover, the SPD wishes to make the Bundeswehr "incapable of mounting offensive operations". This is also a clear reflection of public anxieties over the consequences of a strategy which emphasizes the need for an offensive element. In a country like Germany, which is on the front line of East-West division, public concern is obviously particularly high. As a result, an offensive strategy is often misinterpreted as being an aggressive one. The policy of the SPD is an attempt to give a political expression to these public feelings. The next chapter of this report will describe in more detail the consequences for NATO of the division of European opinion over defence policy and over the transatlantic relationship. Suffice it to stress at this stage that the fact that this division among voters occurs increasingly on party lines is disquieting in the extreme. Temporary differences are manageable, but when they are linked to voting patterns, they can become ingrained in public attitudes and they run the risk of weakening Alliance solidarity in the long term. It is incumbent upon Alliance governments to make sure that Alliance policies do not alienate left-wing supporters, as much as it is the responsibility of Socialist politicians to make sure that their policies do not breed Alliance discord.

DIVERGING TRANSATLANTIC PERCEPTIONS

In recent years, views of the world on both sides of the Atlantic have evolved differently. The economic situation of the United States has until now induced self-confidence, whereas European countries have been beset with economic and social difficulties which have created an increasingly inward-looking attitude. Both in Europe and in the United States, articulate minority views which are getting more influential have seemed to be setting the tone of the transatlantic debate, and may eventually have an effect on policy-making. A vicious circle may have been generated, with the European extreme left-wingers and pacifists hostile to the Alliance, pointing their fingers towards the unilateralist elements in the United States as if they represented the country as a whole, and conversely, with Neo-conservative elements in the United States exaggerating the importance of anti-Alliance groups in Europe. As Lord Carrington himself aptly put it in a speech delivered before the NATO Council meeting in Halifax in May 1986, the cohesion of the Alliance would be affected "if some people in the United States and some in Western Europe continue to indulge in what I might call megaphone cartoonery - Eurowimps in one set of papers and American cowboys in the other".[29] More widely, public views on the grassroots have also been affected by increasingly simplistic respective views of the Allies.

The Europeans and the United States

Many articles have recently been published, especially in the United States, on the rise in Europe of so-called Anti-Americanism. This is most certainly not true if Anti-Americanism is taken in its proper meaning of hostility towards Americans and American culture and society. Indeed, America as a society and as a culture is liked by large majorities of people. The United States is a country which people want to visit, and - more significantly - where many would choose to emigrate if they could not stay in their own country. American cultural influence does not create resentment, except perhaps as far as television programmes are concerned.[30] A major opinion poll conducted in February 1986 in the United Kingdom[31] shows that 66% of British people (against 16%) "like Americans", and that 46% (against 44%) "think we can learn a great deal from the US".

"Anti-Americanism" Is Not the Issue

European criticism of the United States is hardly ever levelled at US culture or at the American way of life. Indeed, over a long period, it is noticeable that the cultural and social differences between Europe and the United States are less and less noticed, probably as a result of what is called "Americanization", which is really a blurring of cultural differences across the Atlantic. It is particularly manifest that this is the case when one takes the example of young people, who recognize very few differences between their way of life and that of their contemporaries on the other side of the Atlantic Ocean. Indeed, it is quite remarkable that protest movements against US or NATO military bases are full of young people who dress in US army surplus uniforms and drink US soft drinks while listening to US pop music. Visiting the United States in ever greater numbers,[32] owing to the cheaper fares offered by (mainly US) airlines, young Europeans are becoming increasingly familiar with US ways. It is indeed more and more difficult to distinguish between the products of American and European cultures. Fashions cross the Atlantic at ever greater speed, and European young people with no experience of two quite distinct and separate cultures have little reason to feel any cultural or social antagonism towards North America.

It would be foolish to claim that there is absolutely no Anti-Americanism in Europe. In small intellectual circles, there is an elitist, quasi-"aristocratic" rejection of US influence. French ex-Minister of Culture Jack Lang's 1981 Mexico Conference programme-speech against "American cultural imperialism" has found a faint echo among left-wing intellectuals. There is also no doubt that influential figures in Germany such as Günther Grass abhor the US way of life as much as US policies. In the United Kingdom, the rise in hostility to Mrs. Thatcher, who is perceived to be too close to the United States, has also rebounded to some extent on the image of the United States, although more in political terms than in cultural and social ones. It is also true that in countries like Spain and Greece, where the United

States is perceived as bearing some responsibility for having maintained dictatorships in power, its image is correspondingly poor, although it has improved in recent years. There again, however, the cause is political, and the feelings towards the United States as a society and as a nation are mere consequences of the image of US state policies, and should never be taken as a sign of a rejection of US ways and customs. It is therefore wrong to label as "Anti-Americanism" attitudes which have nothing to do with a rejection of Americans as a people or the United States as a nation. In his valedictory speech to the Bundestag, Mr. Helmut Schmidt - not an adversary of NATO - drew a valuable distinction: "What did you really expect, when from the beginning you reject every difference of opinion with US policies as damnable 'anti-Americanism', when in fact arguments with the leading power of the Alliance cannot be avoided."

"Equilateralism"

A real trend exists, on the other hand, to equate the United States with the Soviet Union, in terms of international power. In other words, this tendency acknowledges that the Soviet Union is a far less desirable society than the United States, but asserts that the international conduct of both Superpowers is comparable. In this respect, European reactions against President Reagan's rhetoric have played a significant role. Confidence in US leadership has diminished consistently over the past few years. Only France has witnessed an opposite evolution. Over half of the British respondents in February 1986 (before the raid on Libya), and in April 1986 (after the attack), had little or no confidence in American ability to deal wisely with world problems.[33] Other data shows that confidence in US ability has tended to go down in recent months.[34] Even more significantly, the ratings of approval and disapproval of "the role the United States is playing in world affairs" were 28% against 57%,[35] figures which did not differ considerably from the answers to the same question concerning Russia (22% against 52%). The key may be found in the fact that only 14% think that the United States "has done everything reasonable to try to reach agreements with the Soviet Union about controlling nuclear weapons", as against 79% who think the United States "should do more". The figures are almost exactly similar as far as the Soviet Union is concerned (14% and 78%).[36] The mental habit of thinking in terms of "Superpowers" deciding about the fate of the world over the heads of Europeans has certainly played a part in this phenomenon.

The word "Superpowers" itself has a pejorative connotation and implies equivalence. This is particularly evident in questions asked about Superpowers in the abstract, when the judgment takes a moral stance. This is why many American observers have labelled this attitude "moral equivalence", but it is not a purely moral equation, and the term "equilateralism" coined by a British journalist[37] is more suitable, although "parallelism" or "equidistancism" would have been just as effective. In this way of thinking, the two alliances are equated as "instruments of superpower political control, reducing the lesser states to abject cliency. This is as true in the West as in the East of Europe" (note the easy transition from the cautious "tendency" to the unqualified "as true".)[38] The continued occupation of Eastern Europe by Soviet troops is equated with the Vietnam war or the US intervention against Libya. "Challenged on the degree of police surveillance in Eastern Europe (the equilateralist) responds with individual examples of MI5 or CIA phone tapping in Western Europe."[39] The Soviet Union is not considered to be a model; its appeal has vanished almost entirely, but this has not benefited the image of the United States. On the contrary, "A downward reassessment of the Soviet threat is matched by a downward reassessment of the American model and an upward reassessment of the American threat."[40] Diffidence towards the rhetoric of the Reagan Administration explains part of this minority phenomenon, but there are more deep-seated causes. People who think in these terms - and the Rapporteur is convinced that there are an increasing number of them - do so largely out of habit, because it is simple to think of the two Superpowers in equal terms. The Gog and Magog archetype ensures a "balanced" and simplistic vision which puts minds at rest. Obviously, this is a minority viewpoint, however pervasive it may be.

The Europeanization of Europeans

It is increasingly clear that in broad terms, European public perceptions of the world are becoming increasingly different from those in the United States.

This was never so clear as during the aftermath of the US raid on Libya in April 1986. A huge majority of the US people approved President Reagan's decision, whereas equally large majorities in most European countries opposed it.[41] Clearly, feelings on both sides of the Atlantic were considerably at odds. Mrs. Thatcher's authorization to let the US F-111 leave the US bases in Britain for the strike against Libya cost her dearly in public support: 69% (against 27%) of the public opposed her decision.[42] An observer asserted at the time in The Times: "the bombers which flew from Britain to Tripoli could well cost the Conservatives the next general election."[43] In the Federal Republic of Germany and in Italy, very large majorities also disapproved of the US intervention. In France, the public was almost evenly divided (39% in favour, 40% against), but the approval rate for the French government's decision not to allow overflight rights to the F-111 was higher (55% in favour, 26% against).[44] As previous Civilian Affairs Committee General Reports have shown, the image of the United States has improved considerably in France in recent years, and Frenchmen do not share the reservations of many of their neighbours about President Reagan. This is due to the difference between French perceptions of their security and British and German perceptions. The French see their country as being independent from the United States: the French do not have US troops on their territory, and their armed forces are not integrated in the NATO military command. As a consequence, French opinion does not fear that fateful decisions for France will be taken by the President of the United States. They do not dread the involvement of France in a conflict not of her own choosing. The man whom they elect as President of the Republic is seen as the only one who can take France into a conflict. In this sense, if French opinion differs from that of other European countries, it is because France is not "European" as defined by many critical Americans. The public relations difficulties of NATO, the declining image of the United States, "equilateralism" are due to a realization by Europeans that their countries have a limited capacity to take decisions affecting their future in the strategic field, and that the US guarantee cannot be taken for granted. The relative lack of international responsibility induces attitudes which are obviously widely at variance with those of Americans, whose country bears worldwide obligations which are far from the daily preoccupations of many citizens.

The Dependence of Europe

This does not mean that Europe can become more independent in the near future. Western Europe cannot now rely only upon itself. For European opinion to understand the need for the transatlantic relationship, however, NATO has to become a more European institution, where European countries share more equally in the power to ensure their own security. A sense of responsibility has to be restored by the creation of what is usually called a "second pillar" of the Alliance. It is the Rapporteur's belief that public support for the Alliance will be forthcoming if the elected representatives of Western European nations are seen by their electorates to be ultimately responsible for the Old Continent's security. Reforms such as those advocated by Dr. Henry Kissinger for a "Europeanization of NATO" will eventually have to be implemented. This is, however, for the long term.

In the short term, Europe will have to continue to rely upon the US nuclear umbrella without being in a position to make Europe so vital to the security of the United States that the US nuclear deterrence can be seen to be perfect. European public opinion, therefore, will always find it difficult to feel absolutely safe within the present arrangements, and NATO will continue to encounter some difficulties with public opinion. This makes it all the more necessary to improve NATO's public presentation by contributing to the improvement of NATO's message itself. The Civilian Affairs Committee will have to continue to press for such an improvement.

The Americans and Europe

The General Public

Traditionally, pressure on US Administrations to reduce the US military commitment to Western Europe has come from liberal circles. The Mansfield Amendments or certain assertions by George McGovern during his presidential campaign constitute well-known examples of these attitudes. These isolationist tendencies, although they had some support in Congress, have always remained manageable, because the consensus among most policy-makers has stayed hostile to a return to the policies of the 1920s and 1930s which cost the United States and the world so dear. A fear that the Atlantic Alliance would tie the hands of the United States, obliging it to intervene abroad, is traditional, but if distrust towards foreign entanglements is never far from the surface of US public consciousness, majorities of over 60% of Americans have consistently supported sending troops to the rescue of Western Europe in the event of a Soviet attack. NATO is considered as a dangerous trigger by few Americans. US official sources estimate that about 31% of Americans can be classified as "isolationists",[45] but they seem to be less politically active, and therefore less influential, than the other two categories: the "internationalists" and the "unilateralists".

If the post-Vietnam period - a period of doubt and self-deprecation - had been the occasion of a turning in of the United States upon itself, which has been labelled the "Vietnam syndrome", the past few years have witnessed the apparition of a "post-Vietnam syndrome", based upon self-assertion and interventionism. Seen from Europe, United States opinion seems to have been taken over by unilateralism, a position which excludes taking interests of Allies into account when determining US policies. These shifts in public mood between isolationism and global activism would not matter so much if the US political system - because it is so democratic - did not reflect them so directly. The US therefore practises a peculiar brand of foreign policy which swings between two extremes: in some cases, a morally right US ignores the bothersome outside world because it feels it does not need it; in other cases, the US moralistically plunges into the international arena to put it to rights.

In many ways, US opinion has never been so much at odds with European opinion as is now the case. As noted above, US public support for the Libyan bombing was almost unanimous, a fact which has not been fully understood in Europe. The public mood in the United States is one of interventionism. President Reagan's popularity is unique for a second-term President of the United States. Even in the most unfavourable of polls, he is still holding a 60% favourable rating, even though there has been some recent decrease in the proportion who judge him to be "outstanding" or "excellent". This is distinctly at odds with his standing in Western Europe. Although many of the problems which Americans consider to be high priority, like terrorism (80%) or drugs (78%), are at least as serious in Europe, the American public's preferred response is much more robust. 59% of Americans want the Administration to take military action in order to reduce terrorism sponsored by other nations - a rise of 10% in a few months.[46] This rise in the willingness to use military force is most at odds with European attitudes.

The conclusion should not be drawn, however, that Americans are not interested in arms control. 68% want the Administration to pursue a major effort to negotiate agreements to limit nuclear weapons.[47] The difference between Europe and the United States is that in the United States this is not considered to be a number one priority, whereas in Europe - with the possible exception of France, where opinion is more sceptical of arms control than in the United States - the public's attention is almost monopolized by arms control. Clearly, the unilateralist mood in the United States implies that this European concern is of little importance for the US public.

This is reinforced by the fact that Americans feel that Europe is not carrying a large enough part of the burden of its own defence. This is a parallel reaction to that of Europeans towards their own dependence. The 1985 General Report of the Civilian Affairs Committee described the increasingly uneasy attitude among the US electorate and Congress towards the perceived "cheap ride" that Europe "gets away with". The reality is obviously very different, as General Rogers never tires of repeating to US audiences. The calculation of real costs is extremely complex and involves comparing the cost of US professional soldiers with that of European conscripts, and taking land use and loss of tax revenue into account. It is difficult to appreciate at present - before the mid-term elections - how much public feeling against the Europeans has moved, but it would be foolish to hide the fact that the issue will be kept alive in Congress by pressure groups, and that economic pressure will bring to bear upon US military spending in Europe.

It is also remarkable to note how much US public feelings are at odds with those of Europeans on the issue of East-West relations. Increasingly, the Europeans' attention is concentrated on arms control, and this has diminished interest in other fields. There is no doubt, for instance, that human rights concerns have come to play a considerably less important part for Europeans recently, because the overwhelming feeling has been that such considerations should not stand in the way of a possible arms control deal between the Superpowers. It is true that West Germany has her own reasons for keeping an interest in human rights affairs in the East, and that the influence of Solzhenitsyn's writings has created a strong public and political interest in human rights in the East among French opinion, but the pressure of special interest groups and US opinion as a whole on the US Congress and Administration knows no equal in Europe. There is no doubt that politically the perceptions of US and European public opinions have drifted apart in the past few years. The stark difference in attitudes over the Libyan attack has constituted a mere sign of this drift, albeit a particularly obvious and spectacular one. On the US side, the rise of unilateralism has fed upon a popular sub-culture which is based on a popular commercial fashion.

Anti-Sovietism finds an echo in this popular sub-culture - represented in the cinema as well as in television commercials. Here, the implicit assumption predominates that America can solve the complex problems of 1986 simply by resorting to force, as was the case in frontier days. Many Americans look for old-style "warrior heroes" fighting in a clear-cut struggle of good versus evil. This hypersimplistic approach has become the dominant theme of an increasing number of American films. Protagonists like Rocky and Rambo are all muscle and no brains. These characters are fed up with a politically moderate (read: soft on communism) governing elite and, by implication, with those "useless Europeans" who favour detente over confrontation. In "Rocky", one gets the impression that "the big giant is tired of getting his toes stepped on". Rambo is a "noble savage" descended from frontier heroes of yesteryear - men of action, who fought for what was right. Both films do not simply criticize the Soviets, they ridicule them; they subject them to what is known as "red bashing". Rambo pits himself against the scheming East Coast Brahmins who foiled honest military men's efforts to win in Vietnam - the same East Coast Establishment which has for so long focused American foreign policy on Europe. By going back to the jungle to rescue Americans abandoned by the Establishment, and killing a substantial portion of the Vietnamese population in the process, Rambo avenges a lost war, a period of disgrace when the US knuckled under to third rate countries. Rocky represents a new breed of American: tough, disciplined, powerful, forthright. In these films East-West politics are trivialised, brought down to the level of a pantomime. "Rocky is the self-made product of the State. He is a boxer transmogrified into the ultimate cold warrior, taking on the best the Soviets had to offer in a gladiatorial conflict."[48]

"Rocky" and "Rambo" are certainly not alone in perpetrating such an ignorant approach to superpower relations and international affairs. Many other films, as well as TV series, present an image of a resurgent America zealously - and violently - taking revenge on those responsible for past humiliations. Even advertising has entered the fray, reflecting and enhancing widespread popular ignorance and condescension to a Soviet society considered culturally inferior to the United States.

This is not to say either that US opinion is swayed by such gimmickery or that any intelligent person would associate with such sentiments, but that such sub-culture introduces in the public mind an - admittedly extreme and absurd - reference point which pushes back the limit of what is permissible. Obviously, the political influence of such trivia is limited, but the public mentality, especially on matters which are as complex and inaccessible as international affairs, is affected by the mood of the times, of which sub-culture constitutes a part.

US Elites

Since the Second World War, a majority among US elites has consistently supported a strong US connection with Western Europe and the US nuclear guarantee against a Soviet aggression against Europe. As seen above, adversaries traditionally came from a fringe of the liberal wing of the Democratic Party. Recently, however, most liberals have become reconciled to the US military commitment to NATO. Many of the concerns of liberals: no-first use, a nuclear freeze, have found a more sympathetic echo in Europe than in the United States, and this has played a part in this reconciliation. Conversely, many Europeans feel most at ease with US liberals.

Unfortunately, at the same time, the intellectual and, in some respects, the political initiative seems to have eluded liberals. More and more influence is coming from a new brand of political theorists and analysts, many of whom originally came from the quasi-Communist left, but have moved to the right and have formed what is known as a "Neo-conservative" group. Neo-conservatives approve continued US intervention abroad in opposition to the spread of Communism, which they see behind every move hostile to the United States. The US intervention must be unilateral, on US terms and only in the interest of the

United States. The views of Allies should be respected only if they are consistently supportive of US policy moves. Mrs. Thatcher is the only European leader of whom they approve.

Norman Podhoretz, Nathan Glazer, Irving Kristol and Walter Laqueur, amongst others, have said continuously since the mid-1970s that the Soviet threat to US global interests is worse than ever and still growing. They assert that the United States not only suffers from a deficiency in conventional forces, but that the nuclear superiority which it has lost is indispensable. The neo-conservative world view is framed in ideological terms - Democracy versus Communism - and is reflected in President Reagan's "evil empire" approach to superpower relations. It goes back to a traditional American attitude, according to which the supreme good is an ideologically compatible world. In this view, US overseas commitments are interdependent, and damaged credibility in one region harms US interests everywhere. The fact that the United States is seen to have worldwide interests means that US foreign policy is not given a set of priorities, and that global interests form one indivisible whole. In Neo-conservative eyes, the principal battleground of the world struggle between communism and the free world is the Third World, the European situation having long ago become static. Most importantly, they wonder whether the United States' extensive commitment to Europe is worth the enormous expenditures in terms of money and manpower, especially when so many Europeans express strong doubts over NATO policies and the seriousness of the Soviet threat. As for the US commitment to Europe, America should seek to reassert its dominance, while paying little attention to Allies' concerns. The influential Wall Street Journal gives numerous examples of this way of thinking. These thinkers and popularizers devote a considerable degree of attention to the European peace movement and to what they describe as the drift of the Europeans away from the United States. "To aggressive Neo-conservatives who believe America should be less worried about what the allies think, NATO increasingly feels like a ball and chain restraining US foreign policy."[49]

Undoubtedly, Neo-conservatives do not constitute a majority among political thinkers in the United States, but it would be difficult to deny their influence upon the present Administration and some sections of Congress. The Wall Street Journal is credited with having convinced

Ronald Reagan and his advisers to adopt supply-side economics, and some members of the Administration - especially in the Pentagon - are intellectually close to Neo-conservative thinking. Furthermore, their ideas are the new ones, opposed to the establishment-entrenched "Europeanism". They therefore have more dynamism and hence a greater impact than the number of their readers or supporters would superficially lead one to believe.

More significantly, perhaps, voices belonging to the Establishment have recently questioned the wisdom for the United States of maintaining the present level of commitment to Europe. Dr. Henry Kissinger's much publicized proposals in Time magazine in November 1984 included a gradual withdrawal of perhaps up to half of the US forces in Europe. Dr. Zbigniew Brzezinski, President Carter's national security adviser, has recently suggested that the nature of the US military presence in Europe be altered: "the US will have to take the first steps, even perhaps unilaterally, through a ten-year program of annual cuts in the level of ground forces in Europe."[50] The publisher-editor of US News and World Report, Mr. Mortimer Zuckermann, recently advocated a phased withdrawal of 150,000 ground troops in Europe over a period of five to ten years.[51]

These examples show that in the mainstream of US thinking, respected voices wish to reduce the US commitment in Europe. Within a traditional conservative mental framework, this has the advantage of logic. Those conservatives who follow this traditional logic are closer to traditional European thinking than most other Americans. In their view, ideological divisions are largely a fig leaf for rivalry between powers, and all actions in the international arena are defined by specific national interests. The relative power of the US has shrunk since 1945, and traditional conservatives accept the fact that America cannot be everywhere at once - it simply lacks the necessary resources. Budget and trade deficits show US inability to keep global military commitments while putting the economic house in order. A reduced military burden would mean devoting more resources to the domestic economy. European interests are far less important than national well-being. Traditional conservatives do not believe that US credibility in one region is linked to US credibility in another. A policy failure in Africa, where American interests are limited, does not imply that the United States is considered weak in Central America, where the US might be said to have more at stake. In this context, Europeans should look after their own defence, since they have the economic means to do so, and it is up to the United States to stimulate them into doing so, if necessary by unilateral forces reductions.

The Popular Appeal of the SDI

The Strategic Defense Initiative - a US, not a NATO policy - represents another departure from post-war consensus insofar as it is largely construed by US opinion as aiming at creating an impregnable moat around the US and an impenetrable roof over it. This revives the feeling that the US could somehow escape from the ills and dangers of the outside world.

Obviously, many proponents of the SDI and of ballistic missile defence have a more sophisticated vision, in which a defensive system would be used in order to enhance deterrence by protecting missile launching sites, rather than to make it "obsolete". The manner in which the programme has been presented to the masses, however, was aimed at destroying the popular support for the nuclear freeze movement, and therefore stresses the "vision" according to which a nuclear-free world, or at least a nuclear-attack-exempt United States, would be the eventual aim of the programme. From the 23 March 1983 speech by President Reagan, where this vision was first presented to the public, to the rather caricatural advertisements financed by the High Frontier group, this simplistic vision of the SDI has focused the public's attention. This creates the illusion that a perfectly secure US is feasible.

The President's conception of the Strategic Defense Initiative as an impregnable shield against a Soviet strategic strike encourages among US opinion the notion that the United States is progressively ridding itself of international encumbrances in order to pursue its own self-interest more fully. Within the Reagan Administration, a substantial body of opinion focuses on exotic technologies as the means to obtain comprehensive population defences ultimately leading to an abandonment of offensive nuclear strategy. These so-called "true believers" have come to the fore, leaving the more sedate elements, who remain reserved about possible deployment, by the wayside. The President's conception of a total shield, with all its technological and economic implications, brings back historical memories. The SDI represents a challenge in which one finds that ever-recurrent theme of American history: the frontier. The US nation feels duty-bound to push forward the limits of human achievement as a test of national well-being and strength. The simplistic views of the SDI resurrect the mythical challenge of manifest destiny, of conquering a new domain which is rightfully America's.

The SDI enhances the notion of "fortress America" protected from external aggression, and recalls a traditional American dream: the inviolability of American territory. The SDI provides an opportunity to protect America from the Soviet threat and to isolate it from bothersome foreign entanglements, leaving it safe to pursue domestic prosperity. In short, "the SDI recreates the sanctuarisation of the national territory."[52] America's traditional opposition to foreign involvement is integrated with the moral aspect of puritanism which underlies it. On one side, the Soviets threaten to kill millions to obtain global domination. America responds in turn, not by similar immoral threats of mass destruction, but with the moral aim of eliminating the threat of war and of saving humanity through strategic defence.

Congress as a Moderator

Furthermore, by making the SDI the number one priority of all US defence programmes, the Administration runs the risk of playing into the hands of the supporters of unilateral US troop withdrawals from Europe, if only because US resources are limited and will be limited even further by the inevitable reduction in the budget deficit. Whether the Administration likes it or not, it is difficult to imagine that an effective action against the US deficit would not affect defence spending. The most obvious area where cuts could be made is NATO, which is estimated to cost up to 56% of US military resources.[53] This is why it is so important to keep the European connection with the US Congress alive, in order to avoid unilateral measures which could only help NATO enemies in Western Europe.

Congress under the Reagan Administration has often been closer to European viewpoints than the Administration. This is a new development. Traditionally, especially since the US Senate refused to ratify the Treaty of Versailles, Europeans have been circumspect about the role of Congress in US foreign policy. It often introduced in the European relationship with the United States an element of uncertainty which was considered unhealthy. In the recent period, on the other hand, an increase in European uneasiness towards the Administration has been matched by a rise in European comfort with Congressional initiatives. Congress has been far less enthusiastic than the Administration on the SDI, and has cut appropriations correspondingly. Very courageous attempts to prevent the President from going beyond the limits set by SALT II have taken place in both Houses of Congress, and the maintenance of the restrictive interpretation of the ABM Treaty has been successfully defended on Capitol Hill. On all these security matters, Congress was close to the Europeans. This was also true of the resistance of Congress to some foreign policy initiatives of the Administration. The overriding by Congress of President Reagan's veto on sanctions towards South Africa showed that on this issue public moods on both sides of the Atlantic were similar. The moderation of Congress on US relations with Central America also won it many friends in Europe.

The real danger is that the most spectacular positions on both sides of the Atlantic and therefore the most reported ones, are also the most extreme and irresponsible. Extreme feeds upon extreme. Seen from Europe, the Neo-conservatives in the United States may be becoming the visible part of the American iceberg, at a time when the peace movement and the extreme left become inflated in American perceptions of Europe. These polarized images lead to hyper-reactions, which in their turn polarize images further. A very dangerous vicious circle is thus created, by a spiral chain of reactions of the extremists on both sides. It is essential that governments on both sides of the Atlantic refuse to enter this "megaphone diplomacy" contest. It is also all-important that NATO participation be advocated by more effective means.

CONCLUSION: NATO INFORMATION MUST BE REFORMED

The North Atlantic Assembly, at the initiative of the Civilian Affairs Committee, has made far-reaching proposals to reform the present information structure of

NATO, which has to be regarded as unsatisfactory. There is no doubt that many of the present difficulties in communication between NATO and the public are due to political causes which no publicity, however well-packaged, could overcome. The dependence of Western Europe is a fact which only European leaders can address effectively.

However, progress can and should be made. The North Atlantic Assembly has recommended the creation of NATO Information Offices in member-countries, either under the responsibility of NATO, or under that of the government of the member country, or at the initiative of a voluntary group. The NATO Council has welcomed this Assembly's appeal, and some offices have indeed been created in some member countries.

The Civilian Affairs Committee is clearly making a contribution to the reform of the NATO information structure. The two-day meeting held in Brussels in February, where Permanent Representatives to NATO and NATO senior officials discussed the Committee's recommendations with its members, was successful in establishing the Committee as a source of pragmatic ideas for an improvement in the NATO information and public relations structure. Every speaker, including the Secretary General, was aware of the substance of the Committee's recommendations. Some national delegations, the United Kingdom in particular, voiced reservations, but a considerable degree of support was forthcoming on the part of, for example, the United States and the German missions. The Rapporteur has since received signs of additional interest on the part of some other delegations. It is essential to make NATO member countries face their responsibility to inform their opinion on Alliance matters. The fact that information on NATO is primarily a national responsibility should be taken to mean that member governments should be as active as possible. This principle should not be taken as an excuse for preventing NATO from acting from Brussels without the public being informed from individual capitals.

A particular difficulty comes from the fact that unanimity is necessary for any NATO Council decision concerning the NATO structure. This is why the NATO Council was unable to heed the Secretary General's proposal to increase the NATO information budget above inflation, a demand which the Assembly has been making repeatedly for the past two years, notwithstanding the fact that some savings could be made. This recommendation will have to be made again, but it is difficult to avoid the impression that NATO is as flexible and as fast-moving as a dinosaur. The question must squarely be asked: can political goodwill be consistently forthcoming when the NATO machinery proves to be so incapable of adapting itself to the most obvious needs?

In this respect, the Rapporteur has come to the conclusion that it would probably be easier if the NATO information structure - now called Information Directorate - were to be extracted from the NATO bureaucracy and attached directly to the Secretary General's private office, in order that it may escape somewhat from the weight and slowness of the NATO structure.

The fact that the NATO Council has authorized the Secretary General, following the North Atlantic Assembly's recommendation passed at the initiative of the Civilian Affairs Committee, to start preliminary work to undertake a review of the NATO classification rules, is satisfactory. The hope which the Rapporteur expresses at this stage is that decisions will be taken soon. The image of NATO suffers from its excessive habits of secrecy. Obviously, security rules must exist, but communication with the public must always be given high priority. The impression which one now has is that large sectors of the NATO machinery are assigned public information as the least important of all their tasks, and are told to interpret classification rules in order to pay mere lip-service to information duties. NATO would gain greatly from more openness, with due respect to its security requirements.

Finally, more emphasis has to be devoted to transmitting NATO information to people in member countries. The testimony given in frank and open terms to the Civilian Affairs Committee on 24 May 1986 by Ambassador Jean Béliard, Secretary-General of the Atlantic Treaty Association,[54] shows that it is not enough for NATO to rely on its present network of correspondents. Activity varies considerably from country to country, and communications between countries is not ensured properly by ATA (Atlantic Treaty Association), for want of funds and because the national Atlantic Committees have not been interested in exchanging information among themselves. If NATO has to rely on voluntary bodies, let these bodies be a reflection of the main political forces in each country, separately if there is not enough consensus or in a single body if consensus exists. The Civilian Affairs Committee of the North Atlantic Assembly will continue to put forward precise recommendations towards widening the network of NATO correspondents, so that they include people of all political persuasions. NATO will not survive electoral changes in member countries if it is closely identified with governments in office.

NOTES

1. Quoted in The Guardian, 11 September 1986
2. Associated Press, 18 June 1986
3. Alef poll, El Pais, 6 March 1986
4. MORI survey, Sunday Times, 23 February 1986
5. Epoca, 10 March 1986
6. Alef poll, El Pais, op. cit.
7. Ibid.
8. Gallup, private
9. Jonathan Steele, The Guardian, 14 March 1986
10. Newsweek, 23 July 1985
11. Times, 6 June 1986, Christian Science Monitor, 28 June 1986
12. Washington Post/National Weekly, poll, 9 September 1985
13. Ed., G. Flynn and H. Rattinger, The Public and Atlantic Defence, Totowa N.J.: Rowman & Allanheld, 1985
14. US News and World Report, 18 November 1985
15. Marplan, published in The Guardian, 22 October 1983
16. G. Flynn and H. Rattinger, op. cit., p. 159
17. ibid. p. 176
18. ibid.
19. Letter by Bishop Simonis in Disarmament Campaigns, December 1985, p. 31.
20. Disarmament Campaigns, December 1985, p. 3

21. Albert Wohlstetter: "Bishops, Statesmen, and Other Strategists on the Bombing of Innocents", Commentary, June 1983, p. 15

22. Jean Klein, "Esquisse d'une Communication sur les Religions et la Paix", unpublished Paper, 1985

23. Cf. his letter to the Heads of State of France, the Soviet Union, the United Kingdom and the United States in December 1981, and his statement at the United Nations on 7 June 1982

24. Klein, op. cit.

25. Father René Coste, "Les Evêques allemands et américains et la promotion de la paix", Défense Nationale, July 1983, p. 11

26. Coste, op. cit., p. 13

27. 1) only under "present conditions"
2) "superiority should never be the aim"
3) "deterrence must be a step on the road to progressive disarmament"
4) "it is indispensible not to be satisfied with the present situation"

28. Father René Coste, "Les Evêques français et la Construction de la Paix", Défense Nationale, January 1984, p. 13

29. Financial Times, 28 May 1986

30. SOFRES survey, 18-24 October 1984, SOFRES Opinion Publique 1985, p. 259

31. MORI survey, Sunday Times, 23 February 1986

32. Polls in The Economist, 26 April 1986

33. MORI opinion poll, Sunday Times, 23 February 1986 and MORI opinion poll, The Times, 17 April 1986

34. Gallup poll, June 1986

35. ibid.

36. ibid.

37. Timothy Garton Ash, "Superpowers and Gog and Magog - an exercise in equilateralism", The Spectator, 19 July 1986, and reproduced in The New Republic, 29 September 1986

38. E.P. Thomson, quoted in article by Timothy Garton Ash, ibid.

39. ibid.

40. ibid.

41. See comparisons of opinion polls in the US, Britain, France, West Germany and Italy in The Economist, 26 April 1986; also Newsweek, 28 April 1986

42. Gallup poll, The Daily Telegraph, 17 April 1986, confirmed by MORI poll, The Times, 17 April 1986

43. Ronald Butt, The Times, 17 April 1986

44. IFOP poll, 15-16 April 1986, published in Le Point, 21 April 1986

45. US State Department briefing, 16 September 1986

46. All these figures come from State Department briefing, ibid.

47. ibid.

48. Newsweek, 23 December 1985

49. Gar Alperowitz, "America's Europe problem: Naked NATO", The New Republic, 29 September 1986

50. Quoted in Alperovitz, ibid.

51. ibid.

52. Georges-Eric Touchard, "Candide et l'IDS", Défense Nationale, January 1986

53. Source: US Government Accounting Office, 1984

54. Cf. Minutes of the meeting of the Civilian Affairs Committee of 24 May 1986 (Document AD 68 CC (86) 7), p. 11-14

2

The Economics of Atlantic Security

Ludolf-Georg von Wartenberg

GENERAL ECONOMIC DEVELOPMENTS IN ALLIANCE COUNTRIES IN 1985

Two years ago, in 1984, the economic recovery within the Alliance countries was very uneven. That year, the United States witnessed inflation-adjusted GNP growth of 6.6%, whereas the average growth rates of the European Alliance countries showed a rise of about 2.75%. This gap narrowed in 1985, not because the growth rates of the European Alliance countries rose to match the rapid growth in the United States, as would have been desirable, but because the expansion in the United States slowed down, while the average growth in the European Alliance countries continued at a modest pace.

Clearly, the very high dollar exchange rate up to last autumn put the US economy at a considerable disadvantage. For a long period of time, the strength of the dollar caused competitive distortion, boosted the price of American goods abroad and made imported goods more attractive to American consumers. Although the dollar exchange rate declined over most of the year, changes in spending patterns, which typically lag behind movements in exchange rates, were not yet evident in 1985 and imports made further inroads into the US domestic markets. At the same time, the sluggish growth in much of the rest of the world failed to provide strong markets for US exports.

Inflation continued to slow down in most Alliance countries, aided, particularly in the European Alliance countries, by the marked decline in the dollar exchange rate. Prices in the international energy and commodity markets continued to fall in 1985 and in the first half of

1986. In the OECD area, inflation has been in decline for more than five years now - the longest period of disinflation since the Second World War - and the combination of economic growth and falling inflation clearly underpins the recovery.

Although great differences in national inflation rates persist, ranging from approximately 2% to about 45% among the Alliance countries, this gap also narrowed in 1985. The Federal Republic of Germany (2.0%) and the Netherlands (2.3%) were able to further reduce their already very low inflation rates. However, two-digit inflation rates remained a major economic problem for Turkey (45.5%), Iceland (32.5%), Portugal (19.8%) and Greece (18.9%).

Concern grew over the increasingly uneven current account positions among major OECD countries, with the United States deficit and Japanese surplus each reaching 3.75% of their respective GNPs in 1985, and the surplus of the Federal Republic of Germany heading for 3% of the country's GNP. This configuration, regarded by most observers as unsustainable, contributed to heightened protectionist sentiments and trade frictions between the world's three big trading blocs, the United States, the European Community and Japan.

A second unsatisfactory feature of the Alliance economies in 1985 was the continuing high level of unemployment. Given the considerable slowdown in economic growth in 1985, unemployment in the United States fell only slightly, from 7.5% to 7.2%. In Canada, which also witnessed a slowdown in economic growth, unemployment fell from 11.3% to the still very high level of 10.5%. In Europe, efforts to cut joblessness proved disappointing. The unemployment rate for the European OECD countries went up from 10.8% in 1984 to 11.0% in 1985, and persistent high levels of long-term unemployment and youth unemployment continued to contribute to a growing polarization of labour markets.

THE WORLD ECONOMY IN 1986

Improved Conditions for Growth

At the beginning of 1986, a significant improvement in economic conditions, which had already set in last year, generated unprecedented euphoria among economic policy makers about the future development of the world economy. The attainment of a more sustainable pattern of exchange rates, the sharp fall in the oil price and a further reduction of interest rates, were the key developments that spurred the overall optimism.

A meeting of the Group of Five leading industrial nations held in New York's Plaza Hotel on 22 September 1985 brought a sudden end to a period of relative calm on the fiscal and monetary front. The participants in the Group of Five meeting - representatives from the United States, Japan, the Federal Republic of Germany, France and the United Kingdom - recognized that exchange rates were not fully reflecting fundamental economic conditions and that further orderly appreciation of the main non-dollar currencies against the US dollar was desirable. This signal, backed up by evidence that the monetary authorities in the countries involved were prepared to carry out significant intervention in the exchange market, soon moved rates in the desired directions.

At the time this report was written, at the beginning of October 1986, the dollar had declined more than 40% against both the Japanese yen and the West German D-Mark from its peak in February 1985. The bulk of this fall had taken place in the year since the Plaza agreement, during which the dollar lost 30% against the D-Mark and 36% against the yen.

The 22 September 1985 Plaza agreement signalled the abandonment, notably by the United States, of the notion that markets can be left to manage themselves and that policy co-ordination is superfluous. This change, together with the improved configuration of exchange rates which it encouraged, led to what was soon to be labelled as "The Spirit of the Plaza" - a new mood of co-operation between the United States, Japan, the Federal Republic of Germany, France and the United Kingdom, in international economic policy making.

After reaching a peak price of 35 US dollars per barrel in 1981, the price of oil drifted downward quite steadily until December of last year. From then onwards, the Organization of Petroleum Exporting Countries (OPEC) attempted to cut global oil production as a means of boosting the price of oil and securing what the Organization called its fair share of the oil market. However, non-OPEC oil-producing countries did not give in to OPEC demands to curb their production, and OPEC itself proved unable to restore discipline in its own ranks. The combination of these two developments led to an unprecedented fall in the price of oil from 26 US dollars per barrel in January to even less than 10 US dollars in July.

Only at the beginning of August 1986, after many vain attempts in the preceding months, did the oil-producing countries gathered in OPEC reach a temporary accord on production sharing under a ceiling of 16 million barrels a day. The accord had the immediate effect of pushing the price of oil up to about 15 US dollars a barrel, particularly when nations outside the cartel, concerned about the free fall the oil price had experienced and longing for stability, voiced their support.

The decline of the value of the US dollar was accompanied by a steady downward movement in interest rates, abetted by the collapse of oil prices and, as a result, of inflationary expectations around the world. Talk of a co-ordinated round of interest rate cuts surfaced shortly before the January Group of Five meeting in London, but became reality in March, when the Federal Republic of Germany lowered its discount rate, swiftly followed by Japan, the United States and the Netherlands. Cuts in official interest rates in Italy, the United Kingdom, Canada, France, Sweden and Belgium soon followed.

During the first half of this year, as a result of the apparently very favourable developments outlined above, a great optimism about the future development of the world economy prevailed among economic policy makers in the Western industrialized world. The new co-operative spirit which had followed the successful September 1985 Plaza agreement was endorsed at the economic summit in Tokyo in May of this year, where the Group of Seven (the Group of Five, joined by Canada and Italy) underwrote efforts within the IMF to develop improved mechanisms by which the major industrialized countries could monitor their economic performance and try to agree upon complementary economic policies.

From Optimism to Anxiety

In sharp contrast to what many experts expected, the developments briefly outlined in the previous chapter did not immediately lead to a faster, more balanced growth of the world economy. Instead, economic growth slowed significantly and world trade stagnated during the course of the year. The huge current account deficit of the United States did not narrow, but rather became even larger, leading to a resurgence of protectionist pressure in the US Congress. Many developing and heavily indebted countries, already in great problems as a result of weak international commodity prices and creditor-imposed austerity, suffered yet another fall in real income. In parallel, the prospect of new co-operation and coherence in international economic policy-making frequently gave way to bickering between the United States on the one hand and Japan and West European countries on the other. The overall optimism prevailing in the first few months of the year faded rapidly.

Clearly, many economic forecasters misread the effects of lower oil prices on world trade and growth prospects. They expected that the fall in oil prices would impose serious balance of payments constraints on oil-exporting countries, which would require them to reduce their imports from the industrialized nations, continuing a process which began in 1981. Much to the surprise of many experts, however, oil-exporting countries reacted much more quickly to changing circumstances than consumers in the oil-importing countries. Governments of oil-exporting countries, most of them already subject to economic stress, took swift action to cut consumption in line with lower revenues. In the oil-importing countries, on the other hand, demand only responded slowly to the shift of incomes following the fall of oil prices.

In addition, the lower price of oil caused unexpectedly severe dislocations in the economies of oil-producing countries in the Western world, such as Canada, Norway and the United States. In these countries, many oil companies were forced to shut down small "stripper wells" and to slash exploration and drilling budgets. This contraction subsequently generated serious difficulties in other sectors as well.

Over time (and provided the oil price does not rebound again) the net impact of the lower price of oil is still expected to be beneficial. However, the gains may prove to be much smaller than the losses taken during the price-rise shocks of the 1970's.

The sharp fall in nominal interest rates did not translate into significantly lower real interest rates and this also hampered further economic growth. So far, both long and short term real interest rates remain high by previous standards, restraining both demand and investment.

Moreover, until now, the decline of the dollar has not had a real, positive impact on the fundamental imbalance in the world economy: the enormous US trade deficit and parallel surpluses in Japan and the Federal Republic of Germany. Economists the world over expected, and US exporters ardently hoped, that the lower dollar would significantly improve US competitiveness and, subsequently, the American trade performance. So far, however, US companies still feel strong competition from abroad, and the enormous US trade deficit, 148.5 billion US dollars in 1985, is widening even further this year.

Part of the explanation for the apparent lack of reaction to the fall in the dollar can be found in a J-curve effect; trade prices have the natural tendency to react much faster than trade volumes to exchange-rate movements.[1] Another reason is the asymmetry of the dollar's decline. The American currency has fallen sharply against the currencies of countries accounting for roughly half of US trade, but has hardly depreciated against those of nations representing the other half, such as Canada (America's most important trading partner), South Korea, Brazil and Taiwan. Furthermore, the huge Japanese surplus is in part at least a reflection of the structural imbalance between savings and investment opportunities in Japan, and not likely to be rapidly influenced by the recent change in world economic conditions.

By the middle of 1986, the overall optimism concerning the future development of the world economy had been replaced by what could be described as a general mood of anxiety. Many economic experts as well as international economic institutions like the IMF and the OECD, still convinced of the longer term positive impact of improved economic conditions but more cautious than a few months before, somewhat toned down their projections for future economic development. Several other experts and economic policy makers, on the other hand, especially in the United States, saw the omens of a world recession.

TRANSATLANTIC ECONOMIC FRICTIONS - THE ALLIANCE'S CONCERN

According to the same international economic institutions mentioned above, the US current account deficit may reach more than 130 billion US dollars this year, and then fall only fractionally in 1987. Japan's surplus is now projected to be about 80 billion US dollars in 1986, and expected to fall by some 10 billion US dollars next year. The Federal Republic of Germany expects to record a surplus of 25 to 30 billion US dollars in 1986, although this figure is forecast to fall quite sharply in 1987 and beyond.

It is this structural imbalance in the world economy which has seriously dampened the euphoria following the September 1985 Plaza accord, and is at the heart of the serious differences between the United States, Japan and West European countries, which surfaced in the summer of this year.

The imbalance between the world's most important economic blocs, the United States, Western Europe and Japan, is an intricate and deep-rooted problem. Separating one specific area of tension is not an easy task and will not in itself bring us nearer to a solution to the global problem. It is clear, however, that the transatlantic dimension of the problem, i.e. the imbalance between the economies of the United States and its West European allies, is of particular concern to parliamentarians gathered in the North Atlantic Assembly, due to its potential impact on the cohesion of the Alliance. It is for this reason that your rapporteur has decided to make the troubled transatlantic economic relations the focal point of this year's General Report on the Economics of Atlantic Security.

The United States Economy - Slowdown Instead of Acceleration

After World War II, the United States was able to exercise commanding international economic leadership for two decades, while remaining relatively invulnerable to external economic forces. The United States emerged from World War II intact, self-sufficient and determined to remake the world in its own image. It set about the task with massive infusions of capital into the world economy, while impressing on its beneficiaries the virtues of a liberal international trading regime. By the 1960's, the endeavour had proven such a resounding success that the revitalized industrial economies began to provide the United States with serious international competition. By the end of the 1960's, the drain of Vietnam on the domestic economy combined with what had become an increasingly competitive international climate to breach the hermetically sealed US economy.

The invulnerability of the United States evaporated rapidly. The first post-war devaluation of the dollar in 1971, which effectively removed the United States from the gold standard, marked a decisive adjustment to the new forces that had come into play. Since then, the pace of further internationalization of the US economy has been spectacular. US domestic manufacturing shifted increasingly towards export industries and import competition grew rapidly. The stable, relatively open US market presented a hospitable environment for direct foreign investment in virtually every sector of the economy. At the same time, US commercial banks and the US government itself, through the IMF and the World Bank, tethered themselves abroad through hundreds of millions of dollars in loans to developing countries. High dollar values flooded the US market with foreign goods and capital and caused domestic producers to increase their reliance on overseas components and production.

At the beginning of the 1980's the United States acted as the "locomotive" for the world economy. The strong recovery of the American economy and the surge in US imports in 1983 and 1984 helped prevent a far worse recession in Europe and a financial collapse in Latin America. Imports and capital inflows also held down US inflation and eased financing of the American budget deficit. Their enormous magnitudes, however, eventually led to a large trade imbalance and an overvalued dollar which, in turn, slowed the growth of the US economy.

From the middle of 1985 on, US international economic policy underwent major revisions. Firstly, while pressing hard for multilateral trade negotiations within the GATT framework, the US Administration also indicated its intention to explore trade relations on a more selective basis. Bilateral talks with Canada were started in May of this year and in July the United States and Japan concluded a semiconductor trade pact. Secondly, the US Administration toughened its trade stance by establishing a war chest to promote exports and by making unprecedented use of provisions under Section 301 of the US Legal Code, aimed at foreign trade practices deemed to be unfair. Thirdly, the US Administration drastically changed its international financial strategy by promoting co-ordinated

Western action to drive down the US dollar. Moreover, President Reagan directed the US Treasury to explore new approaches to assure greater long-term stability of exchange rates. Fourthly, the US Administration acknowledged that trade alone would not generate sufficient foreign exchange earnings for the indebted countries to relieve increasing strains on the international financial system. Therefore, in October of last year US Treasury Secretary James A. Baker proposed fresh infusions of capital and far-reaching structural reforms to spur growth among the developing countries.

However, the US Administration's more engaged and assertive international economic policy did not pay off as quickly as policymakers had expected. In spite of the lower dollar, imports made further inroads into the domestic markets. At the same time, the lower oil price stunned energy-producing regions and hurt a wide range of industries. As a result, economic growth slowed, disappointment turned into impatience and even anger, and protectionist claims by various industries and the US Congress mounted rapidly.

The US Administration tried to boost economic growth by a further lowering of the US discount rate. After two co-ordinated cuts earlier in the year the United States unilaterally cut its rates both in July and August to 5.5%, the lowest level in nine years.

Simultaneously, the US Administration increased its pressure on Japan, the Federal Republic of Germany and other West European countries, asking them to adopt more expansionary economic policies. While Japan made some concessions by announcing a now almost familiar package of expansionary measures, the Federal Republic of Germany and other West European countries, trading partners and, at the same time, NATO allies of the United States, showed themselves unimpressed by the American pressure and were still standing firm at the beginning of October, when this report was written. It was already clear at that time, however, that the increasingly bitter exchanges had not exactly improved relations among the NATO allies.

Bitter Exchanges Among the Allies

Disappointed by the slow growth of their own economy, the Americans, during the summer, asked their European allies to adopt further stimulative measures, such as tax cuts and interest rate reductions, to increase their domestic consumption. This, the Americans contended, would offer new opportunities for US exports as well as for domestic companies, which would otherwise focus more effort on the US market.

To encourage their allies to act, the Americans have a potent persuader: the US dollar. This summer, the US Administration, well aware of its ability to "talk the dollar down", did not disguise its willingness to do so if its trading partners did not change their domestic policies. This strategy clearly involves great risks. If the decline of the US dollar gets out of hand, rising inflation and higher interest rates in the United States could ensue. This may send the country into a recession which would drag down the whole world economy. The Americans need not be reminded of the dangers of a currency war. They maintain, however, that, apart from political pressure, the "dollar weapon" is the only means they have of influencing the economic policies of their European allies.

West European governments, however fearful of a free fall of the US dollar, were not very willing to implement the expansionary measures the United States asked for. They tried to explain to their American allies that, after a slow start at the beginning of this year, their economies are now picking up and that further stimulation would be dangerous, jeopardizing painful progress in strengthening public finances and reducing inflation. In the course of the year, forecasts published by the Organisation for Economic Co-operation and Development lent force to these arguments. France, for example, is expected to achieve 2.5% growth this year as well as next. The Federal Republic of Germany will speed up to about 3.5% growth this year, slowing to a more moderate 3.0% in 1987. On average, the European OECD member countries are expected to score 2.7% growth this year.

The countries resisting the American pressure for economic policy changes received support from another international economic institution as well. In its 1986 World Economic Outlook, the International Monetary Fund predicted that even a sharp 1% annual boost in growth in the Federal Republic of Germany and Japan, sustained for three years, would reduce the US trade deficit by only 5 to 10 billion US dollars. The IMF also argued that the sharp fall in the value of the US dollar would not, by itself, narrow the US current account deficit. A significant decline in the US current account deficit would require a considerable reduction of the US budget deficit, which has exceeded 200 billion US dollars in three of the past four years.

Restoring Order at Home - US Tax and Spending Reform

A severe imbalance between domestic savings and investment hampers economic growth in the United States and aggravates economic problems throughout the world. In recent years, heavy government and private demand for capital in the United States, combined with a low private sector savings quota, resulted in an enormous influx of foreign capital. Investors from all over the world tended to put their assets in the United States, as the profits expected by high interest returns on investment in the United States were larger than presumable revenue from productive investment elsewhere. The United States is now a net debtor for the first time since 1914. Last year, its net international investment position fell into deficit by 107.4 billion US dollars, and analysts expect the position to worsen by a further 140 billion US dollars this year.

Upon assuming office in 1981, the Reagan Administration moved to stimulate economic activity through substantial tax cuts. A large budget deficit was helpful then, because private spending and investment were weak. By 1984, however, robust economic growth had made a large deficit inappropriate. The US Administration hoped that further economic growth would generate revenues sufficient to reduce the deficit, and that spending reductions would do the rest. Unfortunately, this projection did not materialize. Economic growth slowed down considerably and government spending only increased. As a result, the deficit for fiscal year 1985 reached a record 212 billion US dollars.

In what can only be labelled an act of desperation, the US Congress last autumn approved the Gramm-Rudman-Hollings Budget and Emergency Deficit Control Act, which was subsequently signed into law by President Reagan on 12 December 1985. The legislation sets deficit targets of 171.9 billion US dollars in fiscal year 1986, 144 billion US dollars in 1987, 108 billion US dollars in 1988, 72 billion US dollars in 1989, 36 billion US dollars in 1990 and budget balance in 1991, and requires automatic cuts designed to reach these levels if ordinary budget procedures miss the mark by 10 billion US dollars or more. These automatic cuts, or sequestrations, are to be split equally between defence and non-defence spending.

Legislating under the lash of the anti-deficit law did not turn out to be quite as advertised when the law was enacted. In February of this year, a special federal court found the key feature of Gramm-Rudman-Hollings - its automatic spending cut mechanism - to be unconstitutional. The mechanism was to be activated in mid-August each year if deficit re-estimates showed Congress and the President had not managed through conventional legislation to hold deficits below the targets set by the Act. Without the automatic device, the deficit re-estimates would still be made, but any spending cuts necessitated by those estimates would take effect only if approved by Congress and the president.

On 7 July the US Supreme Court upheld the lower court ruling that the automatic mechanism violated the separation of powers doctrine, because it assigned executive-type responsibilities to the General Accounting Office, which the court found to be a legislative branch entity. The ruling brought firm assurances from sponsors of the anti-deficit law that its remaining procedures requiring congressional and presidential approval of spending cuts would work. Yet almost immediately, the original sponsors of Gramm-Rudman-Hollings I began pushing a revised version of the automatic procedure which, they said, was needed to eliminate "uncertainty" in deficit cutting. Gramm-Rudman-Hollings II gave the authority to determine the final shape of automatic spending cuts to the Office of Management and Budget. The actual implementation of cuts, however, would still have to be approved by Congress and the President.

Right from the inception of Gramm-Rudman-Hollings, it was clear that the complex legislation would work as planned if the bleak prospect of draconian cuts forced a compromise between Congress and the President. It was also clear, however, that such a compromise would be extremely difficult to reach.

The fiscal year 1987 budget proposal, which President Reagan transmitted to Congress on 5 February 1986, made clear that the President was still standing by the budget priorities he had advocated so strongly in previous years: real growth in defence spending, deep cuts in other domestic programmes, and no tax increases. In line with the schedule set in the Gramm-Rudman-Hollings legislation, but based on rather rosy economic assumptions, the deficit would fall to zero by 1991. For fiscal year 1987 the President's budget proposal aimed for a deficit of 143.6 billion US dollars.

By 1 October 1986, the beginning of fiscal year 1987, US legislators had failed to complete action on any of the 13 regular annual appropriations bills that fund government programmes. Only on 15 October, Congress, ignoring the deficit reduction target set by Gramm-Rudman-Hollings, approved a 576 billion US dollar omnibus appropriations bill to fund the Government through fiscal year 1987. However, the bill cut 28 billion US dollars from the President's requested defence budget, bringing it down to slightly more than 290 billion US dollars, to give the smallest percentage increase in defence spending since the President took office in 1981.

The cut in defence spending follows sharp cuts in the rate of growth of the defence budget last year. This may have succeeded in setting the budget deficit on a downward trend from the record level of more than 230 billion US dollars expected to have been spent in fiscal year 1986. However, only die-hard optimists expect next year's budget deficit to come within reach of the Gramm-Rudman-Hollings target of 144 billion US dollars. Until now, there have been no real plans - more importantly, there seems to be no political will to make this happen.

Of course, it is easy to blame the Supreme Court, because it ruled invalid the provision mandating automatic spending cuts. But even if the court had left the automatic spending cut mechanism intact, legislators would probably have found a way to circumvent it rather than make unpopular cuts. In a critical article recently published in the New York Times and the International Herald Tribune, Benjamin M. Friedman, Professor of Economics at Harvard University, called the Gramm-Rudman-Hollings law not just ineffective, but even counter- productive.[2] Last year, according to Friedman, the legislation eased the pressure on the President and Congress by letting everyone claim that the deficit problem had been solved. This year, Congress and the President will likely escape political pressures by devising a way to pretend that the deficit will be within the legislated limit. It is clear, however, that tough questions, like the balance between defence and non-defence spending priorities and the explosion in agricultural subsidies, can not be put off indefinitely.

It is as yet uncertain to what extent the US budget deficit will be affected by the comprehensive tax-reform legislation adopted recently. The legislation was not intended either to raise or reduce revenues, but could very well have a negative impact on the budget deficit. Economists have praised such features of the bill as the lowering of the top tax rate from 50% to 28%, the lifting of all tax liability from some 6 million poor Americans and the abolition of many non-productive tax shelters. There are fears, however, that the abolition of investment tax credits and hikes in capital gains taxation rates might dampen investment. At the same time, if West European countries do not increase their efforts to lower tax rates there will be yet another attraction for investment funds to leave Europe and flow to the United States, which would be an unwelcome development both for Europe and for the United States.

Europe's Unfulfilled Potential

With these remarks we have entered the scope of another important aspect of the troubled transatlantic relationship: Western Europe's apparent inability to make full use of its enormous political and economic potential. Western Europe's size, educated people, and inherent political and economic strength could make it a confident leader in the struggle to shore up the world economy. Indeed, the demands the US Administration has made on Western Europe, both in the political and in the economic spheres, clearly indicate that Americans feel that Europe can achieve a lot more than Europeans themselves believe. Regrettably, however, West European governments have not yet made much progress towards greater political cohesion and the creation of a more invigorating economic climate, and this clearly hampers Western Europe's ability to play a more important international role.

For much of this decade, the majority of West European governments, uncertain about the effectiveness of expansionary economic policies, pursued financial policies aimed at reducing their budget deficits, as well as tight monetary policies designed to restrict inflation. These policies were successful inasmuch as they sustained the economic recovery of the respective countries. However, structural problems, both within the individual countries and in their economic interrelationship, have remained.

Clearly, a true common European internal market would improve efficiency and economies of scale, and result in greater importing and exporting capacities. In December of last year, the leaders of the European Community, at their Luxembourg summit, set the end of 1992 as the deadline for achieving the reduction in internal barriers, harmonization of standards, and elimination of nuisance regulations necessary to make the Community live up to its name as a region in which goods, services, workers and competitive forces can move about freely. Now, almost one year later, it is clear that the timetable agreed upon last year is far from being followed and that, therefore, the 1992 deadline is not likely to be met.

Meanwhile, Europe's resources are still being wasted. Within the framework of its Common Agricultural Policy, the European Community spends huge amounts of money on its surplus production and then has to subsidize the products down to the level of world market prices. Clearly, this extremely expensive policy not only impairs the sales prospects of poorer countries, but also places strains on relations with the United States.

What Europe needs and what its American trading partners would like to see developing in the old continent, is a more invigorating economic climate, in which obstacles to change and innovation have been reduced, more capital is attracted and domestic investment stimulated. More constructive steps towards a true common European internal market will help to create such a favourable climate. However, such an approach can not be counted on to generate increased economic activity right away. At the present time, however, progress in stabilizing prices, coupled with the windfall of lower oil costs and the lower US dollar, offers West European governments greater scope for expansionary policies with less inflationary risk.

The annual economic report of the European Commission, published in mid-October, draws the conclusion that member countries of the European Community fail to take full advantage of the improvement in the international economic climate, and that they must boost their combined economic growth rates to make a significant reduction in unemployment. According to the European Commission, investment must be raised to contribute at least 3% more in terms of its share of value added, and the relationship between growth and the creation of jobs must also improve. This can be done by keeping real wage growth "moderate", while governments exploit whatever budgetary flexibility they have for demand stimulation.

At this point in time, a high degree of inaction is discernible in Western Europe, not just with regard to response to improved macro-economic preconditions, but also with regard to further political and economic integration. European governments almost seem paralyzed, uncertain whether success in the field of economic and political integration would give the United States an alibi to reduce the degree of its commitment in a then more powerful Europe. At the same time, however, more and more Americans are becoming annoyed with a Europe bogged down in national rivalries and apparently unable to fulfil its potential. Clearly, a more determined effort on the part of West European countries to overcome their differences and achieve greater political and economic resilience would be in the interest of both Europeans and Americans, and would thereby certainly contribute to the cohesion of the North Atlantic Alliance.

Greater Understanding Is Not Enough

After the increasingly bitter exchanges which had taken place over the summer, the annual conference of the International Monetary Fund and the World Bank, which took place in Washington at the end of September, at least brought greater understanding. Patience was shown with West European countries, on the way to adjustment, and the Americans were applauded for their bids to balance the US budget.

However, greater understanding alone will not have a tremendous impact on the profound imbalance between the economies of the United States and its West European allies. Only a firm commitment on both sides of the Atlantic to remove obstacles to economic growth, which would ideally be underpinned by improved macro-economic policy co-ordination, will eventually correct the imbalance between the economies of the United States and its West European allies, and generate a lasting improvement of transatlantic economic relations. Such an improvement would not only be of benefit to the individual countries involved, but also to the other actors in the world economy, particularly the numerous countries in the developing world so dependent on Western industrialized countries for their own economic progress. A consideration not to be overlooked by those countries directly involved, is that the North Atlantic Alliance would be further strengthened by improved transatlantic economic relations.

PERSISTENT PROBLEMS IN THE WORLD ECONOMY

The Threat of Protectionism

The volume of world merchandise exports rose by 3% in 1985, following a 9% rise in 1984, which was the highest recorded increase since 1976. The value of world merchandise exports, influenced by the decrease in world market prices in dollars, increased by less than 1% as against an increase of 5.5% in 1984, settling at 1,922 billion US dollars. These figures conceal the fact that major imbalances and frictions in world trade persist. Last year's growth of world trade is almost completely attributable to a 5% rise in trade among the industrialized nations. There was an absolute decline in the value of imports and exports of the developing countries in 1985. Low commodity prices, in particular, reduced the level of trade both among developing countries and between developing and industrialized nations. This was a key factor for the slowdown in the growth of world trade last year.

The growth of world trade could very well slow down even further this year. The General Agreement on Tariffs and Trade, in its 1985-86 annual report, draws particular attention to the threat posed to world trade by protectionism and calls on countries to take a hard look at the damage protectionism is causing to the world trading system.

In recent years, a shift in the basic technique of protectionism has occurred, which has severely undermined the regulatory power of GATT. The emphasis has moved on from tariffs, from which GATT draws its name, to subsidies and to market-sharing agreements (including so-called voluntary export restraint agreements). Market-sharing goes against one of GATT's main tenets by ushering in selective protectionism. It permits the victims of protectionism to be singled out in flat contradiction of the GATT principle of non-discriminatory behaviour, i.e. that a tariff against one country must be a tariff against all countries.

Originally, exceptions from GATT's trading rules and disciplines remained confined to agriculture, textiles and clothing, which at present account for nearly 20% of world trade. However, the hope that special treatment for these sectors would remain exceptional and truly temporary turned out to be an illusion. Subsidies and market-sharing deals have also occurred in other sectors. The semiconductor agreement negotiated with Japan to protect American chip manufacturers is a recent example. However, protectionism is also spreading in steel, motors, entertainment, electronics and machine tools.

The 1985-86 GATT report points out that, even if current policies do not lead to open trade warfare, a continuation of managed trade and market sharing would invite a prolonged stagnation, or decline, in world trade through the cumulative effect of distorted competition on investment decisions and business confidence. Such a development would cripple efforts to deal with such pressing problems as job creation, debt servicing and promoting economic growth.

Unemployment

Unemployment remains a serious concern for Western industrialized nations and is not likely to be wiped out in the near future. An OECD study on "Prospects for Employment" made public at the end of September, revealed that unemployment in the Western industrialized world may stabilize over the next year, but that it is unlikely to show any significant improvement. Some 31 million people may remain out of work in the OECD member countries over the second half of 1986 - an unemployment rate of 8.25% - and the number is unlikely to change in 1987. The number of jobs is expected to grow in almost all OECD countries next year, but so is the size of the working population.

Of the Alliance countries, the United States and Canada are likely to see unemployment remaining stable or even declining slightly. A slight decline is also likely in the Federal Republic of Germany and the United Kingdom. However, marked rises are expected in Italy, Greece and Turkey.

Youth unemployment remains a particularly serious problem, despite some improvement over the past two years, which is likely to continue over the coming year. The OECD report suggests that the young may be suffering from the effects of the Baby Boom, which brought a "bulge" of new applicants on the the job market at the same time as the economies of Western industrialized nations were slackening.

Long-term unemployment is the other main area of concern. The position continued to deteriorate last year in Europe, where more than 45% of the jobless have been out of work for more than a year. There was some improvement in North America. In most countries where the rise of unemployment has slowed recently or where unemployment has begun to decline, this has been accounted for mainly by a reduction of people entering the job market rather than by more unemployed people finding jobs. This means that the number of short-term unemployed has stabilized, but that there has been further growth in the numbers of longer-term unemployed, especially those out of work for a very long period. The OECD projects a further fall in long-term unemployment in North America this year and into 1987, but no significant improvement in Europe.

Once again, the OECD stressed the need for faster economic growth to improve the employment situation in its member countries. It is also important that nominal wage growth remains moderate if the recovery is not to be stifled. With low inflation, this need not mean that real wages have to be kept down.

Economic growth is not enough, however. There must also be a shift towards the kind of growth that promotes employment. Over the decade from 1973, GNP grew by 18% in Europe and by 22% in the United States. The United States, however, created nearly 16 million new jobs in the process, whilst employment stagnated in Europe. In the old continent, capital was used overwhelmingly to increase the capital intensity of production, not the labour intensity. The OECD now calls for policies that would help to spread capital more widely both to the employed and to those who would otherwise remain unemployed.

The Debt Crisis

The high debt of many developing countries and its disruptive impact on their development are persistent dangers facing the world economy. According to a World Bank study published in March 1986, the total debt in developing countries could climb to 1,010 billion

US dollars in 1986. This would be an increase of 6.3%, a rate of debt growth considerably higher than in 1984 and 1985, when debt growth was 4.2% and 4.6% respectively. Developing countries spent 100.1 billion US dollars on interest payments and capital repayments in 1984, thus improving their debt servicing capacity by 13%. In 1985, developing countries spent 102 billion US dollars on interest payments and capital repayments. Also last year, the servicing of the 12 most heavily indebted countries exceeded their capital receipts by 22 billion US dollars and these 12 countries were thus net exporters of capital.

On 8 October 1985, during the IMF and World Bank annual meetings in Seoul, Mr. James Baker, Secretary of the US Treasury, put forward a set of proposals for strengthening the debt strategy. Mr. Baker called on developing countries to adopt a new form of economic adjustment that would secure growth for their economies. In return, creditors were to commit themselves to supplying extra finance, with commercial banks and multilateral development institutions such as the World Bank each agreeing to provide a net 20 billion US dollars over three years to a specially selected group of 15 countries with a combined foreign debt of 429 billion US dollars.

So far, the Baker Plan has not achieved any of its stated objectives. According to the 1986 World Bank annual report, growth in developing countries slipped to 4.3% last year from 5.4% in 1984. The consensus is that the rate will fall further in 1986. Mr. Baker's call for commercial banks to increase their lending to developing countries has met a similar fate: lending has been falling. The Bank for International Settlements recorded a drop of 5.2 billion US dollars in such lending during the first quarter of 1986 and there has been no sign of a pick-up since. New loan commitments by the World Bank did rise by some 1.8 billion US dollars to 13.2 billion US dollars in its fiscal year which ended on 30 June 1986. They are scheduled to rise further to between 13.5 billion US dollars and 17 billion US dollars this year, but disbursement of loans by the Bank actually fell last year, as did its net transfer of resources to current borrowers, which stood at 3.2 billion US dollars in 1985-86 compared with almost 5 billion US dollars a year earlier.

The 12 billion US dollar Mexican loan package announced at the end of September was hailed by many as the initial success story for the Baker Plan. However, the commercial banks, putting up almost 6 billion US dollars in fresh money, were able to fend off many of the concessions for which Mexico struggled, for instance, the direct linking of loans to the fall in the oil price. Moreover, it is unlikely that the Mexican agreement will yield the kind of result the Baker plan contemplated, i.e. a spur to economic growth. In its overall approach, the loan package may very well serve as compensatory financing for the collapse of Mexico's oil revenues, by about 9 billion US dollars in 1986 alone.

Confronted with the disappointing results of the Baker strategy, several experts now argue that the plan of the US Treasury Secretary should be blended with the ideas of US Senator Bill Bradley, who, earlier this year, proposed to cut debt-servicing costs by a substantial reduction in interest rates and to write off part of the existing debt. Such a blend would at least partially justify initial criticism of the Baker plan. Right at the inception of the plan, critics argued that it would probably improve the servicing capacity of those countries burdened by huge debts, but that only a lowering of interest rates and freer access to the markets of the Western industrialized countries would spur growth in the debtor countries.

THE NEED FOR CLOSER CO-OPERATION

The Quest for Co-ordination

Tensions in the world economy may ease if next year brings faster economic growth, and if the recent fall in the value of the US dollar is reflected in the US current account deficit. Even then, quarrels over trade, exchange rates, developing country debt and other economic matters will not stop, unless the world's most important economic powers suddenly find an ideal scheme for closer co-ordination of their macro-economic policies. This, however, seems highly unlikely.

The 22 September 1985 Plaza agreement, made possible by an abrupt change in the international economic policy of the United States, was an unexpected outburst of co-operative spirit on the part of the world's five leading industrialized nations. Now, however, more than a year later, one has to recognize that the Plaza agreement was indeed an outburst, and that little progress has since been made towards closer co-ordination of economic policies.

At the Tokyo economic summit in May of this year, the United States, Japan, the Federal Republic of Germany, France, the United Kingdom, Italy and Canada underwrote efforts within the IMF to develop improved mechanisms through which they could monitor their economic performance and try to agree upon complementary economic policies. This co-ordination would be ensured by a close multilateral surveillance of the evolution of ten "objective indicators" which each country undertook to submit to the IMF. These ten indicators are: GNP growth rate, inflation rate, 3-month interest rate, unemployment rate, fiscal deficit, current account and trade balance, monetary growth, exchange rate, foreign exchange reserves, and savings ratio. During the annual meetings of the IMF and the World Bank in Washington at the end of September, participants once again endorsed the need for closer co-ordination and encouraged the IMF to continue its study of "objective indicators". Few experts dared to admit, however, that this particular exercise has very little chance of succeeding.

The indicators have many drawbacks, which make symmetry and objective evaluation practically unattainable. Should the indicators be forecasts or targets? And why should the figures submitted by a national government be accorded any special status compared with the views of sceptical outsiders? Furthermore, many of the indicators are beyond the power of governments to determine, certainly by conventional instruments of financial policy. Moreover, the indicators are technically "overdetermined", i.e. not free to vary independently. A suggested breakdown of the indicators between policy instruments, intermediate objectives and policy goals is also controversial, because the distinctions will depend on the economic strategy and implicit economic model followed by the government concerned.

Even if the IMF should prove to be capable of gathering objective indicators and, with the help of those indicators, to make previsions and evaluate the consequences of the mixing of policies, that would still leave the problem of the actual implementation of measures and adjustment of policies in conformity with the IMF surveillance. In the final analysis, successful international co-ordination of economic policies depends on the political will of the individual governments to subordinate their policies to co-ordination. However, the recent exchanges between the world's most important industrialized nations are still a far cry from such a policy consensus.

The Uruguay GATT Round

After a preparatory committee had spent six months trying to draw up a workable agenda, officials from GATT's 92 member countries, at the beginning of September, engaged in 30 frantic hours of non-stop discussions at the seaside resort of Punta del Este in Uruguay, to launch the eighth round of talks on the General Agreement on Tariffs and Trade. Two crucial compromises, ending disputes which had defied the preparatory committee in Geneva for six months, opened the way for trade ministers to launch the "Uruguay Round" of trade talks.

The first compromise was forced upon the European Community by the United States and a group of 14 "freetrading" farm exporting countries led by Australia. Trade negotiators will, for the first time, be empowered to examine domestic farm support programmes and export subsidies which have so damaged poorer nations and undermined free trade in agricultural products.

Mr. Clayton Yeutter, US Trade Representative, and the Australians sought a clear commitment to negotiate the phasing out of export subsidies over a set period. In the end, the convoluted language did not pinpoint the EC's export subsidies, but opened the way for them to be tackled in the negotiations, along with "other measures" affecting agricultural trade. No timetable was mentioned except for the four-year deadline for the round as a whole, but a "phased reduction" of the "negative effects" of the subsidies and other distorting measures is to be achieved.

The second compromise resolved a protracted battle between the United States and a caucus of developing countries headed by Brazil and India. Trade negotiators will attempt to frame rules to prevent a proliferation of import barriers to service transactions (insurance, tele-communications, banking etc.) on which richer countries depend increasingly to balance their external accounts.

During the September conference, developing countries, afraid of their service sectors being swamped by foreign competitors, aimed to avoid a situation in which they could be forced to trade off concessions on services for advantages in their exports of goods. The solution turned out to be a hybrid. The ministers, as GATT signatories, declared the start of a new round to deal with trade in goods, and as sovereign governments, they set in motion parallel talks on services.

The September conference of trade ministers was a big success in several respects. The agenda for the "Uruguay Round" is the broadest in the GATT's history, and has all the marks of positive consensus, not merely of defensive compromise. Moreover, the result was achieved without voting and without abstentions among leaders of developing nations, thus preventing a North-South polarization.

Restoring the regulatory powers of the GATT by rewriting the rules and negotiating mutual concessions which will liberalize trade will be a painful and protracted struggle. However, the zeal with which trade ministers worked on the completion of a very comprehensive agenda, at the meeting in Punta del Este at the beginning of September, suggests that the political will is not lacking to make the "Uruguay Round" a success.

NOTES

1. "J-curve" effect. The phenomenon whereby the initial consequence of currency depreciation is a deterioration in the current account as the terms of trade worsen, and conversely for an appreciation. It is only gradually that the impact of the change in relative prices generates real supply and demand responses, which, assuming that the elasticities involved are sufficiently large, gradually outweigh the price effects.

2. Benjamin M. Friedman, "The Gramm-Rudman Sham Has Gone Far Enough", International Herald Tribune, 17 October 1986.

Table 2.1 GROWTH OF REAL GDP/GNP IN THE OECD AREA [a)]

(percentage changes from previous period, seasonally adjusted at annual rates)

	Changes from previous year				1982 shares in total
	1984	1985	1986	1987	OECD
Alliance countries					
Belgium	1.3	1.1	1.75	1.5	1.1
Canada	5.0	4.5	3.75	3.25	3.8
Denmark	3.5	3.1	2.5	2.5	0.7
France	1.5	1.2	2.5	2.5	7.0
Germany	3.0	2.4	3.5	3.0	8.0
Greece	2.6	1.7	0.0	0.0	0.5
Iceland	2.5	2.8	3.0	2.25	0
Italy	2.8	2.3	2.75	2.75	4.5
Luxembourg	4.9	1.9	2.0	2.25	0
Netherlands	1.8	2.0	1.5	0.75	1.8
Norway	5.6	4.4	4.25	2.25	0.7
Portugal	-1.5	2.8	3.75	3.75	0.3
Spain	2.2	2.1	3.0	3.0	2.4
Turkey	5.9	4.9	4.75	5.0	0.7
United Kingdom	2.8	3.2	3.0	2.25	6.3
United States	6.6	2.2	3.0	3.75	41.1
Japan	5.1	4.6	3.25	3.0	14.2
Total OECD	4.8	2.8	3.0	3.25	100.0
OECD Europe	2.6	2.4	2.75	2.5	38.5

a) Aggregates were computed on the basis of 1982 exchange rates

Source: OECD, July 1986

Table 2.2 INFLATION IN THE OECD AREA [a)]

(Percentage changes from previous period, seasonally adjusted at annual rates)

	1985	1986	1987
Alliance countries			
Belgium	5.0	1.5	0.75
Canada	4.0	3.5	2.5
Denmark	4.7	3.25	2.0
France	5.5	2.75	2.0
Germany	2.0	0.0	0.25
Greece	18.9	20.5	12.5
Iceland [b)]	32.5	20.5	20.0
Italy	9.4	5.5	3.5
Luxembourg	4.1	1.5	0.75
Netherlands	2.3	-0.25	0.5
Norway	6.1	5.5	5.0
Portugal	19.8	13.5	10.5
Spain [b)]	8.3	8.0	5.5
Turkey	45.5	32.0	30.0
United Kingdom	5.4	4.0	3.75
United States	3.2	2.75	2.5
Japan	2.2	0.5	0.0
OECD Europe	7.3	5.0	4.75
Total OECD	4.8	3.5	3.0

a) Aggregates were computed on the basis of 1982 GNP/GDP values expressed in 1982 US dollars

b) Consumer price index instead of national accounts implicit private consumption deflator

Source: OECD, July 1986

Table 2.3 CURRENT BALANCES OF OECD COUNTRIES

($ billion : seasonally adjusted, at annual rates)

	1984	1985	1986	1987
Alliance countries				
Belgium - Luxembourg	0.0	0.1	3.25	3.5
Canada	2.0	-1.9	-5.25	-3.0
Denmark	-1.6	-2.6	-2.5	-1.75
France	-0.8	0.3	7.5	5.5
Germany	6.3	13.1	28.5	21.75
Greece	-2.1	-3.3	-1.5	-1.25
Iceland	-0.1	-0.1	0.0	0.0
Italy	-3.0	-4.1	4.0	3.25
Netherlands	4.8	5.9	8.5	7.5
Norway	3.2	3.0	-3.0	-4.75
Portugal	-0.6	0.3	0.5	0.0
Spain	2.4	3.0	5.0	3.75
Turkey	-1.4	-1.0	-0.75	-1.0
United Kingdom	1.2	3.8	4.0	-0.75
United States	-107.4	-117.7	-132.0	-124.75
Japan	35.0	49.3	76.5	70.75
Total OECD	-69.0	-59.2	-8.25	-22.5
EC	5.6	16.0	57.25	41.0

Source: OECD, July 1986

Table 2.4 TRADE BALANCES OF OECD COUNTRIES

(Seasonally adjusted, $ billion)

	1984	1985	1986	1987
Belgium-Luxembourg	0.2	0.4	3.5	4.0
Canada	16.6	12.6	10.0	12.75
Denmark	-0.2	-0.8	0.0	0.25
France	-4.1	-4.6	2.75	1.5
Germany	23.3	29.1	49.5	47.25
Greece	-4.2	-5.0	-3.5	-3.25
Iceland	0.0	0.0	0.0	0.0
Italy	-6.1	-7.0	0.25	0.25
Netherlands	5.5	5.5	8.25	7.0
Norway	5.1	4.8	-0.5	-1.75
Portugal	-2.1	-1.3	-1.5	-2.0
Spain	-4.0	-4.0	-2.0	-2.75
Turkey	-2.9	-3.0	-3.5	-4.0
United Kingdom	-5.8	-2.7	-4.25	-9.75
United States	-114.1	-124.3	-138.25	-130.25
Japan	44.3	56.0	84.75	80.75
Total OECD	-48.9	-44.4	11.0	7.25
EC	2.6	9.9	53.75	43.5

Source: OECD, May 1986

Table 2.5 UNEMPLOYMENT IN THE OECD AREA

(National Definitions in %)

	1984	1985	1986	1987
Unemployment rates				
Alliance countries:				
Belgium	14.0	13.1	13.0	12.75
Canada	11.3	10.5	9.5	9.5
Denmark	10.0	8.9	8.5	8.75
France	9.9	10.2	10.25	10.25
Germany	8.2	8.3	8.0	7.25
Greece	8.0	8.3	8.75	9.25
Iceland	1.3	1.1	1.0	1.0
Italy	10.3	10.6	11.0	11.5
Luxembourg	1.7	1.6	1.5	1.5
Netherlands	15.4	14.4	14.0	14.25
Norway	3.0	2.5	2.0	2.25
Portugal	10.5	10.2	10.25	9.75
Spain	20.6	21.9	21.75	21.25
Turkey	12.4	13.1	13.5	13.75
United Kingdom	11.7	11.9	12.0	11.75
United States	7.5	7.2	7.0	6.75
Japan	2.7	2.6	2.75	3.0
OECD Europe	10.8	11.0	11.0	11.0
Total OECD	8.4	8.3	8.25	8.25
Unemployment levels (millions)				
North America	9.9	9.6	9.5	9.25
OECD Europe	18.4	18.9	19.0	19.0
Total OECD	30.6	30.8	31.0	31.0

Source: OECD, July 1986

Table 2.6 YOUTH UNEMPLOYMENT IN SELECTED OECD COUNTRIES+

(Per cent of total youth labour force)

	Actual					Forecast	
	1981	1982	1983	1984	1985	1986	1987
Youth unemployment rates[a]							
U.S.	14.3	17.0	16.4	13.3	13.0	12.5	12.0
Japan	4.0	4.3	4.5	4.9	4.8	5.5	6.0
Germany[b]	6.5	9.5	10.7	9.9	9.5	8.25	7.0
France[c]	17.0	19.0	19.7	24.4	25.6	25.75	26.5
U.K.[d]	18.1	23.1	23.2	21.8	21.7	21.75	20.75
Italy	27.4	29.7	32.0	33.4	31.7	35.5	37.0
Canada	13.3	18.7	19.9	17.9	16.5	14.75	15.25
Total	13.7	16.4	16.6	15.4	15.3	15.0	14.75
Four European countries	16.5	19.7	20.9	21.6	21.7	21.5	21.25
Australia[e]	10.8	12.9	17.9	16.1	14.3	12.75	12.5
Finland	9.7	10.5	11.3	10.4	9.1	9.5	9.5
Norway	5.8	8.1	9.7	7.6	6.8	5.0	5.75
Spain[f]	33.7	36.9	38.9	44.5	44.1	43.25	42.5
Sweden	6.3	7.6	8.0	6.0	5.8	6.0	6.25
Total of twelve countries[g]	14.5	17.2	17.7	16.8	16.6	16.25	16.0

\+ no data available for the other Alliance countries

(Continued)

Table 2.6 (Cont.)

	Actual					Forecast	
	1981	1982	1983	1984	1985	1986	1987
Youth unemployment levels (millions)							
Seven major countries	7.7	9.2	9.2	8.5	8.4	8.25	8.0
Four European countries	3.3	4.0	4.2	4.3	4.4	4.25	4.25
Twelve countries	9.1	10.7	10.9	10.4	10.2	10.0	9.75

a) The term "youth" generally refers to the 15-24 age group with a few exceptions: the age group is 14-24 in Italy and 16-24 in the United States, United Kingdom, Norway, Spain and Sweden. Data refer to the total youth labour force in all countries except Canada and Australia where the armed forces are excluded from the youth labour force. Data for the United States, Japan, Canada, Finland and Sweden are the average of monthly figures while data for Italy and Norway are averages of quarterly data.

b) Unemployment figures refer to the registered unemployed at the end of September of each year. Labour force figures are annual averages based on various national sources including the microcensus.

c) Data refer to March of each year except 1982 when the data refer to April-May. Conscripts are included in the labour force aged 15-24.

d) Unemployment figures relate to July each year and are based on registrations up to 1982 and claimants from 1983 on. The figures for 1983 and later include non-claimant school leavers registered at Careers

Offices. Labour force data are estimated from several sources including the EEC Labour Force Sample Survey and refer to June of each year.

e) Data refer to August of each year.

f) Data refer to the last quarter of each year.

g) These countries accounted for about 85 per cent of the youth labour force in the OECD area in 1979.

Source: OECD, 1986
Data for almost all countries are from household surveys. The sole exceptions are Germany and the United Kingdom where the data come from both registration and household survey sources.

Table 2.7 INTEREST RATE DEVELOPMENTS IN SELECTED OECD COUNTRIES

	1983	1984	1985	1986[a]	1987[a]
Short term rates					
United States	8.61	9.52	7.48	6.10	5.50
Japan	6.39	6.07	6.47	4.60	3.75
Germany	5.78	5.99	5.44	3.96	3.71
France	12.54	11.74	9.94	7.25	5.60
United Kingdom	9.59	9.30	11.56	10.25	8.75
Italy	18.31	17.26	15.26	11.50	8.25
Canada	9.45	11.19	9.56	8.91	6.50
Long term rates					
United States	12.04	12.71	11.37	8.78	8.00
Japan	7.52	7.08	6.78	5.60	4.75
Germany	7.97	7.79	6.94	5.64	5.24
France	14.36	13.41	11.87	8.60	7.25
United Kingdom	10.81	10.69	10.62	10.60	9.55
Italy	18.52	15.09	13.12	10.50	8.50
Canada	11.79	12.75	11.04	9.71	8.40

a) OECD projections

Source: OECD, May 1986

Table 2.8 VALUE OF WORLD MERCHANDISE TRADE 1985

(in billions of dollars and percentages;
by main areas)

	EXPORTS (f.o.b.)			IMPORTS (c.i.f.)		
	Value	Change over previous year		Value	Change over previous year	
	1985	1984	1985	1985	1984	1985
WORLD TRADE	1,922	5½	1	2,000	5½	1
Developed countries	1,275	6½	3½	1,375	8½	2
Developing areas	440	4	- 5½	410	-1½	-6½
- Fuels	195	-4½	-10½	68	-6	-8½
- Other products	245	13	- 1	342	-0	-6
Eastern trading area	207	3	- 1½	215	4	9½

Source: GATT, 1986

Table 2.9 REGIONAL COMPOSITION OF WORLD MERCHANDISE TRADE

(% shares in the value of world exports and imports)

	Total trade			Trade excluding fuels		
	1963	1973	1985	1963	1973	1985
Developed countries						
-Exports	67½	71	66½	72	77	75
-Imports	67½	72	68½	66½	71	68
Developing areas						
-Exports	20½	19	23	16	13	15½
-Imports	21	18	20½	21½	18½	21
Eastern trading area						
-Exports	12	10	10½	12	10	9½
-Imports	11½	10	11	12	10½	11

Source: GATT, 1986

Table 2.10 ANNUAL RATES OF CHANGE AND ANNUAL RATES OF SWING IN COMMODITY PRICES
(Percentage)

	Change		Swing
	1978-1980 (1)	1980-1984 (2)	1980-1984 (3) = (2)-(1)
Non-oil commodity export prices	13.9	-4.2	-18.1
By commodity group:			
-Food	14.6	-7.4	-22.0
-Agricultural raw materials	12.5	-2.0	-14.5
-Minerals	15.8	2.3	-13.5
-Metals	21.5	-7.0	-28.5
By country group:			
-Developed market-economy countries (b)	14.2	-4.1	-18.3
-Developing countries	13.8	-4.6	-18.4
Crude petroleum export prices (a)	58.8	-2.4	-61.2
Non-oil commodity import prices of developed market-economy countries (c)	18.1	5.8	-12.3

(a) in terms of US dollars
(b) OECD countries
(c) in terms of national currencies

Source: Unctad Trade and Development Report, 1986

Table 2.11 DEVELOPING COUNTRIES' ECONOMIC PERFORMANCE

	1982	1983	1984	1985
GDP growth (%)	2.0	2.0	5.4	4.3
Export volume growth (%)	-0.5	4.7	10.7	2.3
Current account deficit ($bn)				
-Oil importers	64.6	41.4	32.2	35.0
-Oil exporters	35.8	11.0	1.9	5.5
Total medium and long term debt outstanding ($bn)				
-Oil importers	378.2	421.7	450.9	484.7
-Oil exporters	173.8	209.9	224.7	226.5

NB Years refer to fiscal year ending on June 30

Source: World Bank, 1986

Table 2.12 OFFICIAL DEVELOPMENT ASSISTANCE (ODA) PERFORMANCE OF ALLIANCE COUNTRIES IN RECENT YEARS+

	$ million		% of GNP		Annual growth rates of ODA 1979/80 - 1984/85
	1984 actual	1985 actual	1984 (a)	1985	
Belgium	442	430	0.57	0.53	1.1
Canada	1,625	1,638	0.50	0.49	4.3
Denmark	449	440	0.85	0.80	4.3
France					
(incl.DOM/TOM)	3,788	4,022	0.77	0.79	5.7(b)
(excl.DOM/TOM)	2,552	2,768	0.52	0.54	10.1
Germany	2,782	2,935	0.45	0.47	1.2(b)
Italy	1,133	1,099	0.33	0.31	21.0
Netherlands	1,268	1,135	1.02	0.91	0.8
Norway	543	555	1.03	1.00	4.5
U.K.	1,430	1,531	0.33	0.34	-3.7
U.S.	8,711	9,555	0.24	0.24	3.3
Total DAC Countries	28,743	29,580	0.36	0.35	3.6

+ no data available for the other Alliance countries

a. Figures are influenced downward, with the exception of the United States, by the appreciation of the dollar in 1985.

b. To maintain statistical comparability, the growth rates exclude the recent inclusions in aid statistics of imputed student costs.

Source: OECD, June 1986

Table 2.13 DEFENCE EXPENDITURES AS PERCENTAGE OF GROSS DOMESTIC PRODUCT IN PURCHASERS' VALUES

Country	Average 1974-84	1980	1981	1982	1983	1984	1985 (e)
Belgium	3.3	3.4	3.5	3.4	3.3	3.2	3.3
Denmark	2.4	2.4	2.5	2.5	2.4	2.3	2.3
France (a)	4.0	4.0	4.2	4.1	4.2	4.1	4.1
Germany (b)	3.4	3.3	3.4	3.4	3.4	3.3	3.3
Greece	6.6	5.7	7.0	6.9	6.3	7.2	7.1
Italy	2.5	2.4	2.5	2.6	2.7	2.7	2.7
Luxembourg	1.1	1.2	1.2	1.2	1.2	1.2	1.2
Netherlands	3.2	3.1	3.2	3.2	3.2	3.2	3.1
Norway	3.0	2.9	2.9	3.0	3.1	2.8	3.2
Portugal	3.6	3.5	3.5	3.4	3.4	3.3	3.2
Turkey	5.0	4.3	4.9	5.2	4.8	4.4	4.4
U.K.	4.9	5.0	4.8	5.0	5.3	5.3	5.4
NATO Europe	3.7	3.7	3.8	3.8	3.8	3.8	3.8
Canada	1.9	1.8	1.8	2.1	2.0	2.2	2.2
U.S.	5.9	5.5	5.8	6.4	6.6	6.5	6.9
Total NATO	4.7	4.4	4.7	5.1	5.3	5.3	5.6

(a) France is a member of the Alliance without belonging to the integrated military structure; the relevant figures are indicative only.

(b) These percentages have been calculated without taking into account the expenditures on Berlin; if these expenses were included, the percentages would be as follows:

1980: 4.1 1982: 4.3 1984: 4.1
1981: 4.3 1983: 4.2 1985: 4.1

(e) Estimate

Source: NATO, 1986

3

Alliance Security and the Military Balance

Jules de Waart

INTRODUCTION

This year the Committee's General Report reverts to the traditional practice of presenting an overview of Alliance security developments for the year. This follows last year's special report of the Military Committee which focussed exclusively on the compliance and verification aspects of arms control. It was a most useful contribution to the work of the Assembly, and my predecessor deserves the Committee's highest commendation.

In chapter one of the report, an attempt is made to illuminate some of the key developments affecting the NATO-Warsaw Pact military balance in the categories of conventional, chemical, theatre nuclear and strategic nuclear forces. Special attention is focussed on the debate which has taken place in the Alliance during 1986 on the proposed US modernization of its chemical weapons stockpile.

Because the Assembly's Special Committee on Nuclear Strategy and Arms Control has devoted special attention to the Geneva Nuclear and Space Negotiations, as well as to the implications for the Alliance of the Strategic Defense Initiative (SDI), your Rapporteur has purposely limited his comments on these two important aspects of arms control. Developments in the MBFR, CDE and chemical disarmament negotiations are discussed in turn. In addition some comments are offered on the debate about the future of SALT II following President Reagan's May 27 announcement that the US intends to breach its numerical limits, as well as the discussion proceeding in the United States about the future of mobile intercontinental ballistic missiles (ICBMs).

Nuclear testing has once again emerged as a major issue in East-West relations following Soviet leader Mikhail Gorbachev's moratorium initiative and his sustained campaign for a comprehensive nuclear test ban. For this reason your Rapporteur considered it appropriate to examine some of the salient issues involved in this debate in a special chapter.

The final chapter of the report addresses the question of ATBMs, which is beginning to emerge as a major Alliance issue.

THE NATO-WARSAW PACT MILITARY BALANCE

Ascertaining an accurate picture of the military balance between NATO and the Warsaw Pact involves a detailed comparison of many quantitative and qualitative factors. This task is rendered extraordinarily difficult and complex due to the asymmetrical nature of the armed forces of the two sides. From the outset, therefore, it is important to keep in mind that no single measurement can possibly give a comprehensive and accurate representation of the military balance between the two alliances. Comparing quantitative factors such as manpower and equipment is relatively straightforward, but even this exercise can be unexpectedly difficult. In addition to static indicators, a number of dynamic measures bear significantly upon the relative effectiveness of the forces. For example, an assessment of how NATO and Warsaw Pact forces would compare in combat requires consideration of such important variables as morale, training, military strategy, organization, political cohesion and military technology. Other intangible factors in this context include reinforcement potential, readiness and logistical support. A much neglected, but increasingly important, variable is electronic warfare capabilities.

This chapter will confine itself to a static assessment of the military capabilities and trends in the two alliances. Four categories of military capabilities - conventional, chemical, theatre nuclear, and strategic nuclear - will be addressed in detail, and some additional comments will be made about the nature of electronic warfare.

Conventional Forces

Since there will be no NATO-Warsaw Pact Force Comparison published for 1986 (heretofore produced every two years, the last one in 1984) this year's assessment of the conventional force balance is based on data contained in the 1986 edition of Soviet Military Power, which is produced annually by the US Department of Defense.

It should be pointed out that this year's edition of Soviet Military Power employs significantly different criteria to that used in previous editions and also that used in the compilation of Force Comparisons. US Department of Defense officials contend that by utilizing US counting rules and performance criteria one ascertains a more accurate global picture of the Soviet threat.

This new calculation does, however, produce certain anomalies when one compares specific categories and levels of forces with previous years' estimates. For example, the number of Warsaw Pact combat aircraft in place and rapidly deployable appears to have decreased some 33% from the 7,430 aircraft figure quoted in last year's Force Comparisons to the 4,970 listed in Soviet Military Power. This is because NATO, in its 1984 report, counted all aircraft west of the Urals in place and rapidly deployable while the US 1986 report counts only those aircraft in Eastern Europe up to the Soviet border as in place and rapidly deployable.

Similarly the numbers of Warsaw Pact armoured personnel carriers and fighting vehicles shows a significant reduction from those cited in the NATO 1984 report. Again, different data bases account for the differential. The NATO count included armoured command vehicles and other non-fighting carriers while the 1986 US report counts only armoured fighting vehicles west of the Urals.[1]

It is therefore important to bear in mind that any assessment of the conventional balance between NATO and the Warsaw Pact must be set in the wider political and strategic context of the balance of worldwide force deployments, the reinforcement potential of the respective sides and the relative strengths of the respective navies and long-range tactical and support air forces.

In response, NATO has continued to modernize its air forces with the introduction of F-15, F-16 and the Tornado aircraft, which have ensured that it maintains a qualitative superiority in terms of training and weapons systems. It should be pointed out that the F-15 Eagle has many more performance advantages over the MIG-23 than the F-4 has over the MIG-21.

Indeed it is almost certainly the case that the F-15 is the best all-round fighter on either side of the East-West divide. The F-16, which is operated by the United States, Belgium and the Netherlands, has comparable capabilities to the F-15 in terms of dogfighting, using guns and heat-seeking Sidewinder missiles. The F-15, however, has the added advantage of being able to fire radar-guided munitions much more effectively.

Though NATO has far fewer numbers of combat aircraft overall than the Warsaw Pact, training of both aircrews and groundcrews is vastly superior on the Western side. In recent years the total number of Pact tactical combat aircraft has been falling (although still well outnumbering NATO's force), but their quality has increased markedly. Many experts insist that the new MIG-29 and SU-27 (designated respectively Fulcrum and Flanker by NATO) are almost the equal of new NATO fighters in important respects. Equipped with true lookdown/shootdown radar, they carry both the beyond-visual-range AA-10 and the short-range AA-11 air-to-air missiles.

The Pact's defences are an impressive array of interceptors, air-combat aircraft, as well as artillery and surface-to-air missiles. These systems ensure that NATO aircraft would have to operate in an increasingly hostile environment. The Soviet Union, since the 1950s, has made enormous investments in a wide array of defence capabilities and it now maintains the world's most extensive early warning system for air defence. A network of ground-based radars is linked operationally with those of the Warsaw Pact allies. The US Department of Defense estimates the total number of air defence radars on the Warsaw Pact side as standing at 10,000. It also estimates that the Soviet Union and its allies have approximately 9,000 strategic SAM launchers and over 4,000 tactical SAM launchers. Tactical SAMs are designed to counter low-altitude threats and are inherently mobile. They are principally designed to move with the front and organic elements of combined arms formations.

The principal elements of the air defence system on NATO's side include the land-based radar system NADGE (NATO Air Defence Ground Environment); the anti-aircraft missiles; AWACS capabilities; and the fighters. The NADGE system was developed in the 1960s and is composed of a belt which stretches from northern Norway to Turkey. The French ground-radar system, STRIDA, is closely tied into it.

In NATO there are two belts of anti-aircraft systems: one a medium-range (approximately 25 miles) capability equipped with conventionally armed Hawk missiles, complete with radars; the other composed of several dozen Nike Hercules long-range batteries. Most Nikes have nuclear warheads, but these are gradually being phased out in favour of the mobile, conventionally-armed Patriot system. The Federal Republic has agreed to deploy these new missiles under an arrangement with the United States, and it is likely that the Netherlands and Belgium will conclude similar deals.

In addition to these two missile belts all the main NATO armies are in possession of short-range missile defences to cover key military troop installations.

Naval Forces

Since 1971, the Pact navies have made both numerical increases and qualitative improvements. Qualitative improvements are particularly noticeable in the large number of new classes of surface vessels and submarines. Included in these are the first nuclear-powered 25,000 ton guided-missile cruisers of the Kirov-class and the Kiev-class V/STOL aircraft carrier which facilitates the deployment of sea-based fixed-wing aircraft. The 37,000 ton Kiev-class carrier is the largest operational ship in the Soviet navy's inventory and is, in fact, the first modern Soviet-built ship designed to carry fixed-wing aircraft. According to Soviet Military Power, four such vessels have been constructed to date and the last one is currently in the process of being fitted out.

Two guided-missile destroyer construction programmes continued during the last year. The fifth Sovremennyy-class guided-missile destroyer began sea trials in August 1985, and there are believed to be five more in the pipeline. The Sovremennyy is designed for anti-surface warfare and is particularly useful for cruise-missile housing. The Udaloy-class guided-missile destroyer will carry eight long-range cruise missile-delivered ASW weapons. Two more _Udaloys_ came into service during 1985, bringing the active total to seven. In the last three years, the Soviet navy has introduced higher performance submarines: the _Oscar_-, _Typhoon_- and new _Akula_-class.

Qualitative improvements by NATO have taken place in the following areas: shipborne aircraft, command and control detection systems for anti-submarine warfare, and submarine noise suppression. Other notable acquisitions include the introduction of the _Ohio_-class submarine and the Trident missile system.

A comparison of NATO and Pact naval forces indicates that NATO is strong in the sea-based tactical air category, land-based ASW/surveillance patrol aircraft, anti-submarine systems, long-range and amphibious forces. The Pact on the other hand is notably strong in submarines, mine warfare, torpedo attack submarines, land-based attack aircraft and anti-ship missile-equipped ships. The Pact has the geographical disadvantage associated with choke points and long access routes from Murmansk. Despite this, it is undeniably the case that the Soviet Union possesses a global naval capability which is increasingly calling into question NATO's traditional ability to secure vital shipping lanes. As the last _Force Comparison_ study concluded: "NATO does not have the numerical advantage necessary for a satisfactory or safe balance of maritime forces."

Electronic Warfare Capabilities

Admiral Gorshkov's much quoted statement that "the next war will be won by the side that best exploits the electro-magnetic spectrum" reminds us that electronic warfare (EW) capabilities need to be factored into any equation about the balance of forces between East and West. Increasingly, EW is becoming a primary battlefield preoccupation as countries in both East and West come to recognize its force multiplication potential.

It is not the intention of this Rapporteur to discuss in depth the precise balance between Eastern and Western EW capabilities. An accurate assessment in today's complex and fluid technological environment would be a practical impossibility. The intention here is merely to draw attention to an increasingly important (perhaps decisive) variable which is managing to change the whole spectrum of modern warfare with bewildering speed. It is hoped that the Military Committee of the North Atlantic Assembly will place greater emphasis on EW in its work over the coming years.

What is EW? According to the US Department of Defense, EW comprises three divisions: electronic countermeasures (ECM); electronic counter-countermeasures (ECCM); and electronic-warfare support measures (EWSM). Respectively, these three divisions mean, in layman's language: actions taken to reduce or prevent hostile use of the electro-magnetic spectrum; actions taken to ensure friendly use of the electro-magnetic spectrum; and actions taken to intercept, identify, analyze and locate hostile electro-magnetic emissions to support ECM and ECCM.[2] It should be pointed out that NATO's EW definitions are broadly consistent with those of the United States. An overall definition for EW might therefore be the military employment of electro-magnetic energy designed to exploit the battlefield environment in full.

We know from Soviet military literature and from observance of their military exercises that electronic warfare, known as radio-electronic combat (REC) or *Maskirovka* in Russian, is a central component in Soviet modern warfare concepts. It is understood that the Soviet Union has three divisions similar to those of NATO and the United States, but these are supplemented by a fourth category, which is referred to by some analysts as physical countermeasures (PCM) - the physical destruction of NATO emitters and ECM equipment.

The Soviets reportedly train their REC troops on a constant and systematic basis. According to Soviet military literature one such training exercise for REC troops is know as "fox hunting"; this bears a striking resemblance to a training activity in the US forces called a "transmitter hunt".

Throughout NATO the ever-growing dependence on the electro-magnetic spectrum to provide the means for effective communications, target detection and weapons guidance is now universally recognized and appreciated. The diversity and scope of the electronic warfare challenges to NATO are vast. EW systems are essential to protect platforms for tactical aircraft, helicopters, ships, tanks, infantry and manpower. Moreover, they all require countermeasures to warn of attack, decoy capabilities to mitigate threats, as well as anti-radiation missiles to destroy the emitters that guide incoming missiles.

The sheer quantity of the weapons in NATO's threat inventory against which EW needs to be deployed is bewildering. According to one analyst, in the central region of Europe NATO faces 2,000 hostile air-to-air fighters, over 4,000 enemy radar-and-electro-optically-directed surface-to-air missile systems and upwards of 7,000 infrared-seeking missiles[3].

As a direct response to this awesome challenge, NATO established in March 1984 the Multi-Service Electronic Warfare Support Group (MEWSG), the main operating base of which is in southwest England. The MEWSG's mission is "to provide a realistic, hostile electro-magnetic environment in which NATO forces can conduct training and exercise their units in all aspects of warfare."

The training unit was established as part of NATO's Long-Term Defence Programme in 1977 and its original mandate was only for maritime units. It subsequently enlarged to provide a base for other services.

In June of this year NATO announced that agreement had been reached on the development of Phase IIA of MEWSG, which involves the joint financing and purchasing of three jet aircraft to train Allied military personnel in electronic warfare in the 1990s. Training includes activities such as jamming and missile simulation in land and naval exercises.

Conclusion

The Supreme Allied Commander of NATO, General Bernard Rogers, in a recent article[4] has alluded once more to "the widening gap" between NATO and Warsaw Pact conventional capabilities, a gap, he insists, "which grows wider each year". Despite improvements to NATO's conventional force posture in recent years, General Rogers does not believe that it "provides our nations with adequate deterrence against non-nuclear intimidation and aggression by the Warsaw Pact. If attacked today, NATO would be forced fairly quickly to decide whether it should escalate to the non-strategic nuclear level."

SACEUR points primarily to NATO's shortage of trained replacements, ammunitions and theatre war reserve stocks of repair parts and major equipment items as the reason for the excessive reliance on nuclear weapons. He identifies three priority tasks to rectify NATO's conventional deficiencies: the need to enhance sustainability; the need to continue to modernize weapons systems; and the need to add to force structure, primarily with trained mobilizable reserves.

General Rogers' insistence that a widening gap in conventional capabilities continues is not supported by everyone. For example, the widely respected International Institute for Strategic Studies (IISS) concludes in its 1985-1986 assessment that the "numerical balance, although genuinely in favour of the Warsaw Pact (particularly in equipment) appears to have stabilized over the past year." The IISS extrapolates from its overall assessment that the conventional balance in Europe is still such as to make general military aggression a highly risky undertaking for either side. It adds that

> "though possession of the initiative in war will always permit an aggressor to achieve a local advantage in numbers sufficient to allow him to believe that he might achieve limited tactical successes in some areas, there would still appear to be insufficient overall strength on either side to guarantee victory. The consequences for an attacker would still be quite unpredictable, and the risks, particularly of nuclear escalation, incalculable."

Table 3.1 NATO-WARSAW PACT AIR FORCES *

	NATO	WARSAW PACT
AIRCRAFT		
Fighter bomber ground attack	2,100	1,400
Interceptor ++	900	2,800
Reconnaissance	260	380
Bombers	-	390
Total Aircraft	3,360	4,970

(Continued)

Table 3.1 (Cont.)

* Soviet Military Power, p. 89. The figures represent US estimates of 1985 data.

++ Excludes strategic interceptors.

Table 3.2 FORCES IN PLACE IN EUROPE REINFORCED BY RAPIDLY DEPLOYABLE FORCES *

	NATO	WARSAW PACT
Military Manpower (including Naval Forces)	2,600,000	4,000,000
Division Equivalents	90	113
Main Battle Tanks	19,600	33,000
Anti-Tank Guided Weapon Launchers	13,370	18,000
Artillery/Mortars	14,200	18,600
Armoured Personnel Carriers and Fighting Vehicles	32,850	47,000
Attack Helicopters	650	900 +
Transport/Support Helicopters	1,960	1,850

* This table is based on Soviet Military Power (5th Edition 1986), p. 91. As they do not participate in NATO's integrated force structure, French and Spanish forces are not included in the NATO figures. The figures represent US estimates of 1985 data. Between them France and Spain have approximately 20 divisions, 2000 tanks, 3000 artillery/mortars, 1000 anti-tank launchers, 450 helicopters, 900 aircraft and 100 naval ships.

\+ Excludes transport helicopters that can be configured for attack roles.

Table 3.3 NATO AND WARSAW PACT MARITIME FORCES IN THE NORTH ATLANTIC AND SEAS BORDERING EUROPE **

	NATO	WARSAW PACT
Aircraft Carriers/V/STOL Carriers	10	-
Kiev-class Ships	-	1
Helicopter Carriers	6	2
Cruisers	16	21
Destroyers, Frigates, Corvettes	303	199
Amphibious Ships		
-Ocean-going	50	21
-Other Ships/Coastal Craft	69	181
Mine Warfare - Ships/Craft	264	360
Total Submarines (All Types)	209	265
-Ballistic Missile Submarines	35	47
-Long-Range Attack Submarines	70	150
-Other Types	104	68
-% Submarines Nuclear-Powered	50%	50%
Sea-Based Tactical ASW and Support Aircraft including Helicopters	831	145
Land-Based Tactical and Support Aircraft including Helicopters	379	575
Land-Based Anti-Submarine Warfare Fixed-Wing Aircraft and Helicopters	462	220

** *Soviet Military Power*, p. 90. The figures represent US estimates of 1985 data.

Chemical Weapons [5]

The Balance of Stocks

The Warsaw Pact's chemical warfare capability is generally believed to be in excess of that possessed by the United States. Soviet chemical stockpiles are variously estimated at anywhere between the low tens of thousands to the high hundreds of thousands of tons by US intelligence agencies. In 1980 the US Defense Secretary, Harold Brown, informed the US Congress that the different estimates which had been produced by US agencies varied by a factor of about 20; they ranged from a low estimate of 30,000 agent tons to one of several hundred thousand tons.

The latest British Government Defence White Paper puts the Soviet capability at about 300,000 tons. But estimates of the level of Soviet chemical weapons stockpile are notoriously unreliable; a few days after the British MOD figure first appeared in the 1982 White Paper on Defence, a senior Pentagon spokesman was informing Congress that the US DOD was incapable of putting a precise size on the stockpile.[6]

As far as the deployment of Soviet stocks is concerned, there are apparent differences within the US intelligence community. A 1985 Defense Intelligence Agency report asserts that the USSR has stationed CW weapons on the territories of its Warsaw Pact allies. This evidence is unconfirmed by other US agencies. In January of this year General Secretary Gorbachev denied the existence of Soviet CW outside of the Soviet Union.

A similar dispute has arisen between US agencies on the question of Soviet chemical weapons doctrine. There are known to be profound differences of opinion between different United States agencies on the potential Soviet threat to use chemical weapons against NATO forces in Europe. According to testimony presented to the US Congress in March 1985 (to a closed session of the House Appropriations Defense Sub-Committee, made public in early 1986), the Army Chief of Staff Gen. John A. Wickham, Jr. said that the CIA believes "there is less (Soviet) intention to use chemical weapons and therefore probably less of a threat." In classified briefings CIA analysts apparently reported that the Soviet military had cut back its reliance on chemical weapons on the grounds that there was little tactical advantage to be gained from initiating use of chemicals over conventional weapons if NATO forces were in possession of protective gear.

In contrast to the CIA assessment, the US Department of Defense concluded in a recent three-year study that the Soviet chemical weapons threat "is serious, (and) the potential for use is likely". The study was part of a major contract initiated in 1983 which was purposely designed to overcome Congressional opposition to the building of chemical weapons. The Deputy Assistant to the Secretary of Defense for chemical weapons, Thomas J. Welch, apparently authorized the contract in response to questions raised by sceptical Congressmen, as well as to a General Accounting Office report which was critical of the Pentagon's overall chemical weapons programme.

When one turns to the American CW stockpile (only France among other NATO countries possesses CW in modest quantities), one is on safer ground with one's estimates, although estimates are all they are. According to one expert[7] the current US stockpile amounts to some 30,500 tons of nerve and mustard gas; it is stored at eight principal locations in the United States, one location in the Federal Republic and on the Johnston Atoll in the Pacific. All of the American CW munitions were produced before 1969.

The U S Modernization Programme

The first point which needs to be made is that the United States has not produced chemical weapons for 17 years. Despite repeated requests by the Department of Defense as well as SACEUR, the US Congress consistently blocked attempts to re-open production plants during the 1970s and early 1980s. In December 1985, however, Congress granted conditional approval for new chemical weapons production. The Reagan Administration had requested funding for the production of new and safer "binary" weapons, including 155 mm shells and the "Bigeye" aerial bomb.

Congress, however, set two conditions to the legislation. One restricts the expenditure of funds appropriated for this purpose until 1 October 1986. The other stipulated that the expenditure (either on production facilities or on the munitions themselves) was contingent on the prior NATO approval of binary weapons as a "force goal". The key passages of the legislation referring to NATO consultation stated that the President must certify to Congress that the United States:

(a) has submitted to the North Atlantic Treaty Organization a force goal stating the requirement for modernization of the United States' proportional share of the NATO chemical deterrent with binary munitions, and said force goal has been formally adopted by the North Atlantic Council;

(b) has developed in co-ordination with the Supreme Allied Commander, Europe, a plan under which the United States' binary chemical munitions can be deployed under appropriate contingency plans to deter chemical weapons attacks against the United States and its Allies; and

(c) has consulted with other member nations of the North Atlantic Treaty Organization on that plan.

On 22 May the NATO Defence Planning Committee (DPC) in ministerial session adopted an agreement on CW as part of the US chapter of the NATO Force Goals for 1987-92. Although the NATO communiqué does not make any reference to any discussions about the CW programme, it is understood that the secret CW force goal invites the United States to modernize its chemical weapons stocks with binary munitions.

According to press reports at the time, there was no dissenting footnote attached to the binary force goal, but a majority of the Ministers who spoke at the meeting questioned the wisdom of resuming the manufacture of chemical weapons. Apparently the only countries fully supportive of the US plan were Canada, the Federal Republic of Germany and the United Kingdom.[8] There had been intense debates in most European parliaments in the weeks before the DPC Meeting and some legislatures passed resolutions opposing the binary modernization programme.

The following day in Washington the Chairman of the House Foreign Affairs Committee, Representative Dante Fascell, let it be known that he would lead a fight to revoke funds for the new chemical weapons on the grounds that the Administration had failed to comply with the Congressional mandate requiring prior approval by the North Atlantic Council. But on 29 July President Reagan in a letter to Congress certified that the three conditions imposed by Congress on the release of binary weapon production funds had been met. According to the White House spokesman, Mr. Larry Speakes, the DPC action "completes the established NATO procedure for adopting force goals in the Alliance." In response the House Foreign Affairs Committee produced a legal opinion which maintained that the President's certification did not meet the letter of the Congressional legislation.

Congressional opposition to the binary programme has also focussed on two other issues: (a) the nature of the agreement concluded between the Reagan Administration and the European Allies, notably the Federal Republic of Germany and (b) the nature of the chemical munitions themselves, both those on the ground in Europe and the new binary munitions being proposed by the Administration.

It is understood that President Reagan at the Tokyo Summit on May 4-6 reached a compromise with Chancellor Kohl in which the United States agreed to the withdrawal of all existing stockpiles of chemical weapons in Europe by 1992 in exchange for West German support for the binary programme. The Adminstration has said repeatedly that the new binary weapons will not be stationed in Europe, but in the United States. Under the Reagan-Kohl agreement Bonn has the right to refuse, even in times of crisis, the new binaries.

Chairman Fascell has stated that Congress "never intended that funding for the new binary weapons would lead to a unilateral abandonment of our chemical retaliatory capability." Indeed President Reagan's agreement to withdraw the old US CW stockpile in Europe without a clear assurance that the new binary stockpile would be allowed to take its place seems to be in direct contradiction with the 1986 Defense Authorization Act which states that:

> "It is the sense of Congress that existing unitary chemical munitions currently stored in the United States and in European member nations of NATO should be replaced by modern, safer binary chemical munitions."

Some NATO officials are known to have severe reservations about the unilateral withdrawal of the chemical deterrent in Europe and have suggested this may mean that the Alliance could be forced to resort to nuclear weapons even more quickly in the event of a surprise attack by the Warsaw Pact. There is also concern that in a crisis situation the dispatch of binary weapons to Europe may be a negative signal which could increase tensions further.

Congressional critics also question whether the proposed binary munitions have even been thoroughly tested to date, worry that they are more complicated to handle and fire, and insist that they are much bulkier and heavier to move than the existing unitary munitions. It sees the relative safety of binaries as essentially a peacetime asset which is purchased at the cost of usefulness in war. Particular criticism has been directed at the Department of Defense's Bigeye bomb programme. In June a highly critical report was released by the US General Accounting Office on the Bigeye programme which concluded that the munition was not ready for production and that the entire programme should be abandoned.

Underlying the debate about the issue of binaries lies the question of whether or not the existing unitary weapons are insufficient to meet the task assigned to them. Many sceptics inside and outside of the US Congress dispute the frequent claims made that the existing stocks are unsafe and obsolete. Indeed, on the admission of President Reagan's Chemical Warfare Review Commission, which released its report in June 1985, such claims are "exaggerated and inaccurate". The practical arrangements for getting binary weapons over to Europe have also been commented on. According to one expert (utilizing US DOD information) it would take 40 sorties of C-141B aircraft (the cargo aircraft used by the US Military Airlift Command for intercontinental shipments of ammunition) to move 20,000 155 mm binary projectiles into Europe and 19 sorties to move 1,000 Bigeyes. To get half of the total quantity envisioned by the Pentagon to Europe would take 1618 C-141B sorties. There are 270 C-141B aircraft in the US military arsenal.

This same expert states that because of the impracticality of airlifting binaries and in view of European insistence on veto rights on deployment, the US Government is becoming favourably disposed towards the option of using Maritime Prepositioning Ships outside of European territorial waters to house binary weapons.

At this time of writing the future of the binary programme is very unclear. On 13 August the House of Representatives voted to delay CW production by a further year and for a prohibition on the withdrawal of existing European chemical weapons "unless they are replaced with binary chemical munitions stationed on the soil of at least one European member nation of the North Atlantic Treaty Organization." By contrast the US Senate rejected an amendment to the Defense Authorization bill calling for a halt to Bigeye production and also rejected an amendment which would have invalidated President Reagan's July 29 certification.

The agreement reached in the Conference Committee represented an uneasy compromise between proponents and opponents of the binary programme. The ambiguous language adopted, together with the fact that the key outstanding issues have not yet been resolved, ensures that the debate is likely to continue through 1987.

Theatre Nuclear Forces

Theatre nuclear forces refer to those delivery systems capable of delivering nuclear weapons at a range less than intercontinental. They are further subdivided into short-range nuclear forces (SRF), having a range of less than 200 km, and intermediate-range nuclear forces (INF), having a range between 200 and 5000 km. Longer-range intermediate nuclear forces (LRINF) are considered to have a range between 1,800 and 5,000 km. INF and SRF consist of land-based missiles, aircraft and artillery.

Until quite recently the pace of modernization of LRINF has been considerably greater for the Pact than for NATO. By the middle of 1986 the Warsaw Pact had deployed in the Soviet Union a formidable force of SS-20 and SS-4 missiles. The introduction of the mobile SS-20 is of particular significance, since each SS-20 has three independently targetable warheads. At a NATO Special Consultative Group (SCG) meeting on 24 July in Brussels it was announced that the Soviet SS-20 force stood at 441. The Soviet Union is also believed to have retained some 79 SS-4 single-warhead missiles. SS-20 missiles are currently deployed in the Western, Central and Eastern regions of the Soviet Union; more than two-thirds are deployed in the Western and Central region. The range of the SS-20 enables missiles located in the Western and Central region to strike all of NATO Europe; those sited in the Central and Eastern region are capable of striking substantial parts of NATO Europe. Since SS-20 missiles are readily transportable, it may be possible to relocate them westward at short notice.

In addition, it is estimated that the Soviet Union has about 1600 tactical and shorter-range intermediate-range nuclear force ballistic missile launchers in its inventory. During 1985 the Soviet Union began deployments of its new SRF missile system, designated the SS-23 by NATO. This missile has a longer range and more improved accuracy than the SCUD, the system which it is expected to replace at army and front levels.

At the division level the predominant SRF weapon is the unguided free rocket over ground (FROG) which is found in battalions of four launchers. The Soviets have begun to replace the FROG with the more accurate, longer-range SS-21 missile in some divisions opposite European NATO.

Some analysts assert that these new generations of Soviet shorter-range missiles can be employed effectively with conventional warheads because of increased accuracy. It is further maintained that deployments in this mode will give the Soviets a formidable deep-strike system. Sceptics doubt whether the Soviets have attained the accuracy levels which would make such deployments cost-effective (see chapter IV on the debate about ATBMs).

In 1983 NATO began its first deployments of Pershing II and ground-launched cruise missiles (GLCMs) in Europe. These systems, each of which carries one warhead, are owned and controlled by the United States. The mobility, range and high-accuracy characteristics are designed to enable these munitions to reach targets in the Soviet Union. Their forward deployment is consistent with NATO Flexible Response strategy and is designed to fortify the policy of deterrence by conveying the message to the Soviet Union that these nuclear systems may be employed in the effort to prevent a Soviet invasion of Western Europe.[9]

In the Federal Republic of Germany (FRG) the stationing of the 108 Pershing II launchers was completed in December 1985 at former Pershing I bases in Schwaebisch Gmuend, Heilbronn and Neu-Ulm. It is understood that no reload missiles will be accepted in the FRG. In addition, the FRG began deployments in 1986 of 96 cruise missiles at the Wuescheim air base in Bitburg. As a condition of deployment the German government insisted that at least one other continental European Government also deploy cruise missiles.

When the decision was made to modernize the NATO LRINF arsenal four other European countries agreed to deploy cruise missiles: the United Kingdom, Italy, the Netherlands and Belgium. The United Kingdom is scheduled to deploy 160 cruise missiles at Greenham Common and at Molesworth by 1987. These have been deployed at a steady rate through 1986. Italy is to station 112 cruise missiles in Comiso, and the first 16 became operational on 3 April 1984.

On 1 November 1985, after a protracted debate, the Dutch coalition Government agreed to deploy 48 GLCMs in 1988, and an agreement was signed with the United States which governs control of the weapons. The parliamentary elections, which took place in the Netherlands on 21 May 1986, confirmed the ruling Conservative coalition in office, thus putting to rest the acrimonious missile debate which had been a feature of Dutch politics for several years. The Dutch Labour Party had threatened to "renegotiate" the agreement if it were elected to office.

The Belgian government formally made its decision in March 1985 to begin stationing part of its assigned force of 48 GLCMs at Florennes air base. To date 16 have been deployed, with the balance scheduled for deployment in 1987, assuming that an INF agreement does not obviate their requirement. The Belgian government has deliberately staggered the deployment dates in the hope that the Geneva arms control negotiations might produce an agreement which will make such additional deployments unnecessary.

Strategic Nuclear Forces

Several sets of criteria exist to measure the balance of strategic forces between East and West. These include delivery vehicles, equivalent megatonnage, numbers of warheads and accuracy of the systems. In terms of delivery vehicles, the Soviet Union enjoys a clear advantage - 2,497 vehicles compared to 1,997[10] for NATO. In terms of numbers of warheads NATO forces retain a lead of more than 11,200 to 10,084 strategic warheads.[11] With respect to equivalent megatonnage, the advantage remains with the Warsaw Pact: Soviet strategic missiles tend to be larger than NATO's and are therefore capable of delivering a greater explosive megatonnage. The Soviet Union currently holds a more than two-to-one advantage over NATO in the area of "hard-target kill" capability. This advantage is offset somewhat by both the number and the accuracy of NATO strategic warheads.

Both the United States and the Soviet Union are engaged in across-the-board modernizations of their strategic arsenals. The Soviet Union is continuing to produce existing strategic systems such as the Backfire bomber and the *Typhoon*-submarine (3 are now believed to have been deployed, each with 20 SS-N-20 SLBM, (9x20 KT MIRV)); a new SLBM (SS-NX-23) and a new strategic bomber, the Blackjack, which is reported to be similar to the US B-1 bomber. The Soviets have also been engaged in the development of several air- and sea-launched long-range cruise missiles which are expected to be operational this year.

One aspect of the Soviet strategic modernization programme - the development of the mobile single-warhead system, designated as the SS-25 by the United States - has caused considerable controversy over the last two years. The superpowers disagree on whether the SS-25 is permitted under the provisions of the 1979 SALT II Treaty. The United States insists the Soviet Union is in violation of the provision in the Treaty which limits each side to one "new type" of ICBM. A "new type" is defined as differing from an existing missile by 5% in any of the following characteristics: length, diameter, launch weight and throw weight.

In October 1982, the Soviet Union began testing a new multiple-warhead ICBM, the SS-X-24, and informed the United States that this new missile represented its new type of ICBM permitted under the SALT II Treaty. In February 1983, the Soviets began a testing programme on the SS-25. Moscow has consistently claimed that the SS-25 is a permitted modernization of the existing SS-13 and therefore does not constitute a violation of SALT II. Despite limited data regarding the SS-13, the United States remains adamant that the deployment of 45 SS-25s constitutes a clear violation of the Treaty.[12]

The modernization of NATO's sea-based strategic force focusses on the deployment of Trident submarines and the introduction of sea-launched cruise missiles (SLCMs).

To date, 13 Ohio-class submarines have been authorized in fiscal years 1974 through 1986. The first 8 submarines are being equipped with Trident I SLBM and will be retrofitted with Trident II missiles starting in 1992. On the assumption that a Trident submarine would carry 216 warheads, a force of 24 (estimated for the year 2002) would carry 5,184 warheads. These figures represent a several-fold increase in the number of US ballistic missiles capable of striking Soviet hard targets. The justification for the D5 missile, with its greater accuracy and increased range/payload, represents a shift in rationale from the traditional argument of SSBN survivability for assured second-strike capability, to one concerned with substantially enhanced hard-target kill capability.

A special study of the Trident programme carried out by the United States Congressional Budget Office (CBO) [13] estimates that by the year 2000, when 20 Trident submarines will be deployed, the US inventory of all classes of hard-target warheads will have grown from today's level of 1650 to at least 6,800, including 4,800 warheads on Trident II SLBMs. The aggregate number of US ballistic missile warheads will not change substantially during this time, since older systems without hard-target capability would be retired.

The CBO notes that this growth in the number of hard-target warheads will greatly increase US ability to destroy both small and large sets of hardened targets in the Soviet Union. It estimates that the hard-target kill capability of the US strategic arsenal (against 2,000 targets hardened to 2,000 psi) will rise from 59% in 1986 to around 90% by the year 2000. The hard-target kill capability of warheads on submarines only (presumed most likely to survive a Soviet attack) will rise from a figure of 28% today to over 85% by the year 2000.

Opponents of the Trident programme assert that the expanded hard-target kill capacity may cause the Soviet leaders - since the vast bulk of their ballistic missile force is land-based - to move towards a "launch-on warning" strategy. They insist that the potentially destabilizing implications of the Trident programme have not been fully appreciated or debated.

The United States is also in the process of deploying three types of SLCMs under the US Navy Tomahawk programme: the nuclear SLCM (Tomahawk Land Attack Missile-Nuclear or TLAM-N); the TLAM-C, designed to attack land targets with conventional warheads; and a short-range Tomahawk Anti-ship Missile (TASM). The United States navy is planning to purchase about 4,000 Tomakawks, of which approximately 750 will be nuclear.

The Soviet Union's SLCM programme is similarly formidable. It is expected to deploy soon its own long-range SLCM, designated the SS-NX-21 by the United States, which will have a range of about 3,000 kms. According to CIA estimates the Soviet Union will have deployed some 3,000 nuclear-armed cruise missiles by the middle of the 1990s.

Both the United States and the Soviet Union are also developing follow-on systems for the Tomahawk and the SS-NX-21. Existing systems are dual-capable and therefore present considerable problems for arms control.[14]

In the category of land-based nuclear systems the United States, in response to the growing Soviet capability to threaten American ICBMs, has undertaken to replace the older Minuteman and Titan II missiles with the MX missile (sometimes referred to as the "Peacekeeper"). Possessing much greater range, accuracy and payload, the MX is a significant improvement on the Minuteman III. While the precise number of MX missiles to be deployed is still unclear, development is proceeding with a planned Initial Operating Capability (IOC) for December 1986. The mobile, single-warhead Midgetman is still in the very early development stage and is unlikely to be deployed before 1990, if at all (see chapter II).

The first of the new strategic bombers, the B-1B has been introduced; the first squadron is planned to be operational in late 1986. The major programme for the next generation of attack missiles for US bomber forces is the Advanced Strategic Air-Launched Missile (ASALM). The ASALM is seen as a penetration aid for US bomber forces, for, unlike current generation cruise missiles, ASALM would be supersonic and capable of attacking ground targets as well as directly defending the bomber forces with improved air-to-ground capabilities. A force of 100 B1-Bs will be produced by 1988.

THE FUTURE OF ARMS CONTROL

Arms control negotiations between East and West have been proceeding throughout 1986 across the spectrum of functional categories - nuclear, space, conventional, chemical, confidence-building - but with few substantive breakthroughs. The Geneva Nuclear and Space Talks (NST), in being since March 1985, took centre stage for most of the year before the dramatic Reykjavik meeting between President Reagan and General Secretary Gorbachev. But apart from a brief flurry of activity in February 1986, when it looked as though a separate interim agreement might be possible on INF, this set of negotiations has not produced, to date, any definitive settlement in any of its 3 areas of focus. The superpowers - as was amply demonstrated in Iceland - remain deadlocked on the SDI issue, which is the key to any major breakthrough, at least at the strategic level.* In view of its importance a brief note is offered on the relationship between the SDI and the ABM Treaty, which proved to be the chief stumbling block in Reykjavik.

There has been no formal resumption of negotiations towards a Comprehensive Test Ban during 1986, but talks did begin in July between the US and the Soviet Union centred around the status of the Threshold Test Ban Treaty and the Peaceful Nuclear Explosions Treaty, both of which remain unratified by the US Senate. This status also applies to the SALT II Treaty, the future of which has been a continuing source of debate within the West during the last year. Both the SALT II and the test ban issues respectively are addressed in some depth in chapters two and three of this report. In addition some comments are offered on the future of the US Midgetman missile, which has significant arms control implications.

The compliance and verification debate has, if anything, intensified over the last year, following the comprehensive coverage it received in the 1985 General Report. The new US reinterpretation of the ABM Treaty and the latest Reagan Administration Report on Soviet Violations (RSVP) have been central to this debate. In view of last year your Rapporteur has limited his comments on these issues in this Report.

An overview is given on the progress achieved in three multilateral arms control fora since they were last discussed in the 1984 General Report. The agreement which was reached in September in one of these - the CDE - though intrinsically quite modest may have important and long standing implications for the future of East-West arms control, particularly relating to the European theatre.

The Reykjavik Summit and the Future of the ABM Treaty

For two days in October it appeared that the two superpowers were poised on the brink of the most dramatic

---

* The Geneva Arms Control negotiations and the SDI issue are addressed in some detail in the report of the Special Committee on Nuclear Strategy and Arms Control, and your Rapporteur has therefore restricted his remarks on this issue.

and spectacular arms control deal in the history of the nuclear age. This would have involved immediate reductions by 50% in the strategic nuclear weapons arsenals of both sides - this to be followed by their complete elimination within ten years - together with the complete elimination of intermediate-range nuclear weapons in Europe. Detailed accounts from both American and Soviet spokesmen confirm that for a time this was a realistic proposition.

However, at the eleventh hour the summit collapsed over the question of the SDI, and in particular its relationship to the ABM Treaty. The US position was that "research, development and testing" of defensive weapons was permissible under the 1972 treaty, and therefore would take place during the 10-year agreed extension period of the ABM Treaty. This was unacceptable to General Secretary Gorbachev, who made it clear that all potential offensive arms limitation agreements were once again hostage to progress on the limitation of defensive systems. This was contrary to indications the Soviets had been giving in the run-up to the summit which had suggested that a separate accommodation might be possible on INF missiles.

There were reports in the days following the Reykjavik meeting that the Soviet Union had pushed for a more restricted interpretation of the ABM Treaty even than the one the Reagan Administration has consistently rejected for more than a year.

It is important to recall that in October 1985 the Reagan Administration had dramatically announced a new interpretation of the ABM Treaty approving research, development and testing of defensive systems. Despite the fact that the Administration subsequently agreed to continue to abide, for the foreseeable future, with the restricted interpretation, US spokesmen have consistently maintained that the broader interpretation is now "a matter of law". President Reagan's UN speech in September, which made direct allusion to what is permitted under the ABM Treaty, confirms this.

The American negotiations of the ABM Treaty and those principally involved in its formulation, without exception, have rejected the Reagan Administration's "exotic" interpretation of the treaty; the chief American negotiator Gerard Smith declaring that the ABM Treaty would be rendered a "dead letter" if the reinterpretation persisted. The public record confirms that the Nixon Administration, which negotiated the treaty, intended that a restrictive interpretation be applied.

American Administration spokesmen in the weeks since the Reykjavik Summit have laid great stress on the "new" Soviet restrictive interpretation of the ABM Treaty proposing that all SDI work be confined to laboratory research (some scientists in fact say such a restriction might actually be helpful since much of the SDI programme would be unaffected and "stunts" would be stopped). It seems clear, however, that the chief stumbling block to progress concerns the American attempts to enshrine the broader interpretation.

The role of the NATO Allies in this context is immensely important. It was, in large part, pressure from European governments, worried about the collapse of the ABM regime, which persuaded the Americans to back off from the broader interpretation last October and declare that the SDI would be conducted in accordance with the restrictive interpretation (see speech by Secretary of State George Shultz at 1985 North Atlantic Assembly session in San Francisco). Now, it would seem, the American return to the broader interpretation may be putting in jeopardy an historic arms control package - and for a programme which has a dubious prospect of achieving anything of value in terms of contribution to strategic stability.

It still has to be demonstrated, from an Allied perspective, why a greater - distant - reliance on defensive weapons would be better for European security than a strengthened ABM Treaty and deep cuts in strategic and intermediate offensive missiles. In this connection it is altogether puzzling why the European Allies are now prepared to give their apparent approval to the US interpretation of the treaty; an interpretation to which they were unalterably opposed last year, and one that now seems to stand in the way of a spectacular arms control deal.

The ABM Treaty is due for renewal in 1987. It is imperative that its central tenets be updated and strengthened and its ambiguities ironed out. This would not necessarily be incompatible with a healthy SDI research programme. It is conceivable that, providing its stabilizing elements are strengthened and sustained, it could, in fact, pave the way for a remarkable era of arms control. If the European Allies are not to be portrayed as parties to the wholesale dismantling of the ABM Treaty, it is important that they use whatever weight they have to urge President Reagan and General Secretary Gorbachev to grasp this historic opportunity.

Mutual and Balanced Force Reductions (MBFR)

Since the early 1970s, NATO and the Warsaw Pact have been engaged in discussions aimed at limiting the number of troops in Central Europe. These discussions, formally known as the negotiations on the Mutual Reduction of Forces and Armaments and Associated Measures, constitute one of the longest continuously running arms control negotiations of modern times.

For almost as long as the negotiations have been in being there has been deadlock over two fundamental issues: data and verification. The data dispute centres on the absence of common agreement between NATO and the Pact on the number of forces now in place in Central Europe. Western intelligence sources for some years have estimated anywhere from a 150,000 to 200,000 Warsaw Pact manpower advantage over the West in the reductions area. Years of discussion on this data question have failed to resolve the discrepancy. The West had made reductions contingent upon resolution of the data dispute; by contrast the Soviets have made the adoption of verification measures conditional upon reductions taking place first.

Though there is no common agreement on current force levels, both sides have agreed that reductions should result in a common ceiling of 900,000, of which no more than 700,000 could be ground forces.

Verification has been a highly charged issue and a major stumbling block to progress. Throughout the negotiations NATO has insisted on credible and reciprocal verification measures which include on-site inspection.

In 1985 both sides put forward proposals which appeared to narrow the differences between them. In February 1985 the Eastern bloc suggested an initial agreement on American and Soviet reductions: 13,000 and 20,000 personnel respectively. In addition the forces of the participating states would not be increased for a three-year period, at the end of which negotiations would be undertaken with a view to fixing equal ceilings on force levels.

The West responded to this initiative by tabling in December 1985 a counter-proposal which essentially built on key aspects of the East's framework: a time-limited, non-comprehensive, no-increase agreement. The main element which NATO has added is in the area of verification. Under the new proposal the West removed for the first time its long standing requirement for prior agreement on the number of forces in Central Europe before reductions could take place.

The December 1985 Western initiative called for a reduction of 5,000 US and 11,500 Soviet ground troops in a year; the number of NATO and Warsaw Pact forces in the region would then be frozen for another three years. The relatively small numbers were chosen in an attempt to test the verification measures before larger reductions took place. The proposed package of verification measures provided that there be a detailed data exchange, with each side being permitted up to 30 challenge inspections per year on 6 hours' notice. In addition the proposal envisaged the setting up of permanently manned checkpoints to monitor the movement of forces into and out of the Central region. The verification measures were purposely designed not merely to verify the number of Soviet troops departing the zones, but also the number which remained in the zone. This is regarded as a critical element if the West is to accept a no-increase commitment without prior agreement on current force levels.

In essence, the Western initiative proposed that in exchange for a comprehensive and effective verification regime, NATO would be willing to accept the general framework of the February 1985 model. By giving priority to verification measures this approach offered a potential for tackling the data dispute issue and hence overcoming what had been a major stumbling block to progress.

At a news conference after the plenary in December, Soviet Ambassador Valerian Mikhaylov said that the proposal "would be naturally carefully studied but it does not give cause for optimism ....As a first impression, the West has accepted the model tabled by the East in February but they filled it with dubious content." He went on to refer to the failure to include reductions in armaments and to the stringent verification measures which sought "to impose excessively inflated verification provisions disregarding existing realities. All of this does not contribute to reaching a mutually acceptable agreement."

When NATO and the Pact resumed talks in Vienna on 30 January 1986 the United States expressed optimism about the prospect for progress. A State Department statement said that the talks "hold more promise of progress than at any previous time in their 12-year history."

On 20 February 1986 the Warsaw Pact presented a new draft treaty which accommodated a few of the Western positions articulated in December 1985 but seemed to back away from previous concessions. One of the important differences between the two sides is over the scope of inspection measures. NATO has seen fit to put forward very demanding inspection requirements in order to establish conclusively how many troops the Pact maintains in the reduction area. The number and type of Western inspection trips are seen by the East as excessive.

Another difference concerns the rotation of individual replacement troops into and out of the area. The new Soviet proposal embodies a clause exempting routine troop rotations through the monitoring posts (the Soviet Union rotates over 150,000 troops in and out of the area every year). NATO is concerned that the Pact may utilize the rotation procedure to cover a possible build-up in the reduction area which would violate the agreement. However, as some analysts have already noted, "requiring all military personnel entering and exiting the area to pass through the monitoring would accomplish (NATO's) objective, but such a procedure could become a procedural and organizational nightmare".[15]

There is also the question of what to do about weapons. The Warsaw Pact has maintained that forces withdrawn from the reduction area should be required to take their weapons with them. NATO's position is that this provision would be more of a disadvantage to the United States forces than to Soviet force deployments in Central Europe. Consequently the West proposes that the disposition of arms and equipment of withdrawn forces be left up to the reducing parties and any arms reductions be deferred to a later point.

Thus on 20 March 1986 the 38th round of MBFR, which had started with great hope, ended without any meaningful progress. Western officials expressed regret that the Warsaw Pact had failed to respond constructively to the Western proposal of December 1985. It was pointed out that Soviet General Secretary Gorbachev had also appeared to indicate that progress in the area of verification might be possible in his wide-ranging arms control proposal which was tabled on 15 January 1986.

Gorbachev made similar comments in a major speech he delivered in East Berlin on 18 April 1986. In what he described as "serious proposals" to cut conventional troops from the Atlantic to the Urals, Gorbachev again made direct allusion to the possibility for on-site inspection. The proposal said that "military units should be dissolved and their armaments either destroyed or put into storage on their national territories ... verification could be guaranteed by national technical means and international inspection, including, if necessary, on-site inspection." The vagueness of the proposals convinced NATO officials that the Soviets needed first to prove good faith in the Vienna negotiations before any attempt could be made to tackle "the more ambitious elements concerned with force reductions."

In May NATO Foreign Ministers, meeting in Halifax, Canada, agreed to the establishment of a high-level task force on conventional arms control. It was announced that the task force, which would build on the Western proposals at the CDE conference in Stockholm and on the MBFR negotiations in Vienna, intended to propose "bold new steps in the field of conventional arms control." A final report, with a series of recommendations, is to be prepared in time for the December Ministerial meeting.

To a great extent the Gorbachev initiative and the NATO task force announcement shifted the focus of attention away from Vienna. On 9 June General Secretary Gorbachev in a speech in Budapest provided details of his Europe-wide conventional reduction proposal. He suggested that an appropriate forum for discussing a new Atlantic to the Urals agreement on conventional arms could either be a second phase of the CDE, a new forum for all European States plus the United States and Canada, or alternatively a broadened framework of MBFR.

The main points of the Budapest proposal were the following:

- As a first step NATO and the WTO would reduce by 100,000 to 150,000 men each within a year or two. Tactical air forces would take up a significant part of such cuts.

- Further steps would include phased reductions by some 25% by the mid-1990s. Missiles with ranges up to 1000 km might be included.

- "Reliable and effective verification through national technical means" and "international procedures including on-site inspections" supervised by an international consultative committee" were also proposed. It was envisaged that the committee would set up control posts at large railway junctions, airfields and in ports.

The Gorbachev proposals were received cautiously in the West but NATO Secretary-General Lord Carrington confirmed that they would be taken into account by the task force. It is not known what the basis of the NATO task force recommendations will be, although there does appear to be some support for an enlargement of the competence of the CDE in any second phase of this conference.

As the 40th round of the MBFR negotiations got under way on 25 September, both sides denied that they had lost interest in the forum, despite the flurry of activity which had gone on away from the table during the spring and summer of 1986. The American Ambassador Robert Blackwill publicly stated that the West had no interest in continuing MBFR negotiations in another forum. He emphasized the Western interest in a modest first-phase agreement to be followed quickly by an agreement on reductions in Central Europe. Recalling the December 1985 Western proposal, Ambassador Blackwill said that both sides were closer together than ever before "because NATO has made a series of concessions which have brought us to this point."

There can be no doubt that in some significant senses the two sides indeed have moved closer to agreement, but major differences do remain. Moreover, increasing numbers of Western observers are beginning to ask whether, in fact, an MBFR agreement would serve Western interests. There are known to be powerful forces in the Reagan Administration who question the central purpose of MBFR. They point out that even in the best of political circumstances an MBFR accord would not keep the Soviet Union from massing forces on its borders, nor would an agreement really be consistent with General Rogers' frequent statements that NATO needs more not less active duty personnel to support deployment of new weapons systems in the European area.

Other analysts strongly support the concept of MBFR and maintain that an agreement would be very much in the security interests of NATO in that it would lessen the ability of the Warsaw Pact to launch a "standing-start" offensive against NATO forces, and that associated compliance measures which would accompany reductions would significantly increase potential warning of hostilities. In addition, proponents of MBFR assert that an initial accord would in no way inhibit NATO plans to improve conventional forces in Central Europe. They point out that for demographic and economic reasons it is most unlikely that NATO will, in any event, be able to increase its active duty forces in Central Europe in the near future.[16]

Chemical Disarmament

Since 1980, at the Conference on Disarmament (CD) in Geneva, an Ad Hoc Working Group on Chemical Weapons has been working on drafting a multilateral convention designed to prohibit universally the development, production and stockpiling of chemicals, and on their destruction. In addition, the United States and the Soviet Union have been engaged in bilateral negotiations on the subject of chemical weapons since 1977. The bilateral talks have intensified during 1986 in response to commitments made by President Reagan and General Secretary Gorbachev during their summit meeting in Geneva in November 1985.

In 1984, the United States proposed a draft comprehensive treaty. The convention prohibits the production, possession, transfer and use of chemical weapons. The proposal includes a package of rigorous verification measures including "a system of international on-site inspection" to monitor and confirm destruction and to monitor the commercial production of permitted chemicals.

This US draft convention was rejected outright by the Soviet Union. To date, the degree of intrusiveness envisaged in the US draft has proved unacceptable to the Soviets. The key provisions of the draft will exceed anything the Soviets have even shown a hint of accepting, a fact recognized by most West European governments, some of whom reacted with incredulity to the proposal. The chief Soviet delegate to the conference commented that "demands for unimpeded access to the territory of other states continues to block the way for agreement."

What <u>has</u> been agreed at the CD by all parties is that the eventual convention should contain the following elements:

- a broad prohibition on production, use and possession;

- a system for destroying the present stocks and production facilities; all parties agree that the destruction should take place over a ten-year period;
- controls on remaining chemical facilities ensuring that no new chemical weapons are produced, but permitting production of chemicals for non-hostile purposes: industrial, agricultural, research, medical, law enforcement or other peaceful purposes;
- a consultative committee to oversee the above activity, including verification activities.

Destruction of Stocks

In its 1984 draft treaty the United States indicated a wish to have the destruction of existing stocks verified by continuous on-site inspection. The USSR has agreed that destruction could be monitored by continuous on-site inspection but only for nerve agents and mustard gas.

Destruction of Facilities

Up until the 15 January 1986 Gorbachev comprehensive proposal, the Soviet position had been that the USSR reserved the right to convert facilities to commercial use. However, Western observers noted a change in the Soviet position when Gorbachev said that the Soviet Union supported the total elimination of chemical weapons "and of the industrial base for their manufacture itself."

All parties agree that though actual production of chemicals should be permitted for non-hostile purposes, the precise terms of this constraint have been difficult to draw. Detailed discussions have been taking place in Geneva on the following categories: super-toxic lethal chemicals and their key precursors, other lethal chemicals, other harmful chemicals, and chemicals posing a particular risk.

The Declaration of Stocks and Facilities

The United States and most Western countries want all declarations to be made immediately and to include the locations. The USSR is willing to make all declarations immediately but does not want to disclose the location of stocks until they have reached the destruction site; it maintains that prior disclosure will give away a military advantage.

However, in his January speech Gorbachev made a reference to "prompt declaration" actions which could be watched through "international on-site verification". This was interpreted by some American officials as a modification of former Soviet positions.

Verification and Compliance

All parties to the negotiations appear to agree that three types of inspection will eventually need to be employed to monitor any agreement: continuous on-site, periodic or random on-site, and challenge on-site inspection. However, there is disagreement on which procedure should be employed and for what activity.

Disagreement also exists on when challenge inspection may be refused. The USSR's position is that each state should be able to refuse any inspection on national security grounds, although Moscow has also said that that state must furnish sufficiently convincing appropriate explanations.

The Soviet Union has also expressed its complete disapproval of the American proposal that a special on-site procedure "anywhere, anytime", without right of refusal, be part of any negotiated package.

The absence of common agreement regarding appropriate verification measures has been the principal impediment to meaningful progress in the negotiations. Because of the ease with which chemical munitions can be produced, the United States has continued to insist on rigorous verification provisions. That said, however, it would be virtually impossible to have full and complete verification of chemical disarmament. Even assuming that one could institute a regime of "anywhere, anytime" on-site procedures, the task of first ascertaining that a violation had possibly occurred would be extremely difficult to achieve, given the widespread dispersal of potential production plants. It is worth pointing out that unlike nuclear missile sites, chemical munition plants are not readily identifiable with existing technologies.

On 22 April the Soviet Union tabled its long-awaited new proposals in the CD:

- elimination of stockpiles to begin not later than 6 months after entry into force and be completed not later than 10 years after that date;

- declaration to be made on the precise locations of production facilities 30 days after entry into force;

- cessation of all activities at production facilities immediately after entry into force except activities required for the closure of the facilities and closure of facilities three months after entry into force;

- the cessation of operation to be verified by strict verification, including systematic on-site inspection;

- destruction or dismantling of production facilities to begin not later than 1 year after entry into force;

- procedures for destruction and dismantling of the facilities to be developed with regard to the nature and special features of the facilities;

- the conversion of facilities to the destruction of stocks, their elimination upon completion of this task, to be carried out under the supervision of international verification personnel;

- "the presence of inspectors" under systematic international on-site inspection "would be ensured at all important operations for the destruction or dismantling of a chemical weapon production facility";

- measures to apply irrespective of whether state-owned, private enterprises, or transnational corporations are involved.

In June President Reagan met with his Ambassador to the CD and issued a statement saying that the United States was ready to intensify the pace of negotiations. One month later the United States tabled a 53-page document at the CD detailing the domestic locations of its chemical weapons, and challenged the Soviet Union to do likewise.

On 15 July the United Kingdom tabled a challenge verification paper which had been discussed with Soviet Foreign Minister Shevardnadze when he visited London on 14 July. It reads:

> "In summary, our proposals envisage that each State party to the Convention would have the right, in exceptional circumstances, directly to request a challenge inspection of another. The challenged State would then be under an obligation to demonstrate to others, and especially the challenging state, that it remained in compliance....However, in very limited circumstances there would be a right of refusal of direct inspection. In those circumstances a challenged state would propose alternative measures which would then enable the matter under consideration to be resolved.
>
> We are greatly encouraged that the Soviet Union is at least setting out its position in detail, although it must be said that much of this detail does no more than reflect what already seemed to be the consensus view at the Conference. But a serious Soviet statement deserves a serious response. The UK delegation will work to respond fully to all these points.
>
> What must not be forgotten, however, is that Ambassador Issraelyan's statement follows years of negotiation in which Western and non-aligned delegations put forward a range of constructive and practical suggestions for advancing the negotiations, to be met largely by indifference or silence from the Soviet Union. I point in particular to the series of UK papers on the verification of non-production in the civil chemical industry, CD353, CD514 and CD575."

In recent months senior Government spokesmen from both the United States and the Soviet Union have been making optimistic noises about the possibility of an agreement on chemical weapons. For example, on 19 August General Secretary Gorbachev said that new CW proposals "make it possible to sign before this year's end, or next year, a convention on banning chemical weapons and eliminating their stockpiles as well as the industrial base for their production." Then on 20 September, US officials indicated, after the Shultz-Shevardnadze meeting in Washington, that sufficient progress had been made on the question of CW non-proliferation that it might provide the basis of an accord for a summit, should one take place, in late 1986.

Conference on Disarmament in Europe (CDE)

On 22 September negotiators from NATO and the Warsaw Pact signed a CDE agreement which embodied a package of security measures designed to reduce the risk of war in Europe. The agreement, the first major arms control accord since the signing of the SALT II Treaty in June 1979, has its origins in the process which grew out of the 1975 Helsinki Accords on European Security and Co-operation.

US Ambassador Robert Barry, following the conclusion of the negotiations, declared that the Stockholm accord would "help to make the military situation in Europe safer and more predictable" and that "it will make political intimidation much more difficult." From the Western standpoint a central objective of the CDE talks has been to drastically reduce the potential of a surprise attack by the Warsaw Pact. It was only on the final day of the negotiations that NATO and the Warsaw Pact decided on the types of military activity which will require advance notification and which must be opened to outside inspection.

Beginning on 1 January 1987 the two alliances will furnish each other - as well as other non-NATO/Pact participant countries - with detailed advanced information regarding all military exercises and troop concentrations involving 13,000 or more soldiers or 300 tanks. If more than 17,000 troops are involved they must invite all other signatory countries to send observers. The requirements on participatory states are for the provision of written information 42 days or more ahead of military activities. In addition, they must provide an annual calendar of all notifiable activities not later than 15 November of operations involving more than 40,000 troops which are planned for the following calendar year (a year earlier in the case of manoeuvers involving more than 75,000 troops).

The Soviet Union only acceded to the idea of inviting foreign observers to watch its exercises, and "snap inspection" to monitor compliance late in the negotiations. Under the CDE agreement signatory countries are permitted to undertake snap inspections of each other's armed forces if they suspect another country is engaging in military activity which should have been notified in advance. Each country is obliged to accept a maximum of three inspections per year which may not be carried out by any of its military allies. In addition, each country is only allowed one inspection per year, which may be carried out on land or from the air with the inspected country providing the aircraft.

This latter point was only agreed to during the final week of the negotiations when the United States reportedly softened its original position which had called for planes to be provided by neutral countries, not host nations. Apparently the United States made this concession following a direct appeal to President Reagan by the Governments of the United Kingdom and the Federal Republic of Germany, who had feared that the whole deal might collapse over this one issue.

According to the American negotiating team the new requirements embodied in the agreement will mean between 20 and 25 Warsaw Pact military manoeuvers being notified each year, with about ten exercises observed by each side annually. It is hoped that the net result will lead to greater transparency, predictability and a lessening in suspicion between both blocs.

Some Western analysts have suggested that the CDE agreement will increase the political cost to the Soviet Union of trying to intimidate its East European allies, since NATO and neutral European observers will now be able to send observers to witness military activities, and report details to the press. It is hoped that this will act as a powerful disincentive for Soviet action such as that which occurred in 1981 on the Polish border and, in 1968, on the Czech border.

The future of the CDE process will now be discussed at the CSCE Review conference in Vienna on 4 November. This conference is mandated to examine both the Helsinki accords and the Stockholm agreement and propose a framework for the future of the CSCE conferences.

Supporters of the process would like to see the CDE evolve, in time, into the principal forum for East-West conventional arms control, eventually absorbing MBFR. This is more likely to occur if there is substantial progress on the nuclear component of arms control. As former French Foreign Minister Roland Dumas pointed out before the Plenary in January 1986 "... the limitation of nuclear armaments cannot be put forward as sufficient in itself. Security, in all its constituent parts, must be our criterion. For us (Europeans) the problem of conventional armaments cannot receive only secondary priority as compared with nuclear negotiations." A close American follower of the CDE process seems to accept the logic of this statement when he notes that with "its focus on the whole of Europe, and its 35-nation constituency of NATO, Warsaw Pact and neutral and non-aligned states, the CDE offers a potentially promising instrument to execute this ambitious task."[17]

The Future of SALT II Limits

On 27 May President Reagan formally repudiated the US Administration's political commitment to SALT II and let it be known that the United States would exceed its limits later in the year with the continued deployment of B-52 heavy bombers with cruise missiles beyond the 131st aircraft.

The rationale given for the decision was the alleged Soviet non-compliance with SALT II of which the President cited several instances. Critics of the President's decision insist that the Reagan Administration is discarding an arms control agreement which still serves the security interest of the United States and which contributes to international stability. Moreover, they contend that the compliance issues cited to justify the decision are highly ambiguous and that inadequate use has been made of established compliance fora to resolve differences with the Soviets.[18] The President described three key compliance issues - the Soviet development of the SS-25 missile, the Krasnoyarsk radar, and the encryption of ballistic missile technology - as "particularly disturbing".[19]

The SALT II Treaty was signed by the United States and the Soviet Union on 18 June 1979. It logically built on the 1972 SALT I Interim Agreement on Strategic Offensive Arms, and its limitations, in effect, supplanted the key provisions of the SALT I agreement. Although SALT II has never been ratified by the US Senate, each country until 27 May of this year had pledged not to undercut its provisions. Most recently President Reagan reaffirmed US policy of not undercutting of the SALT II limits in December 1985.

Since the Reagan Administration came to office there have been senior Administration officials favourably disposed to dispensing with the SALT II Treaty and abandoning its limits. Regular statements from the Department of Defense, the Arms Control and Disarmament Agency (ACDA), and even the White House have consistently described the treaty as "fatally flawed" and damaging to US national security. Defense Secretary Caspar Weinberger has on several occasions in the past year proposed that the United States discontinue abiding by the provisions of the SALT II Treaty. For example, in a portent of things to come in a November 1985 letter to the President - written on the eve of the US-Soviet summit meeting - Mr. Weinberger made clear his view of the Treaty:

> "A pledge to continue to adhere to SALT II even though the Soviets are violating it could make it difficult if not impossible to do other things we should do to make up for their violations. We can, of course, continue to observe parts of SALT II, at your option, but a pledge to continue observing it all could put rigid constraints on your ability to respond to Soviet violations."

Although the President's May 27 decision did not have an immediate impact on US strategic programmes (Reagan simultaneously decided to retire two Poseidon Submarines on economic grounds) it met with fierce resistance among the NATO Allies and within the US Congress.

In Congress legislation has been passed in the House of Representatives to limit funding for weapons exceeding the SALT limits. A companion measure has been introduced in the Senate sponsored by Senators Joseph Biden and William Cohen. A Senate amendment to the 1987 Defense Authorization Bill requiring a report by 1 October on the military impact of US non-compliance with existing strategic offensive arms agreements, together with the military implications of Soviet violations, passed overwhelmingly. And in October a non-binding resolution was passed by the Congress urging the Administration to stay within the numerical limits of the Treaty.

Reaction to the decision among the NATO Allies has been overwhelmingly negative. This was graphically illustrated at the spring meeting of the NATO Foreign Ministers in Halifax, Nova Scotia on 29 May when Secretary of State Shultz found himself totally isolated amid a torrent of criticism from his NATO colleagues.

There exists in Europe far more scepticism about the military significance of the Reagan Administration's charges of Soviet non-compliance with the SALT Treaty than in the United States. European Governments have been quick to associate themselves with those critics in the United States who stress the positive compliance record of both sides vis-à-vis the SALT limits, and the value of this in terms of international stability and predictability.

Some of the most prominent American critics of the President's decision attended a press conference, sponsored by the private Arms Control Association in Washington on 29 May, to vent their condemnation of the President's decision. They included the former SALT II negotiator Gerard Smith, former ACDA Director Paul Warnke and former Secretary of Defense Robert McNamara. At this same press conference a fact sheet was distributed which explained what action the Soviets had taken in order to comply with SALT II. This is printed for the information of the members of the Military Committee.

The US and Soviet Positive SALT Compliance Record

a) Soviet SALT Deactivations *

The SALT II accords have required the Soviet Union to remove 1,079 ICBMs, 245 SLBMs, 21 bombers, and 21 nuclear missile-carrying submarines:

- In order to comply with the SALT I and II "freeze" on "heavy" ICBM silos, between 1973 -1980 the Soviet Union withdrew 288 SS-9 ICBMs as SS-18 ICBMs entered the force. SALT II also prohibited the USSR from testing and deploying a "new" heavy ICBM and limited the extent to which existing heavy ICBMs could be modernized.

---

* In order for the two parties to remain within the treaties' numerical limits, as new delivery vehicles are deployed, older ones must be dismantled or destroyed.

- Between 1974-1986, the Soviet Union removed 582 SS-11 ICBMs as newer SS-17, SS-19 and SS-25 ICBMs were deployed.**

- Between 1972-1985, the Soviet Union dismantled or converted 14 Yankee-class submarines and 7 Hotel-class SSBNs as new Delta- and Typhoon-class subs were added.

- Between 1975-1978, the Soviet Union dismantled 209 SS-7 and SS-8 ICBM launchers to allow for permitted increases in SLBMs.

- Between 1977-1985, the USSR removed 224 SS-N-6 and SS-N-5 SLBMs as SS-N-18 and SS-N-20 SLBMs were introduced.

- In 1985-1986, the Soviet Union dismantled 21 Bison bombers.

Between 1986-1990, SALT II would require the Soviet Union to remove older ICBMs, SLBMs and heavy bombers, as new ones are deployed. Although the precise number of retirements will depend on the number and character of the new systems the Soviets deploy, they would have to deactivate approximately 500 to 600 strategic nuclear delivery systems.

** Since SALT prohibits the construction of new fixed ICBM launchers, new silo-launched land-based missiles must be deployed in existing launchers and the older missiles removed from the operational forces. US dismantling of 42 Titan II ICBMs, claimed by the Reagan Administration as part of its SALT compliance record, is omitted here because no SALT limit would be violated if the missiles remained.

b) US SALT Deactivations*

The SALT I and SALT II agreements have required the United States to deactivate 320 ICBMs, 576 SLBMs and 13 nuclear missile-carrying submarines:

- Between 1972-1975, the United States removed 260 Minuteman I ICBMs and 60 Minuteman II ICBMs in order to increase the number of Minuteman III ICBMs from 230 to 550.**

- Since 1972, the United States has replaced 176 Polaris A-3 SLBMs on 11 submarines with Poseidon C-3 SLBMs.

- Since 1979, the United States has replaced 192 C-3 SLBMs with Trident C-4 SLBMs on 12 submarines.

- Since 1980, the United States has dismantled or converted 10 Polaris submarines carrying 160 A-3 SLBMs in preparation for deployment of Trident subs.

- In 1985-1986, the United States dismantled three Poseidon submarines carrying 48 C-3 missiles,thereby remaining within SALT II limits as two new Trident missile-carrying subs began sea trials.***

---

* In order for the two parties to remain within the treaties' numerical limits, as new delivery vehicles are deployed, older ones must be dismantled or destroyed.

** Since SALT prohibits the construction of new fixed ICBM launchers, new silo-launched land-based missiles must be deployed in existing launchers and the older missiles removed from the operational forces. US dismantling of 42 Titan II ICBMs, claimed by the Reagan Administration as part of its SALT compliance record, is omitted here because no SALT limit would be violated if the missiles remained.

*** The Reagan Administration states that dismantling of two Poseidon SSBNs starting May 1986 is being done not to comply with SALT but to avoid overhaul expenses.

Between 1986-1990, SALT II would require the United States to remove or retire a number of older ICBMs SLBMs, or ALCM-carrying bombers as new ones are deployed. Although the precise number of deactivations would depend on developments in US modernization programs, approximately 200-300 systems would have to be removed.

July 22-30, two months after the President's SALT II decision, a special meeting of the Standing Consultative Commission (SCC) was held in Geneva. The four sessions ended without progress in an atmosphere of acrimony and polemics. During the meeting the US delegation informed its Soviet counterpart that President Reagan's May decision was final. The Soviet commissioner spoke of the "extremely dangerous consequences of the US refusal to comply" with the SALT II accord.

A report by the Chairman of the House Armed Services Committee, Les Aspin, released two months before President Reagan's decision, while admitting that Soviet arms control violations are a serious political issue, noted that:

> "the costs to American security from the current crop of alleged violations is small potatoes compared to the costs to us if we cancelled SALT. So, as the President constructs his 'appropriate and proportionate responses' he would do well to remember that he is trying to charge "real costs" to the Soviets, not to ourselves."[20]

In the report Aspin asserts that the Soviets have two inherent advantages which permit them to accelerate their force levels quicker than the United States in a SALT-free environment. These are (a) their higher capacity "hot" production lines for strategic forces and (b) the greater throw-weight of the Soviet ICBM force, which could accommodate "fractionation" of warheads to an estimated growth level of 2.2 times current levels.

The Aspin Report's central premise that these two advantages would allow disproportionate increases in deployed Soviet strategic weapons as against American systems (65% to 45% by 1989) is supported by official and private studies which have recently been undertaken. According to national intelligence community estimates, cited in the Aspin Report, by the 1990s the Soviets could have as many as 21,000 strategic weapons in the field. A Congressional Research Service study of 5 October 1984 maintains that the Soviet Union could deploy up to 27,800 strategic weapons in the same time frame.[21]

A major study carried out by the private Arms Control Association notes that the SALT II agreement will require that the Soviet Union, between the years 1985-90, remove at least 500 to 800 ballistic missiles and destroy missile silos equivalent to the number of mobile missiles deployed. In the absence of SALT, the ACA report speculates that the Soviet Union could deploy the SS-24, SS-25 and other missiles in advanced development without retiring any of its fixed land-based missiles (SS-17, SS-18, SS-19, and SS-11). On the US side, the report notes that SALT II will require the removal of between 200 and 300 missiles and bombers from the force as new systems are deployed.[22]

There is little doubt that the United States could in time match the Soviet force levels, assuming that it would be prepared to invest substantial sums in a modernization drive. However, this option must be measured against the costs which may accrue in terms of a diminution in American security. There is also the broader question of whether such steps would be more likely to support or undermine the general state of strategic stability between the superpowers. For instance, the end of SALT II will free the Soviets from the obligation not to conceal activities relating to the SALT II provisions from US national technical means which monitor Soviet military activities. The US knowledge of overall Soviet deployments will undoubtedly be reduced as the Soviets engage once more in deceptive techniques.

In addition, the short-term proliferation of Soviet warheads in a SALT-free environment would exacerbate the already existing apprehension in Washington regarding the vulnerability of US land-based missiles (including future MX and Midgetman systems), thus placing in greater jeopardy the integrity of the strategic triad.

An undercutting of SALT II could also have implications for President Reagan's SDI programme, the feasibility of which, on the admission of US officials, is closely tied to deep cuts in offensive force levels. The US Congressional Office of Technology Assessment has concluded that without substantially reduced numbers of strategic offensive missiles a defensive system could not work. This conclusion is implicitly accepted by the Reagan Administration when it proposes deep cuts as part of an unrestricted SDI policy.

Finally, in the present budgetary environment in Washington, the fiscal implications of such a step would need to be considered very carefully. Matching additional Soviet warhead levels would certainly be an expensive undertaking which would likely run counter to the spirit and intent of the deficit reduction proposals which have bipartisan support in the US Congress.

The Future of Midgetman

Offers made in late 1985 by American arms control negotiators in Geneva to trade away the Midgetman missile, together with doubts by some influential Congressmen regarding its opportunity cost vis-à-vis other weapons systems, has focussed renewed attention on the fate of mobile missiles in general, and Midgetman in particular.

The original rationale behind the development of Midgetman was that it was a "stabilizing" strategic missile which could survive a Soviet attack in sufficient numbers to pose a credible threat of retaliation. It was principally on these grounds that the Scowcroft Commission in 1983 lent its considerable support to Midgetman development. During the same year, a de-facto alliance involving Scowcroft and key Congressional figures, such as Albert Gore and Les Aspin, engineered a White House compromise which featured the single-warhead Midgetman in a package with limited deployments of the MX missile in fixed (vulnerable) mode.

The full Midgetman programme cost is estimated at around $45 billion, and the 1987 budget envisages the outlay of $1.46 billion for development. There is increasing concern in some circles in Washington that the programme is proving to be a very expensive way to obtain 500 warheads. Moreover, there is fear that its continued development may compete with other strategic force modernization programmes and perhaps, also, undermine the rationale for limited deployments of SDI technologies.

Some Administration and Congressional officials are reported to favour a substantial reduction in the numbers of Midgetman missiles, a change in their configuration to facilitate three warheads, and a compensatory increase in the numbers of MX missiles. However, this would appear to destroy the original rationale for the programme, since reducing the number of launchers would mean enlarging the size of the missile, thus rendering it more difficult to move quickly. The net result would be that the missile would become more vulnerable to surprise attack.

In November 1985 the US arms control negotiators in Geneva tabled a comprehensive proposal which included an offer to eliminate mobile missiles altogether. It seems clear that this surprise initiative emanated from the Defense Department, where a number of senior officials are in favour of reductions in the number of Midgetman missiles or their complete elimination. For example, on 19 February 1986 at the London School of Economics, Mr. Richard Perle, Assistant Secretary of Defense, remarked that the $1.4 billion earmarked for development of the missile in 1987 would be better spent on further research in the President's SDI programme.

This unclear state of affairs galvanized some of the Midgetman's original supporters into action. In early April, Congressman Aspin wrote to the Secretary of the Air Force, Russell A. Rourke, requesting clarification and support. In the letter Congressman Aspin cited a recent Defense Science Board panel report chaired by Dr. John Deutch, the Provost of MIT, which supports the findings of the Scowcroft Report recommending a single-warhead missile "small enough to keep the missile agile and to help close down the vulnerability window, but big enough to carry penetration aids to discourage a Soviet ABM breakout or to thwart it should it occur."

The Deutch Commission concluded that the single warhead Midgetman carried by a hardened transport/launcher and deployed on military bases in the western United States met the three critical criteria of survivability, adaptability to future capabilities and cost. It warned against a larger Midgetman missile, supported by some Pentagon officials, on the grounds that it might "seriously complicate mobility of the system."

The debate in the United States on how best to respond to the Soviet mobile missiles has intensified over the last few months. The Soviet Union has deployed about 72 new road-mobile SS-25 ICBMs and is expected to have a railroad mobile SS-24 operational later in 1986 according to the US Department of Defense. The proposed ban on mobile missiles, together with the reports which have emerged during the year that the Pentagon is looking for a new type of nuclear weapon capable of attacking the Soviet mobile missiles, would seem to be two parts of the same strategy to discredit the notion of mobile missiles as stabilizing and therefore in the interests of both sides.

In an August edition of Science Magazine, Senator Gore was quoted as having said:

> "The public rationale given for the arms control proposal was that mobile missiles are inherently unverifiable. I believe and others in the intelligence community share my belief that this is simply not true ... political decision makers have to weigh the military conclusion in a balance which encompasses the need to create an environment in which some of the retaliatory forces on both sides are invulnerable."

There appears to be some danger that the fundamental strategic aspects of the debate about the future of Midgetman may be lost or clouded as a confused and confusing array of forces are pitted against it. Congressman Aspin continues to be its leading advocate and described the missile as our "priority strategic weapon in development" in July. However, the Senate Appropriations Committee voted to halve the Midgetman missile funding for next year. The debate over its future and the future of the entire ICBM modernization programme is likely to continue for some time. This Committee should keep a strong interest in it.

IS A COMPREHENSIVE TEST BAN TREATY IN WESTERN INTERESTS?

In last year's General Report, the issue of a Comprehensive Test Ban Treaty (CTBT) received prominent treatment in the context of a broader discussion of the future verification and compliance requirements for arms control. In view of the sustained public interest, during 1985 and 1986, in this issue, your Rapporteur considers it appropriate and propitious to offer some additional comments in this year's Report. Before doing so, however, it may be instructive to offer a few thoughts by way of background.

A Comprehensive Test Ban Treaty would ban all nuclear test explosions. For this reason, the main interest for the West in general, and the United States in particular, in a CTBT would be two-fold: first, the protection of Western interests through the prevention of other nations developing new types of nuclear explosives and second, a significant slow-down in the qualitative escalation of the nuclear arms race - the declared objective of every nation in the world.

It was in the name of these laudable objectives that every American President from Eisenhower to Carter professed as his stated goal a CTBT, and most engaged in negotiations to this end. Formal negotiations were first actively pursued from 1958 to 1963 between the United States, the United Kingdom and the Soviet Union. Out of these initial talks emerged the Limited Test Ban Treaty which banned nuclear weapons explosions in the atmosphere, under water and in outer space. Later, during the Nixon Administration, further agreement was reached on the Threshold Test Ban Treaty (TTBT) which bans nuclear tests above 150 kilotons. This was followed by an agreement on the Peaceful Nuclear Explosions Treaty (PNET) which regulates the use of multiple nuclear explosions for peaceful purposes. Both the TTBT and PNE Treaties have yet to be ratified by the United States, though all three parties have agreed to abide by the provisions of both treaties.

In 1977, President Carter reactivated negotiations with the Soviet Union and the United Kingdom on a CTBT, and most analysts acknowledge that considerable progress was made before the talks recessed in 1980. Detailed verification procedures were thrashed out and a substantial amount of agreement was reached concerning the emplacement of unmanned seismic monitoring stations on the other party's territory, the concept of on-site inspections by invitation, and data transmission.

On assuming office in January 1981, the Reagan Administration let it be known that it had no intention of resurrecting the talks on CTBT on the grounds that such an agreement would be unverifiable and therefore not in the security interests of the United States. For more than four years the Reagan Administration sustained this position and this rationale.

In August 1985, the Soviet Union attracted international attention when it announced a self-imposed six-month unilateral moratorium on the testing of nuclear weapons. General Secretary Gorbachev announced that the Soviet Union would be prepared to extend the ban if the United States reciprocated. The United States declined to join the moratorium, repeating its belief that such a prohibition was essentially unverifiable. However, in December the Soviets went a significant step further by stating in an editorial published in Pravda that the Soviet Union "stands for coming to terms with the United States on certain measures of on-site verification to remove the possible doubts about compliance with such a moratorium." The Pravda editorial went on to say that Moscow was prepared to accept an offer by the leaders of the six non-aligned countries to help monitor a comprehensive ban on underground nuclear tests by installing seismic devices on their soil in order that "the verification problem thus cannot be seen as an impediment to reaching agreement on a mutual moratorium."

On 29 March 1986 Gorbachev extended the testing moratorium for a further 6 months and called for a CTB summit meeting in Europe. Then on 18 August, Gorbachev announced that the USSR would extend the moratorium again until 1 January 1987, asserting that if the United States were willing to suspend testing, a test ban accord could be completed and signed by the end of 1986.

The Reagan Administration has been forced to publicly confront and explain its alleged "insurmountable" verification problems in the light of the new Soviet overture. The official line in the past had been that the United States lacked the technical means to adequately ensure Soviet compliance. Most experts argue, however, that the Soviets would not be able to evade a CTBT strengthened by the ten in-country seismic stations (agreed to by the Soviets in the past), extra-territorial seismic monitoring stations and, now, on-site inspections. In the last few years advances in seismology have been such that even in the absence of on-site inspection, the verification issue is scarcely a serious obstacle to a comprehensive test ban treaty.

This appeared to be confirmed when in July US scientists with the private US-based National Defence Research Council (NDRC) set up 3 seismic stations in Soviet Central Asia to monitor the Soviet nuclear test programme. This followed an agreement reached in May between the NRDC and the Soviet Academy of Sciences to demonstrate the feasibility of verifying compliance with a comprehensive test ban.

The professed readiness of the Soviet Union to accept effective verification measures has thus thrown the United States on the defensive on the issue of nuclear testing, at least as far as public opinion is concerned. A new set of rationales and justifications explaining the reluctance to engage in serious test ban negotiations has been invoked by senior Reagan Administration officials. Little or no attempt is now made to mask the Administration's outright opposition in principle to the concept of a CTBT.

Within the last several months, a new official policy declaration has been made in Washington which maintains that a ban "in the foreseeable future would not strengthen stability but would lead to a less secure and more dangerous world." The long-term point at which it might be acceptable to stop testing is defined as "a time when a nuclear deterrent is no longer as essential an element as currently for international security and stability."

According to this new policy, as long as US security remains wedded to nuclear deterrence, "testing will be required to ensure the continued reliability and effectiveness of the US arsenal as well as its safety and credibility." This is a remarkable transformation of American declaratory policy vis-à-vis nuclear testing, which appears to be dramatically out of step not only with the previous five US Administrations, but with the declared policy of most, if not all, of its Western Allies (including Britain). Such a fundamental departure requires elaboration, for it has some implications for relations within the Alliance.

The argument that testing is required to ensure the continued credibility and effectiveness of the US arsenal is, at best, debatable. Many prominent Western scientists refute this claim outright. For example, in May of last year, in a letter to the House Foreign Affairs Committee, eight leading American scientists, most of whom had been involved in past US nuclear testing programmes, stated that:

> "Continued nuclear testing is not necessary in order to ensure the reliability of the nuclear weapons in our stockpile. The best way to confirm reliability is to assemble sample weapons and to subject the components to non-nuclear tests. Weapons can also be detonated without their nuclear components in order to ensure that the complete assembly operates correctly.[23]"

In August the Soviet Chief of Staff Sergei Akhromeyev said that "a proportion of nuclear tests is being carried out by them for the purposes of determining the extent to which they are reliable. This proportion is immeasurably small."

Another justification put forward by Reagan Administration officials against a CTBT is that testing is necessary in order to modernize strategic forces (or "catch-up"). However, the United States has already tested designs for a new generation of nuclear weapons, including strategic cruise missiles, MX, Midgetman and Trident II. Indeed, most of these are now either in production or about to enter production. For the MX and the Trident D5, experts agree that main advances lie in accuracy (i.e. in enhancing counter-force capability); potent warheads already exist and additional testing is of marginal value. One incremental improvement in warhead technology which the Pentagon is known to favour is the so-called "earth-penetrating" missile warhead designed to knock out hardened enemy targets such as concrete missile silos and which may have applications against Soviet mobile ICBMs.

Another justification for the need to continue testing, less frequently invoked by Reagan Administration officials, relates to the SDI programme. Critics of the Administration argue that researchers involved in the "Star Wars" programme are eager to ascertain how numerous new materials and equipment perform in conditions that simulate a nuclear battle. Hence, the reluctance to start an arms control process which may result in constraints on key aspects of the programme.

A key element in the current phase of the SDI research effort is the X-ray laser which is in early development. The X-ray laser is essentially a nuclear bomb attached to a series of rods. Simplified, the detonation of the nuclear bomb is supposed to result in the X-ray energy discharge being focussed through the rods, thus creating a laser beam.

In a related development in August it was reported that the SDIO had contracted a study on using nuclear explosives to launch payloads into orbit with a company in San Diego, California known as Creative Enterprises. The theory is that a nuclear explosive device would be placed at the bottom of a 1-kilometre shaft and payloads would be placed on top of it. The device could drive the payload to geosynchronous orbit.

This points to the delicate problem facing President Reagan of explaining to the public that the SDI programme - despite repeated assurances - will not, after all, rely solely on non-nuclear technologies for its success. The Reagan Administration during the first two years of the programme made great capital out of this point; indeed, it appeared to account for much of the programme's popularity with the public.

It may well be that the Soviet Union has already concluded that the best way to set back the US "Star Wars" programme is through attempts at restrictions on nuclear testing. Certainly the persistence with which the Soviet Government has sustained the testing moratorium, despite the defiant gestures by the US Administration throughout 1986, would tend to give a certain credence to this theory. There is good reason to assume that General Secretary Gorbachev believes that a test ban is a popular idea in the West and that eventually the United States will be unable to sustain its negative stance - whether the reasons have to do with "Star Wars" or otherwise - in the face of popular opinion.

Most certainly the Administration has been quite sensitive to recent Congressional motions and resolutions urging a ban on nuclear tests. In March 1986 the President strongly criticized Congress, following the passage of a House of Representatives non-binding resolution calling on the Administration to negotiate a total ban on nuclear testing. In a letter to Senator Robert Dole, the Majority leader, Reagan suggested that the resolution "would undercut the initiatives I have proposed to make on progress on nuclear test limitations issues and they would set back prospects on a broad range of arms control efforts, including the achievement of deep, stabilizing and verifiable reductions." A non-binding resolution to this effect was one of the compromise proposals which emerged out of the Defence Bill Conference Committee in October 1986.

There is little doubt that the issue of nuclear testing is both complex and controversial. However, many of America's Allies remain mystified at Washington's consistently negative reaction to Gorbachev's proposals on verification. It will never be known whether the Soviet General Secretary is serious about his proposals unless Washington begins to respond in a more positive manner; at a minimum, it is argued, a change in the Administration's position might expose the sincerity of Soviet claims that they alone are ready for serious negotiations.

In terms of world opinion the Soviet Union most certainly has the upper hand on this issue. The political benefits to the Soviets of extending their moratorium, despite a succession of US tests and the announcement of more to come, was admitted by the Soviet Chief of Staff Marshal Akhromeyev on 14 April of this year when he said:

> "The level of military costs did not compel us as responsible military men to urge our government to discontinue the moratorium... In our assessment of the situation, political considerations prevailed."

More serious than the public opinion battle which now seems to be a dominant feature of superpower arms control diplomacy is the concern in Europe, as elsewhere, that a real opportunity to put a cap on the qualitative arms race may be spurned. In this regard the Rapporteur would wish to associate himself with the Chairman of the North Atlantic Assembly's Special Committee on Nuclear Strategy and Arms Control, Senator Joseph Biden, who has recently called for the United States to ratify existing treaties limiting nuclear testing (PNE, TTBT) and either to reopen negotiations on a Comprehensive Test Ban or to seek agreement on gradual reductions in the threshold and the number of tests permitted.[24] There have been indications in the last few months - most recently at the Reykjavik meeting of Gorbachev and Reagan - that the Soviet Union would be interested in limiting the numbers and size of tests as an interim step. This opportunity must be seized and not spurned.

ATBMS IN EUROPE: A NEW CHALLENGE FOR THE ALLIANCE?

The announcement in the summer of 1986 that the Supreme Allied Commander General Rogers had forwarded to the NATO Military Committee a set of guidelines for the development of a possible European Anti-Tactical Ballistic Missile (ATBM) defence against shorter-range Soviet threats raised what, hitherto, had been a debate confined to defence experts into a major item on the Alliance's agenda.

The guidelines form part of a broader NATO undertaking to ascertain the threat, feasibility and consequences of a West European air defence system. Two sub-groups of the NATO Air Defence Committee (NADC) which report directly to the Council are also engaged in ATBM work. The Panel on Air Defence Philosophy (PADP) has been requested to develop an "ACE Long Term Counter-Air Philosophy" to identify the relationship between offensive counter-air (OCA) and defensive counter-air options as they relate to the new threats posed by the Warsaw Pact.

The other sub-group, the Panel on Air Defence Weapons (PADW), reportedly began its work on active measures to counter the Tactical Ballistic Missile threat in January of this year. The NADC panels are composed of experts drawn from the different member countries, including France.

The two principal proponents of ATBMs in Europe over the last year have been General Rogers and the West German Defence Minister Manfred Wörner. Substantial pressure is coming from the office of SACEUR where, ironically, there have also been frequent expressions of concern that the American SDI programme might drain attention and funds from the priority requirement of shoring up NATO's conventional defences.

Minister Wörner initially had called for a European Defence Initiative (EDI) which would have used much the same technologies as those being developed in the SDI. He proposed, in this context, European co-operation on an extended air defence system which would provide defences against all aerial threats from conventional fighters and bombers to cruise and ballistic missiles. In recent months Minister Wörner has been less vocal on this matter, calling for an Extended Air Defence System (EADS) specifically against Soviet tactical ballistic missiles using more conventional technologies. There have been reports of significant differences within the German Government on assessments of the true extent of the short-range threat.

Proponents of ATBMs assert that new SRBMs will give the Soviets the ability to concentrate short-range tactical missile strikes on prime NATO targets - nuclear weapon sites, airfields, munitions stockpiles, and C2 centers - and prevent, delay, or obstruct NATO response options. The suppression of NATO air defences by conventional missile strikes would enable Soviet aircraft to conduct follow-up air strikes in NATO's rear area with greatly reduced attrition. It is pointed out that missiles can replace a number of aircraft sorties - sorties which are costly and which otherwise would stand a chance of being destroyed by NATO air defences. Most importantly, the air operation would precede any contact between Warsaw Pact first echelon troops and NATO defending forces.

A study released in July 1986 by the Konrad Adenauer Foundation reported that the Soviet Union has already tested conventionally-equipped SRBMs, potentially giving the Warsaw Pact the ability to launch a conventional pre-emptive strike that would destroy the most valuable military targets in Western Europe. In addition, the study reported that tests of conventionally-equipped ballistic missiles had been so successful that the Soviet Union is expected to begin equipping SS-21 and SS-23 missiles "in the very near future" and would eventually equip 40% of all ballistic missiles with conventional warheads.

Others are more sceptical. Some analysts wonder how many missiles are (or would be) armed conventionally and how many would be assigned for the first phase of operations. They question the accuracy levels of the SS-21s, SS-22s and SS-23s (now and in the near future) projected by proponents of ATBMs. It is important to determine how much the range of missiles is limited both by the required accuracies for conventional use as well as by the heavier weight of conventional munitions.

Sceptics also question whether the conventional arming of short-range missiles would be a cost-effective undertaking for the Soviet Union. Some analysts have their doubts. They also doubt whether this potential short-range ballistic missile threat, should it come to pass, would be qualitatively more ominous than the range of other threats which confront and will confront NATO, such as the several hundred Pact air-to-surface missiles or dual-capable air-launched cruise missiles.

It is questions such as these which require detailed examination by NATO authorities, since the future of the ATBM debate will turn in large part on the answers given and assessments made. To date NATO has no agreed threat assessment on the conventionally-armed short-range ballistic missile question. There are known to be profound doubts harboured in some NATO capitals that the situation is as dramatic or as dangerous as is sometimes portrayed.

There is also the obvious question of cost to NATO of going down the ATBM path. Patriot's current $11 billion price tag can give only a daunting hint of what an eventual workable ATBM system might cost. Should the funds come from new expenditures from already strapped Alliance Governments, or should existing resources be shifted around? Could alternative passive measures, which have in the past proved cost-effective, such as additional runways at airbases, additionally hardened shelters for dual-capable aircraft and improved crisis dispersal, provide a cheaper and more practical alternative to such a program? If the analysis eventually concludes that ATBM is the correct way to address a real Soviet threat, the Alliance must still address the implication of spending on ATBM instead of remedying other glaring deficiencies, such as modernization and ammunition shortfalls. NATO must decide what is more crucial in formulating an overall credible deterrence strategy - it must determine the relative priority to be given to the new short-range missile threat. To wit, ATBM must be introduced into the Conceptual Military Framework and the Conventional Defence Initiative.

This brings us to arms control. Should NATO seek to pursue ATBM within existing treaty constraints, or without? If the Allies do decide to develop ATBM technologies, then they would do well to keep the ABM treaty ambiguous at the upcoming 1987 review conference. If, on the other hand, they reject ATBM, then they must seek to tighten ABM treaty ambiguities which the Soviets may have succeeded in exploiting in constructing their own dual-capable SAM system. Either way, in any case, the outcome may prove crucial for NATO's deterrent strategy.

It is clear that more study must be devoted to answering these questions. Although the early evidence is suggestive of a new potential Soviet offensive capability, public support for any ATBM system must rest on concrete facts.

NOTES

1. For other examples of these discrepancies, see Amy Bodhar and Benjamin F. Schemmer, "Just How Big is the Soviet Threat? It Depends On Who's Counting What?", Armed Forces Journal International, June 1986.

2. For a detailed discussion of these themes see Stephen Johnson, "Soviet Electronic Warfare", in Special International Defence Review, publication on electronic warfare, December 1985.

3. John M. Porter, "Electronic Warfare: Can Everyone Tune In On The Same Frequency?", Armed Forces Journal International, February 1986.

4. Bernard W. Rogers, "NATO's Conventional Defence Improvement Initiative", NATO's Sixteen Nations, July 1986.

5. The information from this section draws heavily from the excellent monograph authored by Julian Perry Robinson entitled NATO Chemical Weapons Policy and Posture, produced by ADIU, University of Sussex, September 1986.

6. See UK Secretary of State for Defence, Statement on the Defence Estimates 1982, Vol. 1 (HMSO 1982), and Statement of R.L. Wagner, US Assistant Secretary of Defense for Atomic Energy, before Senate Appropriations Committee, 6 May 1982, cited in J. P. Robinson, ibid. p.19.

7. J. P. Robinson, ibid. p.25.

8. See article by H. Barnes, in Financial Times, 24 May 1986.

9. For a detailed explanation of the rationale for NATO's LRINF programme, see NAA Special Committee Report on Nuclear Weapons in Europe, 1985.

10. According to figures released in November 1985 by the Arms Control Association of the United States, NATO figures include only American and British (64 Polaris) strategic forces.

11. According to SALT counting notes, all launchers are assumed to carry the maximum number of weapons during testing. An exception is the 288 VS C-3 SLBMs which have been tested with 14 MIRVs but which are actually deployed with 10. Figures do not include US or Soviet SLCMs nor F-111s or Backfires.

12. See the 1985 General Report of the Military Committee of the North Atlantic Assembly for more details of the controversy.

13. "Trident II Missiles: Capability, Costs and Alternatives", Special Study of the Congressional Budget Office, July 1986.

14. For an excellent treatment of this issue, and for general information about US and Soviet SLCM programmes, see James P. Rubin, "Sea Launched Cruise Missiles: Facing up to the Arms Control Challenge", Arms Control Today, April 1986.

15. Stanley Sloan, MBFR: Prospects for An Accord, Congressional Research Service (CRS), Library of Congress, 31 March 1986.

16. For elaboration on some of these points see Stanley Sloan, ibid.

17. See John Borowsky, "Avoiding Surprise Attack" (Unpublished).

18. See, for example, Lee Hamilton, "Soviet Compliance and the Future of SALT" Arms Control Today, July/August 1986.

19. For a detailed discussion of these issues see the 1985 General Report of the Military Committee of the North Atlantic Assembly, Rapporteur Sir Geoffrey Johnson Smith.

20. Les Aspin, Chairman of the House Armed Services Committee, "If You Undercut SALT, You Uppercut Security", Press Release, 31 March 1986.

21. Al Tinajero et al. "US-Soviet Strategic Nuclear Forces, Potential Trends with and without SALT", CRS, 5 October 1984.

22. Countdown on SALT II, Arms Control Association, November 1985.

23. Quoted in Arms Control Association Fact Sheet on CTBT, August 1985.

24. Remarks By Senator Joseph Biden to the National Press Club, Washington DC, The Reagan Administration and Nuclear Weapons: A Smokescreen of Mythology; A Future Less Secure, 10 September 1986.

4

Alliance Political Developments: Maintaining Consensus

Bruce George

INTRODUCTION: A VISIT TO THE PAST - THE FOUNDING OF NATO

It is often true that the closer we come to an object of interest, the more limited our ability to discern its true form. We can thus forgive contemporaries of Christopher Columbus their inability to see beyond the horizon from their vantage on terra firma. Your Rapporteur, in drafting reports on Alliance political developments for this Committee in past years, has developed a keen appreciation for the difficulty this paradox presents to public servants like ourselves. We must stand amidst a whirl of ever changing events, many of which appear to bear little more than temporal relation to one another, and from it we must try to wring coherent, practical policies which will lead us not only through next year but which will show us the way into the next century.

As the experience of Columbus demonstrates, fresh perspectives are the antecedents of bold actions. This is no less true of our world than it was of his. Somehow we must gain a vantage from which to assess the flux of current events and from which we can chart a course which leads beyond the horizon. Your Rapporteur believes that an historical perspective can help provide this vantage. If we take a moment to recall the birth of the Alliance, the unlikely conspiracy of circumstance that brought this group of nations together in a partnership of nearly forty years now, we may rediscover many useful parallels.

The Immediate Post World War II Period

The formative years of the Alliance span the ten years from the end of World War Two to the entry of the Federal Republic in 1955. These are the years during which the post-war order took shape, the time in which nations emerged from a war-torn landscape and sought the best way forward. For many, a security alliance was not the immediate priority. As now, each nation had its own sovereign interests to pursue and the tasks before them were monumental, to say the least. However, other events intervened, and, before long, divergent interests had to be reconciled with a common need. The priorities of the Western democracies changed and with them the shape of Europe and much of the world.

Within this ten-year period, two distinct phases of development occurred. Both were evolutionary in nature and, given the obstacles which had to be overcome, neither was at any time a foregone conclusion. The first, culminating in the North Atlantic Treaty in 1949, involved a gradual, at times grudging, recognition that the Soviet Union posed an increasing threat to a weakened and divided Europe. It became apparent during this period that the political and economic stability necessary to counter the threat could only be brought about through transatlantic solidarity. During the second phase, from 1949 to 1955, the character of the threat to Western Europe assumed a decidedly military cast, necessitating a unified military response. Again, the impediments were myriad. However the Alliance responded and by 1955 had become, in its broad outlines, the organization that it is today.

The world which emerged from the Second World War bore little resemblance to the world of the 1930's. In Europe, both victor and vanquished alike were left with the daunting prospect of reconstructing their lives from the debris left behind by relentless tides of military men and machinery. It was clear that it would take years to reverse the material and psychological damage that had been caused, if it could be done at all. Meanwhile, the redistribution of relative power in world politics began to make itself felt.

The Soviet Union had suffered and benefited greatly. The oft quoted figure of 20 million dead probably only begins to tell the story of the depth of Soviet suffering during the war. However by war's end the Soviet Union had matured into the preeminent military power of the eastern hemisphere, with more than 6 million men under arms and a fully mobilized industrial capacity. She had enlarged her territory by more than 180,000 square miles with the annexation of Latvia, Estonia and Lithuania, and occupation of parts of Poland, Germany, Finland, Rumania and Czechoslovakia. What the Soviets intended to do with their new found power was not immediately evident. The introversion which characterized Soviet society before the war had turned to active concealment in its wake. In a telegram to President Truman on 12 May 1945 Churchill spoke of "an iron curtain...drawn down upon their front. We do not know what is going on behind..."

Of the other pre-war European powers, none had fared as well. France had suffered a prolonged occupation for the greater part of the war, during which her international commitments were suspended or severely weakened. Great Britain had survived the war without direct invasion, but it had stretched its resources beyond breaking in support of the war effort, and as early as December 1945 Britain was forced to borrow 5 billion dollars from the United States and Canada. Germany, of course, had no pretentions to world power after the war, and was concerned more than anything with survival, survival in a national purgatory of indeterminate length and in a divided state with an uncertain future.

The situation across the Atlantic could not have offered a more stark contrast. Alone among the "Big Four", the United States - with the exception of Pearl Harbor - had been spared the direct effects of the war on her home territory. US industry emerged intact and healthier than ever. She found herself in sole possession of the atomic bomb, the "winning weapon". However, US acceptance of the international responsibilities and influence these circumstances entailed was not immediately forthcoming.

At the close of the war America's own brand of isolationism began to reassert itself. The general mood was one of relief at the completion of an unpleasant but necessary job. The temporary alliance had served its purpose, but now it was time to return to the business of running the country. That meant foreign trade not foreign legions. US troop levels were drawn down from over 3 million in 1945 to under 400,000 one year later, and Congress would brook no greater military commitment than the necessary and, it was assumed, temporary occupation forces.

The Four Power Alliance: The Failure to Reach Accomodation

Under the circumstances, a North Atlantic Treaty within four years would have seemed a remote prospect indeed. All indications in the immediate post-war period pointed in the opposite direction, towards a divergence rather than convergence of interests. Britain and France had turned their attentions to rebuilding their own countries and arresting the decline of their respective empires. The United States had begun her traditional withdrawal across the Atlantic. The Soviets were left to tend their wounds and consolodate their wartime gains.

Soviet indiscretions during this early period did not go unnoticed - British Foreign Minister Bevin's indignation at the redrawing of Polish borders in August 1945 and George Kennan's "long telegram" outlining the Soviet mentality in February 1946 typified the growing concern - but, under the circumstances, they were tolerated. The feeling at the time, particularly in France and Britain, was that, certainly, there was enough to do without making enemies of erstwhile allies. The process of rebuilding and the responsibility of dealing with Germany required, if not concert, at least peace among the four central powers. For a time this looked like a reasonable possibility.

Britain and France did their best to placate the Soviets in an effort to preserve the four-power alliance. For example, the UK at one point offered the USSR a fifty-year treaty of cooperation. When the Marshall Plan was first announced, it was the French who insisted on Soviet participation in drawing up the initial European response. As relations between the US and USSR began to sour, Britain and France each tried desperately to supply a moderating influence. For the most part the Soviets remained unresponsive.

There were two primary reasons for believing these gestures might not be in vain. After the war, consultations between the Allies continued in the form of periodic four-power ministerial meetings. In fact, these meetings continued into the mid-1950's, long after they had ceased to serve any useful purpose. In 1946 and into 1947 they offered at least a chance of sorting out differences, but by the time of the Moscow conference in March 1947, the British had begun to lose patience. The March meetings ended in failure and, when the November-December conference met with a similar fate, the British Labour government led by Clement Attlee became convinced that the Soviets were only using the conferences in an effort to sow discord between the US, UK and France.

The second ray of hope came in the form of the United Nations Charter, signed in San Francisco in June 1945. Support for settlement of international disputes by the rule of law instead of the force of arms was understandably strong after the war. However, the problems inherent in such international regimes had not been solved in the interim between the League of Nations and the UN. The UN still did not have the power to enforce its decisions on the very states which gave it legitimacy, and, due to the veto power conferred upon members of the Security Council, it was often prevented from even delivering any decision at all.

With the alternatives to direct confrontation evaporating, it became more and more difficult for Western Europeans to accept Soviet behavior with equanimity. Opposition parties in Poland, Hungary, Bulgaria and Rumania were systematically eliminated in 1947 as communist leaderships became firmly ensconced. Communist activity--whether Soviet inspired or not--began to cause concern in countries like Italy and France.

In January 1948, the British Foreign Secretary Ernest Bevin called for a "European union". On 17 March 1948 the Brussels Treaty creating the Western European Union was signed by Britain, France, the Netherlands, Belgium and Luxembourg. Although the Treaty was ostensibly designed "to take such steps as may be held necessary in the event of renewal by Germany of a policy of aggression", when the first military planning session took place in April 1948, the stated objective was to defend "as far east in Germany as possible..." The Soviet Union had become the obvious aggressor. It would be some time yet before suspicion of Germany subsided, but the Soviets had clearly supplanted them in the British threat assessment and had at least equaled them in the minds of the French.

The Brussels Treaty was a symbol of Western Europe's sincere desire to maintain the peace. But in the face of the clear imbalance of power between the USSR and Western Europe, it was a hollow gesture without support from the United States.

The Increasing Commitment of the United States to Western Europe

If there was one piece of Presidential advice the US

Congress ever took to heart it was George Washington's caution against entangling alliances. But even this time-honored tradition fell victim to the events of 1947 and 1948.

Although the United States had long criticized Great Britain and France for the "undemocratic" nature of their colonial pasts, not even the US was prepared for the consequences of a rapid decolonization process. Britain's financial state had grown much worse by the beginning of 1947 and she had already begun to pare her military forces as a result. A memo from the Chancellor of the Exchequer to the Prime Minister in January summed up the state of the national treasury: "We must think of our national defence, in these hard and heavy days of transition, not only against the more distant possibility of armed aggression, but also against the far more immediate risk of economic and financial overstrain and collapse."

In order to relieve her financial burdens Britain began to pare her international commitments. In February 1947, the British government informed the United States that after March they were withdrawing from Greece and Turkey. Then Undersecretary of State Dean Acheson explained the consequences to a group of congressional leaders: "Soviet pressure on the Straits, on Iran, and on northern Greece had brought the Balkans to the point where a highly possible Soviet breakthrough might open three continents to Soviet penetration." Whether or not Acheson was overstating the strategic implications, the Truman administration was agreed that something had to be done to fill the void left by the UK. On 12 March 1947, Truman announced aid to Greece and Turkey in what was to become know as the "Truman Doctrine".

Coupled with political turmoil, the threat of financial collapse in Europe raised grave concerns in Washington. In June, the US responded with the announcement of the Marshall Plan to help ease the financial strain on European states. Coming as it did, just as US and Canadian loans were running out, news of the Marshall Plan was welcomed by the British government. However, plans for major cuts in military forces continued regardless. The result of these developments was less a security crisis than a crisis of confidence. With the Marshall Plan and Truman Doctrine, the US had taken the first steps toward direct peacetime involvement in Europe but was not yet ready to supply more than financial assistance.

The first six months of 1948 would force the US

hand. In February 1948, one month after Bevin's call for a union for the defense of Europe, communists staged a coup d'etat in Czechoslovakia. On 17 March, within hours of a speech in which Truman announced the "death" of Czechoslovakia, the Brussels Treaty was signed giving tangible evidence of Europe's commitment to the security of the West. On 11 June, Senator Vandenberg, a well know advocate of "America first", offered a resolution calling upon the United States to support "regional and collective" security arrangements. Thirteen days later, events of the first half of 1948 were crowned by a Soviet blockade of Berlin. In September, the first round of the North Atlantic Treaty talks began.

The Need for US Troops in Europe

The North Atlantic Treaty, signed in April 1949, stated that "an armed attack against one or more of [its members]...shall be considered an attack against them all." The twelve original signatories were Belgium, Canada, Denmark, France, Iceland, Italy, Luxembourg, the Netherlands, Norway, Portugal, the United Kingdom, and the United States. Greece and Turkey joined in 1951 and Spain in 1982. The Atlantic Alliance had the strong support of many Socialist and Social Democratic parties in Europe. The British Labour Prime Minister Clement Attlee was a key figure in the negotiations, as was the Belgian Socialist Paul-Henri Spaak. The Labour and Social Democratic governments of Norway and Denmark, after having worked unsucessfully for a Nordic Union, were also founding members of NATO.

The political commitment that this statement represented, especially coming from to the United States, went a considerable distance towards addressing the apparent crisis of confidence which had arisen in Europe. But it left many questions unanswered. The US Congress had given its consent to an association, but one which required no specific commitments of men and materiel to Europe during peacetime. Yet it was commonly acknowledged that the forces stationed in Europe at the time of the Treaty signing were impossibly overmatched by Soviet forces in the region. It was estimated in January 1950 that 54 divisions would be necessary just to "defend a line of retreat at the Rhine river, NATO had only 10 divisions in West Germany." The UK still did not feel able to contribute additional forces to the continental defense, and France, the only other European NATO member with a significant military force, was dividing its attention between Europe and Indochina. Inevitably, the prospects of German rearmament and the commitment of US ground forces rose to the fore.

The contribution which Germany could make to the defence of Europe had been recognized even before the signing of the North Atlantic Treaty. Britain had already accepted the possibility in principle at the formation of the Western European Union. In the US, the Pentagon had not only accepted the possibility but the necessity of German troops if Western Europe were to have any chance of holding off a Soviet attack. France,however, would have no part of German rearmament. When the French National Assembly ratified the North Atlantic Treaty, they did so with the express understanding that the Germans would not rearm.

In 1948, the Germans themselves began to add fire to an already heated debate. There was growing concern about the security of Germany in the face of an increasing threat just across the border in East Germany. In June, several retired German generals issued a critique of Western forces and war plans. Recognizing that, in the circumstances which existed at the time, West Germany was likely to be the battleground of any future war in Europe, they criticized forces in being as woefully inadequate for the task of deterrence. They found the use of the Rhine as the first line of Western defense a disturbing and unnecessary concession of German territory to the potential enemy and called for defense at the Elbe. As for a German contribution, they left that to the discretion of the occupation governments. In December 1948, one of the drafters of the June memorandum, Dr. Speidel, shared these views with Konrad Adenauer.

Officially, the United States remained opposed to German rearmament and additional US troops in Europe until the North Korean invasion on 25 June 1950. The invasion, as far removed from Europe and America as it was, was seen as a radical and deliberate escalation of the Cold War by the Soviets. In addition, US and West European leaders saw parallels between a poorly defended South Korea and the inadequate defence posture of Western Europe. In September Truman agreed to significant increases in US forces in Europe _if_ the Europeans could raise sixty divisions, ten of them German. The proposal was made to the Allies at the North Atlantic Council meeting in New York on 12 September and was immediately rejected by the

French. In October the French proposed a plan of their own for a European army, in which they conceded the inevitability of German rearmament. However, by proposing that German soldiers be integrated in small units under a European command, they sought to maintain some control over their size and independence. A compromise was reached in December and the European Defense Community (EDC) was born.

The Inability to Achieve a Credible Conventional Deterrent

In April 1951 the United States Senate approved Senate Resolution 99 sending four US divisions to Europe. The "entangling alliance" was at last established in full. But it did not come without a catch. Accompanying Resolution 99 was a mandate that the Joint Chiefs of Staff certify the Europeans were making an effort on their own behalf.

Thus, when Alliance Foreign, Defense, and Finance Ministers gathered in Lisbon in February 1952, it appeared the major obstacles had been traversed and no lasting damage had been done in the process. The meeting itself only confirmed the optimistic projections. When the session was adjourned on 25 February, the concept of the EDC had been ratified, an integrated command had been established, and all NATO countries had agreed to substantial military commitments to the Alliance.

By 1953, the French National Assembly had still not ratified the EDC, European countries were finding it extremely difficult to meet the Lisbon conventional force goals, and the United States was being held accountable. However, tight budgets were not exclusive to Europe. NATO's first Supreme Allied Commander was now President of the United States and there was no mistaking his allegiance. The US economy was not what it had been in the post-war years and Eisenhower was determined to gain control of it, through forced austerity if need be. Conventional military forces were inherently expensive and nuclear weapons, pound for pound, were <u>very</u> cheap. Thus, the US military's "new look" was one which relied on massive retaliation with nuclear weapons. Reluctantly, NATO Ministers were convinced of the desirability of the new emphasis.

By 1954, it was looking more and more as if the EDC was headed for defeat in the French Assembly. There was no little concern in Washington that it would take the

German force commitment down with it. The House of Representatives tied US aid to ratification of the agreement, and the White House threw its support behind the legislation. But it was all in a losing effort. When Stalin died in 1953, the Soviet government which replaced him launched an immediate and fairly successful "peace" campaign which resulted in reduced threat perceptions throughout Europe. In France, the Indochinese debacle had ended in armistice in July 1954, and in August, the National Assembly defeated the EDC.

Picking up the pieces after the failure of EDC was surprisingly easy. By the end of October, the Paris agreements had been signed restoring West German sovereignty and extending them an invitation of membership in NATO. With German entry in 1955, the second phase of NATO's development came to a close. The Alliance had assumed the basic form it retains today. Germany had been restored to independence; the US had accepted the commitment of substantial military forces for an indeterminate time in Europe; and the Alliance had become nuclear.

Establishing the Parameters of the US-European Relationship within NATO

The US commitment to Western Europe was thus firmly established, as was the nuclear component of the Alliance's deterrent capability. Both these elements, however, would prove to be sources of apprehension throughout the coming decades, and continue to do so today.

In the late 1950's the US Soviet strategic balance, and in particular Soviet gains in delivery systems, caused the United States to increase its tactical nuclear presence in Europe, raising concern about the future trends and risks involved in maintaing a nuclear balance between the superpowers. Yet the Soviet Union continued to be perceived as a threat to Western Europe following the invasion of Hungary in 1956 and, later, the Berlin crisis. The continuing presence of US troops in Europe and the American nuclear guarantee remained crucial to Western security. During the same period the growing integration of European economic institutions generated the belief in an Atlantic community between equal partners. This "Atlantic Partnership", however, was not achieved, stumbling over French resistance to the US nuclear monopoly and the exclusion of Britain from the process of European integration.

Despite these problems, important and constructive decisions were taken in the late 1960's. Growing dissatisfaction on both sides of the Atlantic with the strategy of massive retaliation led to the adoption in 1967 of the flexible response doctrine. Concern that NATO over- emphasized the military aspects of security resulted in the commission of a year long study on the "Future Tasks of the Alliance" which became known as the Harmel doctrine. It reflected NATO's commitment to maintain a strong defence but also strengthened NATO's political mandate, assigning it the task "to pursue the search for progress towards a more stable [political] relationship" with the Warsaw Pact. The 1967 Harmel report thus planted the seeds of the current dual approach to Alliance security: defence and dialogue.

The changes in NATO's nuclear strategy and the Harmel Report also had a direct impact on the US-European relationship within the Alliance. With the creation of the Nuclear Planning Group (NPG) in 1966, Western Europe obtained the right to influence the planning for the potential use of nuclear weapons. In a crisis, this was particularly important given the number of battlefield nuclear weapons deployed in Europe. Adoption of the Harmel report led the Allies to agree to strengthen NATO's political institutions through the creation of a Senior Political Committee composed of the Deputy Permanent Representatives. This development opened the door to greater intra-Alliance consultations, particularly in the field of arms control.

Conclusion

The Rapporteur hopes that this brief historical analysis has highlighted the continuity of many of the issues facing the Alliance. It could be argued that some of NATO's dilemmas are structural. The need for the US presence in Europe has fuelled quasi-permanent debate on the nature of the US contribution to NATO. The inability to maintain a credible conventional deterrent and the resulting dependence on nuclear weapons has been the source of constant disquiet since the early 1950's. These paradoxes are the focus of intense debate today and the nature of current discussions is addressed in the following section.

Yet past experience has also shown that many of the

challenges to the Alliance, although often related to the points mentioned above, are more transient in nature. The contribution of an independent Federal Republic of Germany to the security of the Alliance, bitterly disputed during NATO's early years, is now taken for granted. Developments outside the NATO area, whether the Suez crisis or the US action in Grenada, have raised tensions within the Alliance but have not caused its collapse. In addition, economic, financial and trade differences have erupted periodically throughout the history of the Alliance, as have diverging US/European perspectives on the conduct of East/West relations. Yet the Alliance has consistently been able to weather the tensions generated by "pasta wars" or by disputes over the appropriate reaction to Soviet activities in the Third World. Thus a certain perspective is necessary when discussing intra-Alliance difficulties.

Finally, the history of the Alliance has shown a remarkable ability to adapt successfully to new situations. Even when the very stucture of NATO was under stress at the time of France's withdrawal from the integrated military command, solutions were found to meet the new situation. In the end, the interests and requirements essential to maintaining the common security of the West have always prevailed. This should be a source of optimism.

THE STATE OF INTRA-ALLIANCE RELATIONS

> "In recent years an air of crisis has hung heavy across the Atlantic. Americans have accused Europeans of harboring anti-American thoughts and of risking "self-Finlandization". Europeans have countered with charges that the US has turned into an irrational Ally with a fascination for military power whose follies could drive Europe into an unnecessary and devasting war." [1]

Introduction

Since its foundation, NATO has relied on both a strong nuclear deterrent and the commitment of North America to Western Europe as two essential elements of Alliance defence against the Warsaw Pact threat. During the last several years political consensus on the desirability of these two components has eroded causing concern that the Alliance may be weakening. Although the credibility of NATO's overall nuclear deterrent has been strengthened through deployment of Cruise and Pershing II missiles, the validity of nuclear weapons as a deterrent is being seriously questioned. The heated debate over deployment of the INF missiles, which occurred in the early 1980's, has contributed to a breakdown in bi-partisan agreement over defence policies in many Alliance countries and has led to calls for a total withdrawal of nuclear weapons from Europe. The debate on this issue is not new. Dissatisfaction over NATO's nuclear strategy emerged in the 1960's, if not before; however, there is fear that it has reached a critical stage.

The closer binding of US and European nuclear vulnerability resulting from INF deployments has also raised concern that the nuclear threshold in Europe is too low. Criticism of the state of NATO's conventional forces focussed attention in the United States on Europe's willingness and ability to contribute substantially to the Alliance defence effort. Calls eminating from the US Congress, backed up at times with threats to withdraw US troops from Europe, led to fears that the transatlantic link was in danger. This has been compounded by US impatience at the perceived European unwillingness to support the US in key foreign policy areas and signs that the growing US trade deficit, coupled with America's budgetary problems could result in the US Congress adopting a "buy America" policy with serious repercussions on co-operative defence ventures with Europe.

For those who are convinced that the continued survival of the Alliance depends on both nuclear deterrence and US involvement in Europe, and who do not see, as some do, the US troops in Europe as an occupation force, the solution to these problems resides in improving NATO's conventional defence capabilities. A stronger conventional defence posture would raise the nuclear threshold, thereby decreasing NATO's reliance on nuclear weapons. In addition, the greater European contribution needed to enhance conventional defence could serve to allay criticisms within the Alliance which have arisen over burden-sharing.

This approach has been adopted by the Alliance to date. A series of initiatives ranging from new conventional strategies such as Follow-On Forces Attack

(FOFA) to increasing opportunities for greater defence co-operation, have been put forward as the best means of achieving the aims discussed above.

On the other hand several Socialist and Social Democratic* parties within NATO have adopted policies which diverge considerably from current NATO doctrine and from some policies they adopted while in office. These parties, particularly those in opposition, have called for the total elimination of nuclear weapons from Europe and in some cases the adoption of new conventional strategies based on concepts of "non-offensive defence". Many of their recommendations are drawn from the Palme Commission. Proponents of this approach share several common characteristics: a perception of the United States as being threatening and isolationist or unilateralist; a more benign assessment of the Soviet threat than is currently accepted by NATO; an abhorrence of nuclear weapons, especially in Europe; opposition to the Strategic Defense Initiative; an intense interest in arms control; and a belief in the utility of chemical and/or nuclear free zones. With elections approaching in several key Alliance nations, fear has been expressed in some quarters that NATO may soon be faced with major challenges to its current doctrine and strategies.

In the United States, President Reagan has offered another radical alternative to nuclear weapons, the Strategic Defense Initiative (SDI), a research programme which he hopes will result in a technologically feasible and financially affordable conventional ballistic missile defence against nuclear weapons. His vision marks a major departure from the strategic doctrine of the last twenty years - that the appropriate relationship between the United States and the Soviet Union is one of mutual vulnerability. Many in Europe and America are highly sceptical of the programme, believing it to be destabilizing, and fearing it could lead to a decoupling of the United States from Europe. The SDI's harshest critics, especially, but not exclusively, those on the

---

* The Rapporteur uses this terminology for the sake of convenience. He realizes that the terms Socialist and Social Democratic do not cover all parties who advocate these policies. In general, these parties are all affiliated with the Socialist International.

left of the political spectrum, see the programme as further justification for developing a new strategic doctrine which would rely on a Europeanisation of the defence effort.

The debate that is now taking place, on these and related issues, has fuelled speculation that the Alliance is heading for a major crisis. Some observers fear that the criticisms of NATO that are emanating from both sides of the Atlantic could lead to a serious erosion of Alliance consensus. A closer examination of the political implications of the problems discussed above is therefore warranted.

NATO's Efforts to Bolster Deterrence

Following the deployment of the INF missiles in Europe, the Alliance governments recognized that the overall deterrent triad - strategic and non-strategic nuclear forces and conventional defence - and particularly the conventional component, needed to be strengthened. General Rogers had declared that the state of existing conventional forces would require him to request the release of nuclear weapons in a matter of days. This situation was clearly unacceptable, and steps were urgently needed to raise the nuclear threshold.

Irritation over this situation was particularly keen within the US Congress. In the Senate, one of NATO's strongest supporters, Sam Nunn, introduced an amendment in June 1984 which, if adopted, would have called for the progressive withdrawal of US troops from Europe unless substantial efforts were made by the European Allies to improve NATO's conventional defence capabilities. Although the amendment was defeated, it sent a strong signal to allied governments that action had to be taken to address the concerns behind Senator Nunn's proposed legislation.

In December 1984, NATO Ministers of Defence agreed to a substantial increase in NATO's common infrastructure in order to improve facilities for US reinforcements in Europe and to increase inadequate ammunition stocks. The following year, in May 1985, Ministers adopted a package for improving conventional defence, the Conventional Defence Initiative (CDI). This programme called for improvements in sustainability, exploitation of technology and long-term planning.

In addition, changes have been made in NATO's

conventional strategies which are designed to enhance deterrence by diminishing the risk that NATO's conventional forces, after withstanding an initial attack by the Warsaw Pact, could be overwhelmed by the Pact's second echelon forces. This concept, known as Follow-On Forces Attack (FOFA), is seen as an extension of NATO's traditional capability to delay and disrupt Warsaw Pact follow-on forces through the use of new technologies. FOFA is not intended to downgrade NATO's other crucial missions, such as fighting the close battle.

The improvements being made in NATO's conventional defences and the use of new technologies in the endeavour is, however, expensive. Recognition of this has led to efforts to improve the return Alliance nations obtain from their defence investments. This approach has resulted in better long-term planning. At the political level, assessments are made on the NATO/Warsaw Pact conventional imbalance. These estimates serve to define and prioritize critical deficiencies in NATO's defence posture. These elements in turn have come together in a conceptual military framework, enabling the major military commands to introduce long-term planning into their procurement decisions.

In parallel with these efforts to identify key areas in conventional defence which require the urgent attention of the Alliance, steps have been taken to facilitate greater defence co-operation - both transatlantic and intra-European - in order to increase the cost-effectiveness of weapons' research, development, and procurement. In November 1984, the Independent European Program Group (IEPG), the only co-operative forum where all NATO European nations are represented, met for the first time at the ministerial level. This and subsequent meetings at the same level have given major political support to strengthening arms co-operation among the IEPG members. Recently, for example, the IEPG proposed six weapons projects for joint US-European development involving close to $400 million.

An environment favourable to NATO arms co-operation also exists in the United States, as evidenced by recent Congressional legislation, a series of decisions within the Department of Defense, and support from the State Department.

In June 1985 the Senate voted in favour of an amendment to the fiscal 1986 budget, sponsored by Senators Nunn, Roth, and Warner, authorizing $200 million for co-operative research and development projects among the

Allies. In addition, the legislation requires the Pentagon to set aside $50 million to test European equipment against similar US systems. This amendment thereby addresses both ends of the arms procurement process: by focussing on R&D it seeks to co-ordinate better the early stages of weapons development; the $50 million will also provide stimulus to US purchases of European manufactured weapons by requiring testing of existing US and European weapons. Similar legislation was also adopted by the US House of Representatives.

In a further effort to facilitate Alliance arms co-operation Indiana Senator Dan Quayle introduced legislation which allows European firms to compete with US corporations on an equal basis. This legislation has been incorporated into the defence budget as well.

In parallel with this Congressional action the Department of Defense (DoD) has taken a number of steps designed to further transatlantic defence co-operation. In the latest Defense Guidance issued by Defense Secretary Caspar Weinberger in December 1985 for the fiscal years 1988-1992, the services are directed to "expedite filling material needs through acquisition of existing equipment from Alliance nations". In addition, the Department of Defense has been instructed to take "full advantages of technologies, including emerging technologies, to improve conventional defences by actively seeking co-operative armament programmes with the Allies".

Secretary Weinberger also established a management team to oversee the DoD's arms co-operation efforts. Called the DoD Steering Group for NATO Armaments Co-operation, this taskforce has been placed under the direction of the Deputy Secretary of Defense, currently William Howard Taft IV. Mr. Taft has made clear that he expects all the military services in the United States to consider seriously joint US-Allied ventures before approving any new development programmes. Among the projects he has designated for possible collaborative ventures are a new deep-strike 200 km-range tactical missile to follow on to the multinational shorter-range Multiple Launch Rocket System (MLRS) currently being co-produced by Great Britain, France, Germany, and Italy; a new joint tactical Information Distribution System; a Joint Surveillance and Targeting Attack Radar Systems for the Air Force, and a short-range air defence command and control system for the Army.

These developments have received general support within the Alliance. Some specific aspects of these policies such as FOFA have generated criticism, particularly among opposition parties, and these concerns will be addressed below. The steps taken to date, however, are seen as part of an overall move away from reliance on early first use of nuclear weapons and towards a truly credible strategy of flexible response.

Other steps taken in an effort to raise the nuclear threshold, however, have generated greater controversy. In particular, plans to modernize the US chemical stockpile have been the cause of deep concern for many NATO nations and several members of the US Congress.

Modernization of US Chemical Weapons

At the May 1986 Defence Planning Committee meeting NATO ministers "formally noted" national force goals for the 1987-1992 period. Included in the US force goals was a plan to end the unilateral moratorium on the production of chemical weapons (CW) established by the Nixon Administration in 1969, and to build a new generation of binary chemical weapons. The US Secretary of Defense stated that the modernization of the aging stock of chemical weapons was essential to apply pressure on the Soviet Union to reach an agreement in the multinational conference on disarmament in Geneva. Nevertheless, the US plan has generated heated criticism within the US Congress, and of the NATO Allies only the UK, West Germany and Canada were reported to support it.

The Department of Defense in the United States has argued for over four years that there are ample military and political reasons to improve the US chemical stockpile. The Pentagon has been concerned by the growing imbalance in US and Soviet CW capabilities. The USSR has not responded to the 17-year moratorium in the United States on chemical weapons production. As a result, while the US stockpile of CW agents is estimated at between 70,000 and 90,000 tons, the Soviet stockpile is believed to range between 300,000 and 700,000 tons. In addition, the Soviets are thought to operate between 8 and 14 CW production facilities with a total annual production of approximately 10,000 tons.

In addition the Department of Defense believes that the current US stockpile is at the end of its useful lifespan and that the aging stocks, over 90% of which are stored in the United States and the remainder in West

Germany, is deteriorating and could constitute a safety hazard.

US military commanders also argue that the modernization of US CW munitions is necessary if NATO is to have a deterrent to the use of CW by the Warsaw Pact forces other than the release of battlefield nuclear weapons. A credible chemical capability is seen as part of the broader effort to raise the nuclear threshold and decrease NATO's reliance on the early use of nuclear weapons. In this context officials refer to the experience of the Second World War when both the Allies and the Axis powers refrained from using chemical weapons as an argument in favour of providing the Alliance with a capability to deter in kind.

Finally, US officials believe that a resumption of production of CW would force the Soviet Union to negotiate seriously on a treaty leading to a global ban on chemical weapons. The total elimination of chemical weapons is, of course, the solution preferred by the Administration to the current imbalance in this area. The United States tabled a draft treaty for a complete ban on CW at the Geneva conference in April 1984. The US is seeking stringent verification procedures including open challenge inspection which would allow suspected treaty violations by government-controlled facilities to be investigated by international inspectors within 24 hours. The Soviet Union has rejected these demands as being too intrusive.

The arguments put forward by the Administration in favour of chemical modernization are far from universally accepted. For many Allied nations, chemical weapons are as controversial, if not more so, than nuclear weapons, largely as a result of the experience of gas warfare during World War I. A number of NATO member countries have expressed opposition or reservations about the American production plan. While acknowledging they could not block the US decision, the governments of Denmark, Norway and the Netherlands have all officially stated their opposition to it. In addition, Belgium, Turkey, the Netherlands, Denmark and Portugal have declared that they will not allow chemical weapons to be deployed on their soil.

Aware of Allied sensitivities to chemical weapons, the US Administration has sought to keep the issue from becoming a "political football" in Europe by limiting NATO discussion to consideration of the US force goal. However, in order to obtain congressional funding authorization for the programme the Administration was required to certify to Congress that NATO governments had agreed that the production of binary weapons would reinforce NATO's deterrent posture and that an acceptable plan had been worked out for deployment of the weapons in time of crisis. Legislation was drafted which the Administration hoped would meet these requirements. Voted in July 1985 by Congress, the law authorizing and funding chemical modernization states that funds cannot be spent for procurement or assembly of binary munitions or for establishing production facilities for those munitions until the following conditions are met:

> That the US has submitted to NATO a force goal requiring modernization of the US share of the NATO chemical deterrent with binary munitions, and that the force goal has been formally adopted by the North Atlantic Council.
>
> That, in co-ordination with SACEUR, a plan has been developed for the deployment of US binary munitions to Europe in a crisis situation.
>
> That the United States government has consulted with other member nations of NATO on that plan.
>
> Final assembly of complete binary munitions may not commence before 1 October 1987 and then only if an international agreement on all chemical weapons has not been entered into by that date.

The law also requires the President to report to Congress on consultations with the Allies concerning efforts to:

> Protect key civilians at support facilities
>
> Upgrade chemical defence
>
> Initiate a study on chemical defence of logistic and command and control installations
>
> Initiate a study of equitable sharing of chemical weapons deterrent responsibilities.

The Administration believes that approval by NATO's Defence Planning Committee of the US force goal meets the first of these requirements. However, ten members of the

Senate Appropriations Committee wrote to the President indicating that they did not believe the DPC approval fulfilled the certification requirements. They argued that the issue was political and that therefore nothing short of approval of the plan by the North Atlantic Council would meet the intent of the legislation.

In addition, some key congressional leaders questioned the deployment plans for the weapons. The Administration had concluded that "the peacetime deployment of binary munitions in foreign countries is not essential because of the safety and speed with which these munitions can be transported." As a consequence of this decision the United States reached an agreement with the Federal Republic of Germany to remove existing stocks of US chemical weapons from the Federal Republic by 1992. In addition, under the terms of the accord, contingency plans for the deployment of binary weapons in time of crisis must include deployment in other NATO countries besides West Germany.

The Chairman of the House Foreign Affairs Committee, Dante Fascell, has critized this accord describing it as "a folly from a foreign policy and national security standpoint". Others have stated that the deal has led to the abandoning of the US chemical deterrent in Europe and makes it difficult if not impossible to deter in kind a first use of chemical weapons by the Soviet Union since it would be politically unfeasible for the West German government to accept a re-introduction of these munitions in time of crisis.

Despite these problems the President certified to Congress that the conditions required by Congress for the release of funds in fiscal year 1986 for the binary weapons modernization programme had been met. Nevertheless in August 1986 the House of Representatives voted narrowly 210-209 to bar production of binary munitions through 30 September 1987. The Senate, however, voted earlier against an attempt to block production. The issue will have to be resolved in a House-Senate Conference.

In Western Europe strong opposition to chemical weapons has led the Social Democratic Party (SPD) in the Federal Republic of Germany to reach an agreement with the East German Communist party on a model treaty which, if implemented, would ban chemical weapons from their two countries. The SPD has pledged to ratify this treaty if elected and to work for the creation of a chemical weapons-free zone in Central Europe. To this end the SPD has drafted a series of proposals on a chemical weapons-free zone in collaboration with the East German and Czechoslovak communist parties. These proposals have been submitted to the governments of Belgium, Denmark and the Netherlands, and Norway, Hungary, Poland and Luxembourg have been urged to consider them as well. The SPD has been criticized for participating in these talks when its status as an opposition party does not give it the authority to negotiate on the future security policy of the Federal Republic.

The SPD committment to a chemical-free zone in Europe is but one element of the party's security policy which differs substantially from current NATO doctrine. The party's defence platform is not unique; other Socialist and Social Democrats in Europe have adopted similar policies, generating concern that not only consensus on defence within the Alliance may be irreparably damaged, but that NATO itself could not withstand the challenges these programmes would pose should they be adopted.

The Debate Over NATO Strategy

Several European political parties are currently engaged in a reassessment of their approach to NATO's strategy and in some cases have adopted policies which differ substantially from current Alliance orthodoxy. These parties are all on the left or centre left of the political spectrum and are currently in opposition. However, increased attention is now being paid to these discussions since future elections in the Federal Republic of Germany and the United Kingdom could bring to power two parties pledged to undertake major reform of their nations' security policy and of the nature of their military contribution to the Alliance.

It should be stressed, however, that the policies discussed in this section are not new, nor have they emerged from a vacuum. In fact, Socialist parties from the Netherlands, Denmark, Norway, Flemish-speaking Belgium and Luxembourg have been meeting since 1981, within the Scandilux group, in an attempt to coordinate their policies towards the Atlantic Alliance. French Socialists, German Social Democrats and Labour members from the UK have attended these meetings as observers. Beginning in 1985, the Scandilux group has met with another group of European Socialists, Eurosud, composed of the French, Italian, Spanish, Portuguese and

French-speaking Belgian socialist parties. In addition to these groups, Socialists and Social Democratic parties discuss security issues within the Socialist International and its Disarmament Advisory Council, and within the Socialist group of several interparliamentary organizations such as the North Atlantic Assembly and the European Parliament. Leading participants in these meetings have expressed the hope that they will contribute to building a consensus on a new strategy for the Alliance.

The various alternatives to NATO strategy have many similarities; they seek to eliminate dependence on nuclear weapons, and a greater Europeanization of defence, with a decreased reliance on the United States. In addition, most of them incorporate some elements of "defensive defence" or "non-offensive defence", a concept which seeks to restructure conventional forces in a way that they can pose no offensive threat. Strongest support for these policies can be found in the defence programmes of the Social Democratic parties in Denmark and West Germany and the Labour Party in Britain.

In August 1986 the Social Democratic Party in Denmark adopted a document which begins by stating: "the Social Democratic Party sees no alternative to the membership of the Atlantic Treaty and NATO, its military organization. It also endorses non-offensive defence, urging Denmark to move to a non-offensive structure "in order to demonstrate peaceful and non-aggressive intentions and to contribute to bilateral détente." The party called for the withdrawal of one of three Danish brigades from the joint Danish-German Command for the defence of Schleswig-Holstein; disarming the airforce's F-16 aircraft of bombs; eliminating the navy's combat capabilities and converting it to a purely surveillance role; consigning seaward defence to mobile land-based missile batteries; and the reduction of peace-time levels of the navy and airforce. The programme commits the party to strengthening the defence of reception areas for incoming reinforcements. As regards nuclear weapons, Denmark already has renounced the deployment of nuclear weapons on its territory in time of peace. The Social Democrats are currently debating whether or not to extend the ban to cover wartime as well, through the creation of a Nordic nuclear-free zone.

At their party conference in Nürnberg in August, while re-affirming their committment to NATO, the West German Social Democrats adopted a platform calling for the creation of a purely defensive-oriented forward defence, incapable of mounting large-scale transborder operations. The party rejects deep strike concepts like Airland Battle and Airland Battle 2000. The party also backed negotiated reductions in NATO and Warsaw Pact force levels in Europe; however, the party rejected by a large majority the concept of large-scale unilateral reductions. The party conference appealed to the United States to halt and reverse the deployment of Cruise and Pershing II missiles in West Germany and requested that the Soviet Union reduce the number of SS-20s aimed at Western Europe to pre-1979 levels and remove the SS-21s and SS-22s stationed in East Germany and Czechoslovakia. The party recommended the creation of a nuclear-free corridor in Central Europe as a step towards a Europe free of nuclear weapons in East and West.

The British Labour Party adopted at its October Party Conference in Blackpool a policy that, while reaffirming its strong committment to membership in NATO, calls for a non-nuclear defence of Britain and the removal of all US nuclear facilities from the United Kingdom. They would cancel the UK's Trident missile programme and decommission the existing Polaris submarines. On the conventional front the party is committed to increasing the UK's conventional contribution to the defence of NATO. Changes in British strategic doctrine include consigning the UK's attack submarines to a coastal defence role, while the Tornado aircraft would be withdrawn from its FOFA tasks and re-assigned to ground support missions in Europe and naval-air patrols in the North-East Atlantic. In addition, as part of its emphasis on non-provocative defence concepts, the Labour Party is pledged to restructure the army, navy and airforce away from offensive towards defensive military roles. Labour has also said it would review the process by which assessments of the Soviet threat are made through a reduced reliance on US intelligence data and a restructuring of British Intelligence services.

Those who advocate the type of security policy outlined above strongly believe that it would promote more stable East-West relations. A non-offensive defence would be perceived by the Warsaw Pact as less threatening, and would therefore encourage reductions in the conventional forces of the Eastern bloc. Nuclear weapons in Europe are not perceived as a credible element of deterrent strategy since their use is inconceivable. Yet their presence in Europe increases East-West tensions. There is therefore a need for their drastic reduction or total elimination in order to ease these tensions and reduce the dangers of miscalculation.

The proposals contained in the defence policies of these three political parties have been heavily criticized. Directly addressing the Labour Party's defence policy, US Secretary of Defense Caspar Weinberger warned that it would be difficult to hold the NATO Alliance together if a Labour government were to impose unilateralist policies and close down US nuclear bases in Britain. This statement was endorsed by the US Administration and echoes similar sentiments expressed by several US Congressmen, and in particular, the liberal Democrat Stephen Solarz.

More generally, it is argued that nuclear weapons have played a crucial role in deterring the outbreak of war in Western Europe ever since 1945. Given the current state of the balance of NATO and Warsaw Pact forces, a potential nuclear response must remain an integral part of the NATO deterrent. Abandoning the nuclear option would destroy the credibility of the Alliance defence posture. In addition, the risks which result from this situation must be shared by all the Allies. US Ambassador to NATO David Abshire has stated "it is a dangerous illusion for anyone to expect that, if they were not willing to share the nuclear risk, the United States will blithely continue its nuclear guarantee." The unilateral renunciation of nuclear weapons will not make them disappear from the international scene, offers no incentives to the Soviet Union to eliminate its own nuclear arsenal, and constitutes in the eyes of many observers an open invitation to invasion, particularly if there is no credible conventional deterrent.

However, these same analysts also believe that the concepts of non-offensive defence are not credible. While some elements of this strategy are seen as holding genuine potential (particularly the recognition of the need for a better organized reserve force, improved reinforcement reception facilities, and proposals for passive defence barriers on the West German Plains), the doctrine as a whole is not seen as capable of genuinely defending against an aggression. There is little detail on how forces would be deployed under the concept, how sea lines of communication across the Atlantic would be defended, or how an invading force would be repelled back to its own territory.

An assessment of these alternatives to NATO strategy highlights a conceptual approach to the Alliance which is vastly different from that currently adopted by Allied governments. Proponents of non-offensive defence see NATO's current force posture as inherently threatening to the Warsaw Pact and are particularly concerned, in this respect, by the new FOFA strategy.

In addition they also disagree with NATO's analysis of the Soviet threat and ascribe to the USSR more benign intentions than does the Alliance. On the other hand, they see the United States as adopting more aggressive policies, citing as examples the US action in Grenada and the raid on Libya. They fear that this trend may grow, particularly if the United States deploys some kind of strategic defence system.

It would appear, then, that the consensus which existed at the time the Alliance was created and which resulted in sovereign nations joining together to face a commonly perceived threat may be collapsing. Of course, the 16 nations of the Alliance retain their sovereignty and are therefore at liberty to modify their policies to meet security challenges in new ways if they believe their defence requirements can be better fulfilled through different strategic concepts. However, the members of the Alliance have also agreed to a collective approach to their security; if this fundamental character of NATO is to be preserved then the implications of a change in one nation's defence policy on that of the other member countries cannot be ignored. One senior NATO military official has expressed the view that it is unlikely that the Alliance could withstand abrupt, fundamental changes in its strategy if they were to be implemented unilaterally by one nation without consultation with its Alliance partners.

The Strategic Defense Initiative

The impact that one nation's defence policy can have on the Alliance as a whole has been demonstrated by the debate sparked off by President Reagan's Strategic Defense Initiative (SDI). The programme, launched by the President in March 1983, is a comprehensive research programme whose aim is to harness new advanced and emerging technologies in an effort to determine whether an effective and affordable defence can be built against attacking ballistic missiles.

The concept itself challenges the strategic orthodoxy that has governed superpower relations for the last two decades. If a strategic defence system is deployed it would entail moving from a situation of mutual vulnerability to - _in extremis_ at least - one of mutual invulnerability. The President has, in fact, called for a move from an offensive environment to a defensive one.

The programme itself involves research into a number of high-tech fields and is divided into five project areas:

1. surveillance, acquisition, tracking and kill assessment;

2. directed energy weapons;

3. kinetic energy weapons;

4. systems analysis and battle management;

5. support programmes.

It is beyond the scope of this report to enter into a discussion of the technical details of the programme. The Rapporteur would refer those colleagues interested in the subject to the General Report of the Scientific and Technical Committee by Mr. Lothar Ibrügger.

It should be pointed out, however, that much of the criticism of SDI has been on technological grounds. Many scientists question whether the complicated problems of surveillance, acquisition and battle management can be solved. A comprehensive strategic defence system would have to perform, in a matter of seconds, a myriad of tasks including early warning of an attack, the tracking of missiles and re-entry vehicles throughout their trajectories, and the distinguishing of targets from decoys. The failure to perform any of these missions successfully would seriously compromise the ability to fend off an attack.

Disquiet has also been expressed over the cost of the programme. The President has requested $26 billion in order to fund the first five years of research. This has caused concern that other more immediate defence requirements, particularly in the conventional field, may be neglected. In addition, no credible estimate of how much it would cost to deploy a strategic defence system has been put forward so far. However, since the programme is still in a research phase it is difficult to imagine any basis for attempting to undertake a cost analysis of deployment.

Whatever the judgement on technological or enocomic factors, primary concern about the programme has, however, been expressed over its strategic desirability. Fears have been expressed that SDI could lead to a decoupling of the United States from Europe by creating a "Fortress America". The Administration has sought to allay these fears by stressing that the SDI is designed to protect the United States and its allies, a statement included in President Reagan's March 1983 speech. In fact, officials at the SDI Organization have expressed confidence that defences could be developed to successfully counter Soviet medium- and short-range missiles which threaten Western Europe. This has led to discussion of an early application of SDI technology to the European theatre and to the development of a European Defence Initiative based on anti-tactical ballistic missiles.

In addition, the Administration has been actively encouraging Allied participation in the programme. To date, the United Kingdom, the Federal Republic of Germany, and Italy have all signed agreements with the US government which establish varying degrees of cooperation in the research stage of the project. Israel and Japan have reached similar accords with the United States.

Nevertheless, other concerns remain. In particular, the prospect that both the United States and the Soviet Union could successfully deploy strategic defence systems has caused some to speculate that the European theatre could become an attractive battleground for conventional war. The two superpowers, certain that their own territory would be invulnerable from nuclear attack, could be less hesitant about waging war in Europe.

Some observers also argue that the strategic doctrine behind SDI calls into question the validity of the flexible response doctrine. The credibility of NATO strategy depends at present on the graduated nuclear escalation from the level of battlefield nuclear weapons up to that of strategic nuclear ones in the event that conventional deterrence should fail. Deployment of strategic defences by the two superpowers would eliminate the effectiveness of the upper end of NATO's nuclear scale, US strategic forces.

Finally, SDI's impact on overall US-Soviet relations has been an additional source of concern. Questions have been raised about the ability to move from an offensive environment to a defensive one without increasing instability by causing one side to believe that the other is in reality trying to achieve the capability to launch a pre-emptive strike. In addition, the consequences of SDI on the Geneva arms control negotiations is uncertain. While there is reason to believe that the SDI was one of the factors which contributed to a Soviet return to the negotiating table, some fear that it may prove to be a stumbling block which could prevent the reaching of any agreements on the reduction of nuclear offensive weapons.

Proponents of the SDI stress that it is at the moment only a research programme and that, before any decision is made to deploy a strategic defence system, not only must technological challenges be overcome, but that the strategic considerations evoked above would have to be taken into consideration. In addition, there is no doubt that the Soviet Union is engaged in similar research, and has been since the mid 1960's. The magnitude of Soviet Ballistic Missile Defence (BMD) programmes is impressive, involving perhaps as many as 10,000 scientists. There is also evidence that some of the Soviet research is at the prototype stage, including a ground-based laser capable of destroying low orbiting satellites. It is maintained, therefore, that as long as the Soviet Union is investigating ballistic missile technologies, prudence dictates that the United States should do so as well, with the support of its Allies. Finally, it is argued that should the research programme conclude that deployment of a strategic defence system is neither strategically desirable nor economically feasible, the work done on SDI technologies may have positive implications for conventional defence improvements.

Transatlantic Frictions

Discussions over the current validity and future directions of NATO strategy are occurring at a time when there are signs of growing transatlantic differences over a range of security, foreign policy and economic issues. The strains crystalized perhaps following the US raid on Libya.

The most obvious result of the US attack on Libya was to emphasize the deep differences between the US approach to the problem of state-sponsored terrorism and that of many European Allies. Traditionally, European nations have preferred political and diplomatic solutions to all types of conflict. Regarding the specific dilemma of Libyan support for international terrorism, European Allies felt that a military intervention would be ineffective and would run the risk of increasing terrorist incidents, which primarily occur on European soil. In addition, although most European governments found evidence linking Libya to international terrorism to be conclusive, at least with respect to the bomb attack against a West Berlin discotheque, they did not view Libya either as the sole or as perhaps the primary terrorist sponsor. Concern was also expressed over the potential damage the attack would cause to Western interests both in the Middle East and among moderate Arab states. The possibility that the use of military force in Libya would put civilians at risk was an additional source of disquiet, and unfortunately proved to be justified in the wake of the US attack.

For these reasons the European Allies issued continued calls for restraint, and urged both the United States and Libya to avoid action which would escalate tensions in the Mediterranean. The United States has also maintained that it would prefer to exercise political rather than military means to try to resolve its differences with Libya. The implementation of economic sanctions against Libya by the US government in January 1986 was one such measure.

The United States also strongly urged its Allies to follow suit, and adopt some form of diplomatic or economic measures in an effort to dissuade Libya from abetting terrorists operating against US and European interests. The twelve European Community Foreign Ministers could not, however, agree to take any such steps, to the great disappointment of the United States.

Despite intensive consultations it became increasingly obvious that the governments of the United States and the European members of NATO were unable to find common ground on this issue. It would appear that the United States decided it would not get the necessary support and therefore would have to take unilateral action. On 15 April, US forces, some of which flew from bases in Great Britain, struck targets in Libya. The United States, citing evidence of Libyan support of past terrorist attacks against American interests and plans to launch future ones, maintained that this attack was undertaken for reasons of self-defence as authorized by article 51 of the United Nations charter.

In addition to the political consequences of the US response to Libyan support of terrorism, the Alliance is faced with possible military repercussions. The British Government allowed the use of British bases leased by the

US Air Force in the raid. The opposition parties strongly condemned this decision, which provoked considerable criticism among British public opinion. Some observers predicted that the public outcry over the use by the United States of its bases in Britain for a non-NATO operation could strengthen the British Labour Party's position that all US nuclear forces in the United Kingdom should be removed.

Moreover, the lack of support for the US operation in other European countries reopened the debate over out-of-area developments. This issue, which had originally focused on Southwest Asia and the impact of possible deployment of the US Central Command, had largely been resolved within NATO. The US-Libyan confrontation, together with the French and Spanish refusal to allow American planes flying from Britain to use their airspace, may reopen this debate both in Europe and in the United States. Already the Social Democratic Party in West Germany is calling for a re-evaluation of the right of the United States to use its forces stationed in Europe for out-of-area operations.

It is not the intention of the Rapporteur to be either overly pessimistic or unduly alarmist. However, it is his view that state sponsorship of international terrorism is becoming, if only by the force of events, an Alliance issue. The lead-up to the US strike demonstrated the failure of Allied consultations on the specific problem of Libya. The Rapporteur very much regrets this. Allied consultations have, in the past, worked rather well, particularly on East-West relations and arms control. The remarkable degree of solidarity among the Allies on these issues provides a striking contrast to the current tensions which surround the Libyan crisis. It is the view of the Rapporteur that there is an urgent need for the creation of an institutional framework for the Allies to discuss both political and operational approaches to the fight against terrorism. Unless such a framework is established it is highly probable that present differences will remain and that transatlantic tensions will worsen.

The immediate consequence of the US strike against Libya was to serve as a catalyst for the emergence of a host of complaints on both sides of the Atlantic. For those members of the general public and of the policy making elites in the United States and Europe who are hostile to NATO, the controversy surrounding Libya has served as a pretext for voicing harsh criticism of the

Alliance and the way it functions. Observers who greatly value NATO urgently called for efforts to limit the potential serious damage that this acrimonious debate could engender. It would appear that these calls have been heeded; the leaders of the seven Western industrialized nations meeting at the Tokyo summit agreed on a series of measures designed to combat the threat of state-supported terrorism. The Rapporteur hopes that this, and other action, will be sufficient to calm recent rhetorical excesses and that the Alliance will emerge relatively unscathed from the controversy that erupted in the Spring of 1986.

Despite the progress made in co-operative efforts to fight terrorism, there is concern that the emergence of a strong current of anti-Americanism in Europe, following the raid on Libya, may erode Alliance cohesion. Anti-Americanism is not a new phenomenon; the view that the United States is unsophisticated, overly aggressive and interfering has been expressed by some European politicians and intellectuals for decades. What is disturbing about the recent attacks on the United States is their virulence and the fact that there would appear to be an increasing tendency in some circles to place the United States on the same moral plane as the Soviet Union.

Furthermore, the way in which these views have been perceived in the United States has also provided ammunition to those in the US who are critical of the American commitment to NATO. Protests in Europe against the US action in Libya have been described as further evidence of Europe's "self-Finlandization" and lack of commitment to the values the Alliance represents.

These developments have given a bitter flavour to transatlantic discussions. Unless many of the misconceptions in both the US and Europe can be dispelled and transatlantic debate placed on a more even keel, these trends may be amplified with profound negative repercussions for the Alliance. This is of particular concern to the Rapporteur, since economic considerations are increasingly influencing the state of the transatlantic defence relationship. The $148 billion US trade deficit has led to pressures in the US Congress to retaliate against perceived unfair trade practices. There are also indications that a new "Buy America" mood on defence procurement is growing in Congress, as exemplified by the Glenn Amendment restricting the ability of the US government to award SDI-related contracts abroad. Although this amendment has not been passed by the House of Representatives, together with similar legislation it could constitute a serious setback to the progress made recently in the United States in improving transatlantic defence cooperation.

Moreover, the size of the US budget deficit and the necessary cuts in spending required to reduce it have not only affected domestic programmes in the United States. The US Congress is also re-evaluating the United States' foreign policy commitments, and aid to several key countries, including Turkey, is likely to suffer as a consequence. There is even concern that attempts will be made to withdraw troops from Europe in order to curtail the size of the defence budget.

Conclusion

It is far too soon to offer any prognosis on what the long term import of the issues discussed in this chapter will be for the Alliance. As indicated earlier, NATO is undertaking a serious endeavour to reduce its reliance on nuclear weapons through improved conventional defences. In parallel with these efforts, major steps have been taken to address concerns related to an equitable sharing of the defence burden. However, these measures may not be sufficient in themselves to counter the growing criticisms on both sides of the Atlantic about Alliance policies and strategic doctrines.

It is the view of the Rapporteur that Alliance political leaders must seek to rebuild urgently the increasingly fragile agreement over defence policies within NATO. To do so will require not only renewed efforts at improving communication to Western publics, but also increased consultations at every level as NATO charts its future course.

EAST-WEST RELATIONS

Intense activity occurred throughout 1986 between East and West. Several events - the Chernobyl nuclear disaster in the Soviet Union, the arrest by the KGB of American journalist Nicholas Daniloff on manufactured charges of spying, the series of expulsions of diplomats undertaken by the United States and the Soviet Union, and the commemoration of the 25th anniversary of the Berlin Wall - served to highlight the tensions which make the search for stability in East-West relations so difficult.

Other developments pointed to a genuine desire on the part of both the Alliance nations and the Eastern bloc countries to try and find ways to promote better relations on a long-term basis. Multilateral negotiations in Stockholm within the framework of the Conference on Disarmament in Europe led to an agreement on a range of confidence and security-building measures. General Secretary Mikhail Gorbachev announced the withdrawal of a small number of troops from Afghanistan, leading to renewed hope of a political settlement and confirming for some analysts the view that a new and more flexible leadership had now taken hold in the Kremlin.

Greatest attention has focussed on the bilateral nuclear arms control negotiations taking place in Geneva between the United States and the Soviet Union. The increasingly detailed proposals put forward throughout the year by both sides indicated that, on several crucial issues, and particularly intermediate-range forces stationed in Europe, the two nations were perhaps close to reaching an agreement. In the wake of the October Reykjavik meeting between General Secretary Gorbachev and President Reagan, it appeared that the two sides had notionally agreed to a broader principle of arms reductions. The prospect of the total elimination of intermediate forces from Europe and 50% reductions in the two countries' strategic forces suddenly became a realistic possibility.

The Reykjavik meeting did not, however, result in the signature of such sweeping accords. The two leaders were unable to resolve their differences over strategic defences; and whatever progress was made on intermediate and strategic weapons, the gap which separates the two sides on ballistic missile defence appears to be as wide as ever. Both nations, however, have stressed their belief that the momentum generated in Reykjavik can be carried over to the Geneva arms control talks.

These and other developments have raised new expectations and generated new uncertainties about the future course of East-West relations. A more detailed review of these events may provide a clearer perspective of their long-term implications.

Mikhail Gorbachev and "The New Political Thinking"

The 27th Congress of the Communist Party of the Soviet Union signaled perhaps a turning point in the country's political life and potentially major changes in the Soviet foreign and domestic policies.

The New Soviet Leadership

General Secretary Gorbachev has apparently gone quite some way toward building a leadership of new puritans - men who share his disgust at the lethargy and corruption of the Brezhnev era. They are equally men who have fought corruption and graft throughout their careers. Many were singled out by Yuri Andropov, often thought of as Gorbachev's mentor. Perhaps the most prominent among this new breed is Yegor Ligachev, Second Secretary of the Communist Party and Gorbachev's effective second-in-command, in charge of party organization and appointments. A teetotaller himself, Ligachev, the most hardline of Gorbachev's new appointees, also leads the anti-alcohol campaign. He seems determined to maintain ideological purity during the uncertain period of economic renewal to come. Before the Party Congress, Ligachev was the only other Soviet official besides Gorbachev to have a voting position in the Politburo as well as the Central Committee Secretariat, a sign of real favour and true power. Victor Chebrikov, KGB chief, is another key Politburo member and so far a key proponent of substantial economic change. Nikolai Rhyzkov, Premier, a technocrat with a background in industrial management, has also advocated innovation in economic decision-making. Before the Congress, it was apparent that Gorbachev, Rhyzkov, Ligachev and Chebrikov dominated Politburo meetings, ranging themselves against three neo-Stalinist holdovers from the Brezhnev era, whom Gorbachev could not find the support to oust. Moscow Party Chief Victor Grishin, one of the three, was replaced at the Congress by Leningrad boss Lev Zaikov, who becomes the third voting Politburo member to also hold a post on the Central Committee Secretariat. Gorbachev is seconded by the rest of his new appointees, non-voting Politburo members Vitaly Vorotnikov, Geydar Alieyev and Foreign Minister Edvard Shevardnadze, all prominent in attempting to root out corruption in their own regions.

The new Politburo is unique for its technocratic expertise. In addition, for the first time since 1973, the Minister of Defence is not a full voting member of the top Party body. This is not so much a punishment, although the military view it as such, as it is a slight by the government, considering the current Minister's lack of party experience. Moreover, the presence of the chief of the general staff at Reykjavik, as well as Mr. Gorbachev's post-Reykjavik comments that his proposals had been ratified by both the bureaucracy and the military, show that the role and influence of the military has not been eliminated.

Economic Reform

Clearly, Gorbachev must attend to the ever-deteriorating state of the Soviet economy, so crucial to providing the muscle power and prosperity necessary to a respectable superpower. The USSR does indeed face critical economic problems. Slow growth has become an endemic malaise which may ultimately threaten long-term damage to the economy. Stagnation and lack of dynamism and innovation throughout the economy characterize a long-run slowdown dating back to the 1950's. Increased growth is crucial if the Soviet Union is to avoid even more intense competition for resources between defence, investment, and consumption. Gorbachev faces the very real possibility that his country will no longer find it feasible to maintain its superpower status in the international arena. Dynamic and consistent growth is the answer to the dilemma. How to achieve it is the burning question for Soviet leaders. Expert opinion in the West differs on what tack Gorbachev will choose. Some see a rather doctrinaire leader, very much a product of his time, seeking to streamline the means of production and distribution, exhorting workers to increase their efficiency and using discipline and some material incentives - in short, "improving the machinery of planning". A smaller body of evidence suggests that Gorbachev, after consolidating his power more fully, will press for bold economic reforms.

In speeches early in his tenure, Gorbachev did indeed allude to "radical reforms" and bold steps needed to reinvigorate the Soviet economy. He has even gone so far at times as to hint at his support for longstanding reform proposals, including partial marketization of the economy along the lines of Lenin's 1921 New Economic Policy - in short, a combination of plan and market. Conflicting signals have appeared on this question. Evidence supporting the latter view appeared in recent remarks by Soviet economist Abel Aganbegyan, who has stressed on several occasions that more radical measures are in order for the Soviet Union to achieve its growth goals. True, Aganbegyan did promise that no radical reform of price structures was in the immediate offing. As the architect of the new five-year programme presented at the recent Party Congress, Aganbegyan outlined innovations including self-financing factories with independent power to invest their profits, linking wages to performance, and some limited freeing of prices. He is equally the architect of the recently unveiled 15-year plan for economic progress. It now appears Gorbachev has three possibilities before him. First, he may pursue the "safe" course of policy and organizational reforms, such as streamlining the economic system and increasing discipline. Secondly, Gorbachev and his supporters may attempt to carry on in the current vein for several years, only to realize in the early 1990's that the continuing deterioration of economic performance will necessitate a turn toward the market. Thirdly, he may actually try a relatively immediate resort to radical reforms. Here, however, it must first and foremost be realized that an oligarchic leadership is ill-suited to initiate and execute a major structural reform, which could in fact reduce that very leadership's control over the country. It must be noted that these reforms are radical by Soviet standards and not Western ones.

In addition, it would appear that Gorbachev is fighting an on-going battle with the government bureaucracy in his attempts at economic reform. In recent public speeches he has attacked the bureaucracy for ignoring his policy prescriptions. These speeches display his frustation at resistance to his economic reforms. This action on the part of the bureaucracy is not surprising, as the General Secretary's plans to devolve some decision-making powers to production enterprises would weaken the bureaucracy's control. Despite the small degree of change involved, Gorbachev is evidently facing considerable opposition. This appeal to the masses would appear to be part of a peace movement to crush bureaucratic protest, involving both the upper echelons of the Soviet hierarchy and the masses. The key question is whether Gorbachev will defeat the system or whether the system will defeat Gorbachev.

Foreign Policy

Mikhail Gorbachev has infused Soviet foreign policy with a new vigour and activism as evidenced by numerous policy decisions, including the withdrawal of small numbers of troops from Afghanistan, the 14-month long unilateral moratorium on nuclear testing, and acceptance of on-site inspections within the framework of the Stockholm agreement on confidence and security-building measures. These and other acts may reflect a new conceptual approach to foreign policy which differs substantially from that of the Brezhnev era.

In his Political Report to the 27th Party Congress, Gorbachev strongly criticized the rigidity of previous Soviet foreign policy, and noted that "the changes in the development of the contemporary world are so profound and significant that they require a rethinking and comprehensive analysis of all its factors". The General Secretary also acknowledged the existence of "global problems" which are not rooted in class or economic rivalries and can only be solved through international co-operation. In this context he also stressed the interdependence of nations in the nuclear age.

Perhaps the most innovative aspect of Gorbachev's approach to foreign policy is his assertion that the security of the USSR cannot be achieved by "military-technical means" alone. This analysis would appear to call for a less central role for the military in the elaboration of security policy and a greater emphasis on political considerations. In this context it is interesting to note that the new Soviet leadership has signaled a desire to constrain levels of military spending. Traditionally the Kremlin has pledged itself to make available "everything necessary to reliably defend" the Soviet Union. However, in several key speeches, both Mikhail Gorbachev and his Minister of Defence, Marshal Sokolov, have declared that the armed forces must be maintained at levels which would prohibit the United States from gaining strategic superiority. Some analysts see these statements as indications of a new ideological criterion for determining the allocations of resources to the military.[2]

In parallel with these declarations, Mikhail Gorbachev has also introduced a number of organisational and personal changes in the foreign policy apparatus of the Soviet Union. He has appointed the former Soviet ambassador to the United States, Anatoli Dobrynin, to head the Central Committee's International Department and created a Directorate for Arms Control and Disarmament, headed by General Viktor Starodubov, within the Department. The directorate has special responsibility for managing the technical and military implications of arms control agreements. These changes are seen as not only streamlining the Soviet foreign policy process, but also as shifting the centre of decision-making away from the Foreign Ministry directly to the Central Committee.

In conclusion, it is clear that the Soviet leadership, at least at the highest level, is undertaking a significant re-evaluation of Soviet foreign policy and is perhaps moving towards a more pragmatic and less ideological approach to international relations. It is equally evident, however, that this process has not led to a redefinition of the USSR's permanent policy goals, the most important of which remain securing the Soviet Union's status as a superpower and reducing, if not eliminating, the US committment to Western Europe. Finally, it is less clear the degree to which the General Secretary's approach has met with the agreement of the majority of the Soviet hierarchy. The resolution on foreign policy adopted by the 27th Party Congress backed away from, or toned down, many of the conclusions Gorbachev made in his speech, including references to global problems and the need to achieve mutual security with the United States.

The Situation in Afghanistan

The announcement in July 1986 that the Soviet Union would withdraw 6,000 troops from Afghanistan was seen as a sign of new flexibility in Soviet foreign policy. Although it was recognized that the number of troops involved was small compared to the estimated 115,000 soldiers occupying the country, some observers saw this decision as an opening to a political solution to the problem.

It should be noted, however, that the announcement made by General Secretary Gorbachev in Vladivostok was addressed as much at the People's Republic of China as the West. The Chinese Government has long made improvements in Sino-Soviet bilateral relations dependent on three things: a political solution to the Afghan situation, a removal of Soviet troops from Mongolia, and an end to the Vietnamese occupation of Cambodia. Mikhail Gorbachev's Vladivostok speech addressed two of these issues: the

Soviet presence in Afghanistan and the level of Soviet troops in Mongolia. The reduction in troop levels in both areas was announced in the context of the "urgent need" to make radical changes in foreign policy and to look at "international policy issues from an Asian Pacific viewpoint".

Moreover, there is no indication that the Soviet Union is planning to reduce substantially its involvement in Afghanistan. Dissatisfaction with Babrak Karmal's failure to consolidate the Government of the Democratic Republic of Afghanistan led to his abrupt replacement in May 1986 by Najibullah, head of the KGB-dominated security service, KHAD. Najibullah is known both for his long-standing and close ties with the Soviet Union and his efficient leadership of the ruthless Afghan security force.

In addition, Moscow has up-graded its military infrastructure in Afghanistan in order to improve its ability to dominate certain regions in the country other than major population centres and to ameliorate its ability to combat the Afghan resistance. These measures include the construction of heavily fortified air bases within range of the Persian Gulf and greater use of small, specialized military commando units, which have been more successful than regular Soviet troops in fighting the Mujahideen.

Domestically the Soviet media is depicting the situation in Afghanistan with greater frankness. This has taken the form of limited discussion of casualties in Afghanistan, the erection of war memorials to soldiers who died "performing their heroic duty" and coverage of the problems returning veterans are having in readjusting to civilian life. Some analysts believe this new candour is part of an effort to generate public support for a long-term involvement in Afghanistan.[3]

The UN-led negotiations continue in Geneva, but remain restricted to indirect talks between the Kabul government and Pakistan. In June 1985 the UN reported tentative agreement on three accords: non- interference in Afghan affairs, international guarantees of a final settlement, and the voluntary return of Afghan refugees. The fourth and crucial agreement necessary to an overall settlement, a schedule for the withdrawal of Soviet troops, remains elusive. Although the Kabul government has dropped its insistence that any discussion of Soviet withdrawal must take place in direct Afghan-Pakistani talks, it still maintains that "outside interference" - the term used by the Soviet Government to describe the

Mujahideen - must cease before troops can be removed. It appears unlikely that the resistance will end their operations unless they can participate directly in the talks, a step Soviet officials have consistently rejected.

In the meantime, the fighting continues in Afghanistan with increasingly heavy costs to the civilian population. Moscow and Kabul have adopted a policy of "migratory genocide", - the deliberate attack on civilians and destruction of crops in areas of strong resistance support, in an effort to weaken the Mujahideen. As a result some 5 million Afghans out of a total population of 15 to 17 million people have fled to Pakistan and Iran.

The Chernobyl Nuclear Reactor Accident

It is far beyond the scope of this report to provide a detailed analysis of the tragic accident at the Chernobyl nuclear power plant which occurred in April of this year.[4] A brief discussion of the disaster may, however, be useful to the extent that the way it was handled by the Soviet Union may provide a further example of new trends in Soviet foreign and domestic policy.

The Soviet reaction to the accident was initially characterized by a steadfast refusal to acknowledge it. Despite concrete evidence from Western governments that a cloud of radiation was spreading from the Ukraine across Europe, Soviet officials denied that an incident had occurred at the Chernobyl power station. A full 24 hours after the accident and only after repeated protests and strong demands for information from Western governments did the Soviets admit to the accident, and then only through brief statements which provided little genuine information. Many analysts took this as evidence that General Secretary Gorbachev's policy of "openness", or glasnost, was either mere propaganda or did not reflect the view of the majority of the Kremlin leadership.

Over ten days after the accident, Mikhail Gorbachev made a speech on Soviet television which, while acknowledging that a serious accident had occurred, was limited in the amount of information it contained. No mention was made of fall-out beyond the Soviet border, either in Eastern or Western Europe, no reference was made to the immediate and long-range health effects of the accident, no regret was expressed over delays in informing other countries about the accident. Instead, Gorbachev attacked the West for taking advantage of the fact that the Soviet Union was stricken by "misfortune" to launch a vicious "anti-Soviet campaign". He also linked the accident to the dangers of nuclear technologies in general and stressed in this context Soviet arms control proposals. Finally, he urged that greater powers be given to the International Atomic Energy Agency.

Despite its limitations, this speech appeared to have marked a turning point in the way the Soviet Union handled the accident. Domestically, the Soviet media began providing more detailed coverage of the disaster, including interviews with accident victims and television pictures of the damaged reactor itself. The Soviet Union also provided greater information abroad, which culminated in a comprehensive report to the International Atomic Energy Agency on the causes of the accident.

Five months after Chernobyl, it would appear that Soviet candour has managed to vastly improve the country's international standing. The August report to the IAEA has been praised for its detail and for its admission of both the human and technical failures that led to the accident. Lord Marshall, head of the British Central Electricity Generating Board, praised the Soviet nuclear scientist who presented the report by saying "he's laying it all out, admitting faults in design, in training, in Soviet safety philosophy".

As a result of the report, the IAEA put forward 13 proposals to improve nuclear safety. They include international training and accreditation for nuclear operators, collaboration on man-reactor "relations", and international cooperation on the long-term effects of radiation contamination. Additional measures taken by nuclear power-producing nations to improve the safety of nuclear reactors have also served to enhance Soviet credibility, since these measures were a direct result of the Soviet report on Chernobyl.

In addition, the Soviet Union did not hesitate to link the disaster to the need for arms reductions. Mikhail Gorbachev referred specifically to Chernobyl when he announced an extension of the Soviet unilateral moratorium in August. By emphasizing this connection, the Soviet Union has shifted attention in the West away from doubts about its ability to manage a crisis and about its trustworthiness. Instead, for many in the West, the primary lesson of the Chernobyl disaster is the world's vulnerability to a possible nuclear mishap and the need for reductions in nuclear weapons.

The openness which the Soviet Union finally applied to its handling of the Chernobyl accident has been confirmed by other events, most notably in October, when a Soviet nuclear submarine sank off the coast of the United States. The policy of glasnost is part of a broader effort to bring attention to inefficiencies and abuses within the Soviet system which have been held responsible for hindering economic growth. This approach is welcomed by Alliance governments and can only be encouraged; it should not, however, be taken as a sign that either the fundamental structure of the Soviet system is about to be altered, or that the basic Soviet foreign policy goals mentioned earlier are in the process of a major revision.

Arms Control Negotiations

The twelve months since the 1985 November summit in Geneva have perhaps witnessed the greatest level of activity in East-West arms control talks since 1981. In fact it can be argued that arms control now so dominates the East-West agenda that all other issues have been relegated to the sidelines. Although the intensity and seriousness of the negotiations are extremely welcome, it should not be forgotten that the arms race is but a symptom of the fundamental differences which separate East from West. Genuine reductions in the nuclear arsenals of the United States and the Soviet Union will certainly contribute to reducing tensions; it is unlikely, however, that such steps taken in isolation can achieve long-term stability in East-West relations.

The Conference on Disarmament in Europe

After two-and-a-half years of negotiations, the 35 nations participating in the Conference on Disarmament in Europe (CDE) reached an agreement on a series of confidence- and security-building measures. It is worth recalling that the CDE began in Stockholm in 1984 during a period of particularly strained East-West relations. The Soviet Union had withdrawn from the bilateral nuclear arms negotiations with the United States just three months previously, and then Soviet Foreign Minister Andrei Gromyko used the opening of the Conference to launch a bitter polemical attack on the United States. The progress made within the CDE is but one sign of the changes in the East-West climate that have occurred since then.

Initially the two sides were far apart, with the NATO countries proposing specific measures to promote stability in Europe while the Warsaw Pact argued for the adoption of general declaratory principles. In essence the NATO position called for an annual exchange of information on forces in position in the CDE region, an annual exchange of forecasts of military manoeuvres, 45 days notice for manoeuvres involving 25,000 or more ground troops in the area, and on-site inspection of all pre-notified activities. The Warsaw Pact position could not have been more different, urging no first use of nuclear weapons, a non-aggression pact, limits on military expenditure, European chemical- and nuclear-free zones, and limited notification of military manoeuvres.

In the end the agreement reached in Stockholm reflected to a large extent the concepts sought by the NATO countries and contained concrete confidence-building measures. The document begins by reaffirming the signatories' committment to the peaceful resolution of disputes and to the duty to refrain from the use of force. The accord then enumerates a series of measures designed to increase stability and lower the threat of war by miscalculation, including:

> 45 days prior notification of manoeuvres involving at least 13,000 troops or 300 battle tanks;
>
> 12 months prior notification of manoeuvres involving more than 40,000 troops;
>
> constraints on the size of manoeuvres that can be carried out without prior notification.

One of the most crucial issues under negotiation was, of course, verification. The Allies placed great emphasis on the need for adequate verification procedures if an agreement was to be reached, and in order to be credible any verification procedures would have to include some type of on-site inspection. The Warsaw Pact nations resisted this approach, maintaining that "national technical means" were sufficient to verify any agreement. The decision taken by the Soviet Union in August 1986 to agree to some form of on-site inspection constituted a major breakthrough for the Conference.

The provisions for verification can be summarised as follows:

> a maximum of three on-site inspections per year;
>
> the state which requests an inspection can designate the territory to be subject to inspection;
>
> inspection from the ground and air;
>
> aircraft for inspection will be chosen by mutual agreement between the inspecting and "receiving" states.

Some analysts believe that the Soviet concessions on on-site inspection within the CDE framework are part of a new and more general willingness within the Soviet Union to agree to such measures. As evidence of this new attitude they point to Soviet statements that, in certain areas, verification issues should be raised at the beginning of the negotiations. This is in contrast to past practice when verification was only discussed by Soviet negotiators when the content of an agreement had been reached. In addition, these same analysts are encouraged by the emphasis which is apparently given to verification within the Central Committee's new Arms Control Directorate.

The agreement reached in Stockholm will be submitted to the third follow-up meeting of the Conference on Security and Cooperation in Europe (CSCE) in Vienna in November. At that meeting the 35 nations will decide what form the CDE will take in the future within the CSCE, of which it is an integral part.

The Mutual and Balanced Force Reduction Talks

There are some signs that at the Vienna Review Conference the Eastern bloc will urge that current discussions on conventional troop reductions be folded into the CSCE process. Negotiations on Mutual and Balanced Force Reductions (MBFR) in Central Europe have been taking place in Vienna between 12 NATO states and 7 Warsaw Pact countries since 1973 and thus constitute the longest running arms control negotiations between East and West. For the Allies participating in the talks the primary objectives are to reach a short-term agreement on the monitoring of US and Soviet troop reductions, followed by a commitment not to increase the remaining forces on both sides. This agreement would then serve as the basis for a broader accord which would establish parity through a collective ceiling on both sides' manpower levels: 700,000 ground troops and 900,000 combined air and ground forces per alliance.

Although the Warsaw Pact states accept in principle this two-phased approach to the talks, progress has been hampered by disagreement over current force levels present in the MBFR zone and over verification issues. The Warsaw Pact maintains that there is virtual equality between the two sides' troop levels instead of Warsaw Pact superiority. Until recently NATO has sought agreement on current Eastern troop levels prior to signing an accord, but deferred this requirement in December 1985.

As for the verification provisions of an eventual treaty, the Warsaw Pact accepts in principle the need for on-site inspection. However, their proposals limit the scope of on-site inspection, particularly by granting each side the right to refuse requests for this type of inspection.

In addition, Warsaw Pact proposals tend to address other issues besides constraints on troop levels. Other long standing Soviet objectives include an expansion of the geographical area to be covered by an eventual treaty beyond the current MBFR zone and the inclusion of tactical and medium-range nuclear systems in the talks.

These characteristics were evident in the Warsaw Pact June 1986 appeal to NATO and other European states made in Budapest. The proposal calls for two stage reductions in the manpower and armaments of NATO and Warsaw Pact conventional land forces and in their tactical aviation and medium range (up to 1,000 km) nuclear missiles. In the first stage each side would cut 100,000 to 150,000 troops over a 12 to 24 month period. In a second step each side would further reduce troops by almost 500,000 men and decrease their tactical aviation and medium-range nuclear missiles by 25% by 1990.

According to the proposal, verification would be carried out by national technical means, mutual exchange of data, and on-site inspection. No details were provided, however, on how the on-site inspection would be carried out or what geographical area would be covered by such inspections.

In addition the Budapest appeal suggested that the framework for the negotiations be modified. The Eastern bloc would like to include other European states in the talks, including neutral and non-aligned nations, either by broadening the mandate of the MBFR or CDE conferences or through the creation of a new forum open to all CSCE participating states.

Western negotiators in Vienna have stated that the Budapest appeal has not been reflected in the MBFR talks. The Eastern bloc position remains the one tabled twelve months ago. Western negotiators are in addition particularly frustated by the fact that the Warsaw Pact continues to adopt a "minimalist" approach to verification. The inspected side's right of veto is maintained and any on-site inspection at short notice is ruled out. In addition, the data provided by the Warsaw Pact on troop levels remains inadequate and too general to ensure compliance with an eventual "no increase" commitment.

Western reaction to the Budapest appeal has been generally favourable, but reserved. Allied governments insist that before the broader concept of Pan-European negotiations can be accepted, concrete progress must be made in the MBFR talks first. In addition, concern has been expressed that, given the verification difficulties which already complicate the MBFR negotiations, it is likely that discussions within a broader framework could become even more complex.

A special task force on conventional arms reductions has been created within NATO to study new approaches to the talks. In particular, some NATO officials have indicated that the task force will attempt to go beyond the formulation of a Western counter proposal and will instead seek to draft an entirely original position. The group is expected to make concrete proposals sometime in the autumn of 1986.

US/Soviet Nuclear Arms Reduction Talks: The Road to Reykjavik

Of all the arms negotiations currently taking place, the bilateral discussions between the United States and the Soviet Union on strategic, intermediate-range nuclear forces and space-based defences have been subject to the greatest scrutiny. The Rapporteur will not review here the details of the two sides' proposals over the last 12 months. This has already been done by Mr. John Cartwright in his comprehensive report prepared for the Special

Committee on Nuclear Strategy and Arms Control. Instead, in light of the Reykjavik meeting, this section will assess indications that the two countries are in agreement on the principle of making substantial reductions in their intermediate and strategic nuclear forces and will discuss their differing approach to strategic defences.

At the November 1985 Summit meeting in Geneva President Reagan and General Secretary Gorbachev agreed to work towards a 50% reduction in strategic nuclear weapons and to the principle of reaching an interim agreement on intermediate-range missiles in Europe. In an effort to achieve these goals, the two leaders also agreed to accelerate the pace of the negotiations in Geneva.

In January 1986, Mikhail Gorbachev, directly responding to President Reagan's vision of rendering nuclear weapons "impotent and obsolete" through strategic defences, announced a plan to eliminate all nuclear weapons by the year 2000. Although much of his proposal was considered to be unrealistic, the provisions to eliminate INF were considered to be promising. By adopting President Reagan's "zero option" it seemed that the Soviet Union was moving closer to the US position on INF. Therefore, the United States centered on this aspect of the Gorbachev plan and put forward a counterproposal in February that would lead to the total elimination of all intermediate nuclear forces in Europe within three years.

The positions of the two sides differed in many crucial respects; the Soviet Union insisted on a freeze on the British and French nuclear arsenals and resisted constraints on SS-20's based east of the Urals. Both these conditions were unacceptable to the United States and its Allies. The US conterproposal, therefore, called for reductions in the SS-20's deployed in Asia and rejected any limits on French and British nuclear forces.

The two sides also had serious differences on other issues, particularly a nuclear test ban. Nonetheless, throughout 1986, prospects for an agreement on INF seemed bright, especially since the Soviet Union no longer made an accord contingent on a settlement of the strategic defence issue. In fact optimism was expressed that an agreement on INF could serve as the basis for a second summit meeting in Washington, possibly to be held in late 1986.

US-Soviet relations became strained in the middle of the year, due to continuing differences over a test ban, to Soviet insistence that a second summit could only take place if the two sides were to sign an arms control agreement, and to peripheral issues, such as the US raid on Libya. Tensions further increased in late August when the arrest of a Soviet UN employee on charges of spying in the United States led to the detention of an American journalist in Moscow, Nicholas Daniloff, on manufactured charges of espionage. As a consequence chances of either a summit or an arms control agreement in 1986 looked increasingly dim.

It was a suprise, therefore, that discussions between US Secretary of State George Shultz and Soviet Foreign Secretary Edvard Shevardnadze in September resulted not only in a resolution of the Daniloff affair, but also in an agreement to hold a meeting in Reykjavik at the level of head of state. The nature of the talks which took place in Iceland between President Reagan and General Secretary Gorbachev proved to be the source of further surprise. Originally described as an effort to generate new "impulses" in US-Soviet relations and to lay the groundwork for a full-scale summit in Washington later in the year, the Reykjavik meeting instead came close to resolving major differences which had been impeding progress in the Geneva arms control negotiations.

In essence, the United States and the Soviet Union reached a series of tentative agreements on reductions in strategic nuclear and intermediate-range nuclear weapons. The two sides fixed a ceiling of 1600 strategic nuclear delivery vehicles (missiles and bombers) for each side with a limit of 6000 warheads. They also agreed to eliminate all intermediate-range nuclear weapons from Europe, although the Soviet Union would be allowed to keep 100 warheads on its SS-20's deployed in Asia and the United States could maintain an equal number of INF forces on its territory.

The talks broke down, however, over strategic defences, the one area of the arms control negotiations which has consistently proven to be the most difficult to resolve. It has been clear since the United States and the Soviet Union resumed arms control talks in 1985 that Soviet concern over the strategic and technological implications of SDI have contributed both to their willingness to negotiate and to their desire to see the programme halted altogether.

In Reykjavik, President Reagan and Mikhail Gorbachev were apparently unable to achieve a formula that would allow the United States to continue its research programme in parallel with reductions in the two sides' intercontinental nuclear forces. Differences centered on the 1972 anti-ballistic missile (ABM) treaty and the type of development and testing of strategic defences permitted by it. The United States has maintained, under a new interpretation of the treaty announced twelve months ago, that the treaty permits the development and testing of ballistic missile defence components and systems based on advanced technologies which were unknown at the time the ABM treaty was signed. This interpretation of the treaty, although not currently applied by the United States, has been rejected by the Soviet Union.

In Reykajvik, President Reagan apparently argued that the ABM treaty should remain in force for an additional 10 years (it is scheduled for review in 1987) provided that there was agreement on its broader interpretation. The Soviet Union also accepted a ten year extension of the treaty but rejected the broader interpretation altogether. Instead, Mikhail Gorbachev proposed a "strengthening" of the ABM treaty which would have confined SDI research to the laboratory.

After extending their talks for an additional 3 1/2 hours the two leaders were unable to achieve a compromise and the discussions broke up. Despite their genuine disappointment that their continuing differences over strategic defences prevented the signing of an arms control agreement, the two sides maintained that significant progress had been made on INF and strategic nuclear weapons. They both expressed the hope that the momentum generated in Reykjavik would be carried over into the Geneva negotiations. In addition, the United States and the Soviet Union will hold high level talks next month.

It is too early to assess the long term implications of the Reykjavik meeting. It would appear that major progress has been made on several crucial issues and there now seems to be a genuine commitment on both sides to work towards reductions in their respective nuclear arsenals. It can only be hoped that divergences over strategic defence will be resolved and that the Reykjavik meeting will prove to be the catalyst to the signing of major arms control agreements.

Within the Alliance attention is now focusing on the possible strategic implications of the tentative agreements reached in Reykjavik for NATO's defence posture. Officials within the West German and British governments, as well as senior NATO military commanders, have expressed concern that the total elimination of INF from Europe would leave NATO vulnerable to the Warsaw Pact's superior, conventional forces and to Soviet short-range missiles. In the final analysis, these legitimate considerations will have to be weighed against the potential advantages of removing some of the more threatening nuclear weapons from the European theater.

Conclusion

One need only recall the tensions that existed between East and West in the early months of 1985 to realize the improvements that have occurred in East-West relations over the last eighteen months. An important multilateral agreement on confidence-building measures in Europe has been signed in Stockholm; the United States and the Soviet Union are earnestly pursuing their bilateral arms control negotiations at several levels, and there are strong indications that the Soviet Union is adopting a more flexible approach to its foreign policy.

The management of East-West relations is, however, a long term and arduous task. The NATO Allies recognized this as far back as 1967 when they agreed to the Harmel guidelines for the achievement of genuine security between East and West. In 1984, a review of the Harmel report which resulted in the Washington Declaration re-affirmed these principles. This approach, based on a strong defence capability to counter the Warsaw Pact military threat and efforts to seek political solutions to sources of East-West tensions, has provided the Alliance with a strong and unified position in its dealings with the Eastern bloc. There are now signs that this resolve may bring significant results in the field of arms control. There are, however, other issues which shape East-West relations, human rights being but one example. Differences over these questions must also be addressed if long term stability between East and West is to be achieved.

NOTES

1. Stanley R. Sloan, Nato's Future: Toward a New Transatlantic Bargain, National Defense University Press, Washington D.C. 1985; p. 55.

2. See for example Charles Glickham, "New Directions for Soviet Foreign Policy", Radio Liberty Research Bulletin, September 6, 1986, RL Supplement 2/86.

3. Craig Karp, "The War in Afghanistan", Foreign Affairs, Summer 1986, pp. 1026-1028.

4. A detailed discussion of the circumstances surrounding the Chernobyl nuclear accident can be founded in the General Report of the Scientific and Technical Committee presented by Mr. Lothar Ibrügger, Rapporteur.

5

Strategic Defence: Technology Issues

Lothar Ibrügger

INTRODUCTION

Since 1983, the Committee's General Report has examined strategic defence technology. In view of the considerable Alliance interest in this subject, your Rapporteur intends to continue to monitor developments in this area. Thus this Report charts some of the recent technological progress made and also presents information about strategic defence programmes which has emerged since the Committee's last meeting. In addition, the Report will explore two associated issues which are of major importance to the Alliance: the manner in which strategic defence programmes relate to the Anti-Ballistic Missile Treaty, and the nature of Alliance participation in the United States' Strategic Defense Initiative.

UNITED STATES STRATEGIC DEFENCE TECHNOLOGY

The American programme of research into strategic defence technology is known as the Strategic Defense Initiative (SDI). The SDI's purpose is to investigate technologies which hold promise for strategic defence applications and to define systems and concepts for incorporation in such applications. The programme is not geared towards actual weapons production but is intended to establish the "technological base" to support future decisions on whether and how to develop strategic defences. In other words, the SDI will produce data on the likely nature, effectiveness, and costs of possible defensive systems. This type of information, plus "non-technical" considerations such as the state of East-West relations, and the presence or absence of an agreed arms control formula governing defensive systems, will be critical factors in determining whether defensive deployments could and should take place and, if so, what form they could and should take. Current assessments suggest that such decisions could take place in the early 1990s.

The research areas in the SDI are divided into five categories:

- Surveillance, Acquisition, Tracking and Kill Assessment
- Directed Energy Weapons
- Kinetic Energy Weapons
- Systems Analysis and Battle Management
- Support Programmes.

What follows is a brief description of these programmes, devoting particular attention to some of the most significant areas of recent progress.

Surveillance, Acquisition, Tracking and Kill Assessment

A ballistic missile defence system must be able to locate and track hostile missiles with sufficient precision to facilitate interception. Interception engagements must also be monitored so that, if necessary, further interception attempts can be made. The technical description given to these tasks is surveillance, acquisition, tracking and kill assessment (SATKA), and investigations into SATKA technologies and concepts are one of the key elements of the SDI. Many specific projects are in progress because each phase of a ballistic missile's trajectory lends itself to different monitoring techniques, though there is some degree of overlap. The sensor technologies being examined include radar, infra-red, optical, and laser radar devices, and ground, air and space basing modes are being studied. Associated with these projects are other research programmes including, for instance, the collection of data on ballistic missile emission characteristics, the study of refrigeration techniques, and the investigation of production techniques for lightweight, high precision mirrors.

In recent months, a number of significant developments have occurred in SATKA programmes. These include the successful tracking of a sounding rocket by a ground-based laser system which successfully compensated for atmospheric distortion of the laser beam. This, incidentally, also has relevance for weapons concepts incorporating ground-based lasers. Advances have also been made in the fabrication of extremely light mirrors, and in cryogenic coolers for infra-red sensors. Substantial progress has been made in techniques to discriminate between heavy and light objects during the mid-course phase of a ballistic missile's trajectory, a task which would enable defensive systems to distinguish warheads from decoys. Other developments in SATKA programmes include the modification of the COBRA JUDY radar based on a surface vessel, and the procurement of a Boeing 767 to serve as a sensor test bed. COBRA JUDY now has an increased capability to monitor Soviet ballistic missile tests, and through being located on a ship, can get close enough to the Soviet Union to collect data from the re-entry phase of Soviet missile tests. The data collected by COBRA JUDY will support the design and testing of new tracking radars. The Boeing 767 is for use in a project known as the Airborne Optical Adjunct. This project is intended to investigate the feasibility of tracking objects in space from high-altitude aircraft. The aircraft will be equipped with optical and infra-red sensors, plus associated data processing, navigation and communications equipment.

Directed Energy Weapons

The SDI is investigating a wide variety of technologies relevant to directed energy weapons (DEWs) with the projects grouped into four categories:
- Space-Based Laser Concepts
- Ground-Based Laser Concepts
- Space-Based Particle Beam Concepts
- Nuclear-Driven Directed Energy Concepts

This categorization reflects current assessments of each concept's potential application but does not preclude the prospect of variants on these themes. For instance, ground-based particle beam weapons may emerge as viable weapons candidates depending upon the outcome of research. Also, some technologies are relevant to several DEW concepts and some DEW and SATKA technologies overlap.

The most mature space-based laser candidate is the chemical laser. Chemical lasers are powered by the reaction between two gases which also act as a lasing medium. Several types are being studied, and those using hydrogen and fluorine, and deuterium and fluorine have achieved the highest power levels. Indeed, the Mid-Infra-red Advanced Chemical Laser (MIRACL) has an output of 2.2 megawatts rendering it the most powerful laser in the Western world.

Despite their relatively advanced stage of development, chemical lasers cannot yet achieve the combination of power and weight necessary for useful weapons applications. Furthermore, because they emit at relatively long wavelengths, their beams disperse more and are not absorbed as well as those of shorter wavelengths. Another type of laser, the free electron laser (FEL), may eventually prove to be a more viable candidate. The free electron laser operates by passing a beam of electrons through a specially tailored magnetic field which causes the electrons to oscillate. This causes the electrons to emit photons of electromagnetic radiation which, by adjusting the magnetic field, can be tuned to virtually any wavelength. Although present free electron lasers are rather cumbersome, and their power outputs cannot yet match those of chemical lasers, they are considered to hold substantial promise as potential space-based laser weapons.

Free electron lasers are also being studied as possible ground-based laser weapons. Indeed the ground-based free electron laser is seen as one of the most promising forms of directed energy weapon and is receiving considerable emphasis in the SDI as a result of substantial recent progress in free electron lasers. For the ground-based application, beam wavelengths would be selected which are transmitted easily through the atmosphere and the weapon would engage its targets through a series of orbiting mirrors. Using this arrangement, it would not be necessary to develop power sources and laser devices compact and light enough to be placed into orbit.

Excimer lasers are also being considered for this type of application. "Excimer" is a contraction of "excited dimer", a dimer being a molecule consisting of two atoms. In this case, one atom is a noble gas and the other is a halogen. The noble gas is ionized by an electron bombardment and then reacts with the halogen to form a gas that can be made to emit a laser beam in the visible to ultra-violet range. The beam tends to be emitted in pulses rather than as a continuous wave and these devices are somewhat inefficient. However, a device known as a Raman cell offers the prospect of coupling arrays of excimer lasers to produce one very powerful beam at a slightly longer wavelength than the excimer input beams.

Ground-based lasers would, of course, have to contend with atmospheric distortion but, as noted earlier, substantial progress has been made in compensating for this problem. Essentially, by measuring the distortion in reflections of the beam, or by measuring distortions of a beam from a space-based laser beacon, the weapon beam can be pre-distorted so that it forms a perfect beam on passing up through the atmosphere.

Space-based particle beams also hold promise as viable DEWs. At more modest power levels than those required to destroy a missile physically, they can severely disrupt a missile's electronic systems, though both physical and electronic destruction techniques are being investigated. Neutral particle beams are being considered for interceptions in space because, unlike charged particle beams, they are unaffected by the Earth's magnetic field. Charged particle beams can, however, propogate through a rarefied gas by being fed into an ionized channel created by a relatively low-powered laser beam. This technique has been demonstrated and may permit charged particle beams to operate between altitudes of 85 and 600 kilometers.

Undoubtedly the most controversial potential DEW is the nuclear-driven X-ray laser. This would involve using low-yield nuclear explosives to generate X-rays which could be directed at hostile missiles using "lasing rods" attached to the device. Each device might be able to power as many as 50 lasers but would destroy itself in the process of firing. These weapons may be fitted to small missiles - perhaps based on submarines - and launched in response to an attack.

The DEW programmes have made remarkable progress though performance levels remain well below weapons requirements. In some areas, goals have been moved almost a decade forward and, according to Lt. Gen. James A. Abrahamson, the Director of the SDI Organization, "world class breakthroughs" have been achieved. The free electron laser, for instance, has achieved an efficiency of over 40 per cent, rendering it the most efficient laser in the world. Substantial advances have also been made in establishing the lethality of laser weapons. The MIRACL laser successfully destroyed a static missile booster placed under simulated launch stresses at a range of about 750 meters. Even though the beam was refocussed onto the booster by a mirror, and the distance between the laser and its target was well below a useful weapon distance, the test facilitates calculations of a laser weapon's design goals. In addition, advances in a variety of optical technologies, and in rapid retargeting and precision pointing, are notable developments. Successful experiments in atmospheric compensation, as noted above, have also taken place, suggesting that ground-based laser weapons are more feasible than hitherto believed.

Demonstrations of enormously powerful electron beams have also taken place, and the atmospheric propagation of an electron beam has been shown. The "White Horse" particle accelerator has also been used to demonstrate target discrimination and beam control techniques as well as contributing to improvements in accelerator technology and the production of negative ion sources. Experiments with the nuclear-pumped X-ray laser have also continued with the "Goldstone" and other subsequent tests underneath the Nevada desert. Controversy has surrounded the utility of these tests as a result of a debate about the accuracy of some of the instrumentation used to measure the "brightness" of the X-rays generated, but the highly classified nature of these tests makes it difficult to assess the actual progress achieved. A test in December 1985 came in for particular criticism based on questions of instrumentation reliability but an investigation by the General Accounting Office concluded in June 1986 that there was no need to have delayed the test.

Kinetic Energy Weapons

Kinetic energy weapons are a more conventional interception method in that they rely on physical impact to destroy their targets. Devices in this category include a variety of guns and missiles intended to perform interception at all phases of a ballistic missile's trajectory. Electromagnetic rail-guns are one of the primary areas of research. These devices operate by passing a current of several megaamps through two parallel rails. A projectile fits between the rails and makes electrical contact across them. When the current flows, the geometry of the magnetic field created causes the projectile to be propelled along the rails. In strategic defensive applications, rail guns might fire either salvos of small, unguided projectiles at each target or just one larger projectile fitted with some form of terminal homing device.

Several electromagnetic rail-gun projects are under way, and progress has been remarkably rapid. A new facility known as Checmate (compact high-energy capacity, advanced technology experiment) became operational in November 1985 and can fire two shots per day compared with other earlier facilities which typically have operational capabilities of one shot per month due to the need to replace their rails after each firing. This improved rate of fire will enable researchers to develop much more rapidly the data base required to improve rail gun technology. Current research goals are to achieve velocities of about 10 kilometers per second with 1 kilogramme projectiles, and repetition rates of 1 shot per second.

Already, new capacitors have been developed with the ability to store 100-200 times the energy that can be stored in "traditional" capacitors, and substantial improvements have been made on power converters known as homopolar generators.

Other kinetic energy projects include small, rocket-powered interceptors based on orbiting platforms, a variety of ground-launched rocket interceptors, and terminal defences using rapid-fire guns or swarms of short-range rockets. Research on these projects is also moving forward, but work on ground-launched rocket interceptors is particularly noteworthy. The Exoatmospheric Re-entry-Vehicle Interceptor Subsystem (ERIS) follows on from the successful Homing Overlay Experiment (HOE) in 1984. HOE demonstrated the feasibility of intercepting a ballistic missile warhead by direct physical interception. The ERIS programme sets out to design, build and test a two-stage rocket to perform interceptions at altitudes between 100 and 160 kilometers. The programme also includes the development of an advanced optical seeker, flight control hardware, and a "radius expander" to enlarge the diameter of the intercept mechanism as it approaches its target. Also under development is the High Endoatmospheric Defence Interceptor (HEDI) intended for interceptions up to altitudes of about 90 kilometers. Unlike ERIS, HEDI will use some form of explosive warhead to scatter small projectiles into the path of an incoming warhead.

Several experiments in recent months have displayed the increasing maturity of direct interception technologies. In late June 1986, for instance, a ground-launched, radar-guided missile fired from the White Sands Missile Range intercepted a simulated ballistic missile re-entry vehicle within the atmosphere. This experiment was the sixth flight in a planned series of nine which is designated the "flexible lightweight agile guided experiment" (FLAGE). (This is the new designation for the "small radar-homing intercept technology programme known as SR-HIT). Previous tests of the FLAGE interceptor had used static targets but the June test used an air launched target vehicle. This vehicle was launched from high altitude and was then boosted into a trajectory akin to that of a ballistic missile warhead. Ground based radars tracked the vehicle and an interception point was calculated. The FLAGE missile was launched, acquired the target with its millimeter-wave radar, and was "nudged" onto the correct trajectory by firing its 216 small steering rockets as necessary. Impact occurred seven seconds after launch, at an altitude of about 3.6 kilometers and both the interceptor and the target were travelling at around one kilometer per second.

Another experiment -- the "Significant Technical Milestones Experiment" -- involved the launch of a Delta rocket on 5 September 1986. The experiment entailed placing the Delta second stage, and a specially-built satellite into slightly different orbits such that the vehicles' orbits periodically crossed each other resulting in very close approaches. During these approaches the instrumented second stage was able to inspect the satellite against space and various Earth backgrounds and the instruments also observed the launch of an Aries sounding rocket. These experiments will facilitate the development of sensors which can discriminate warheads and boosters against a variety of backgrounds. Finally, the Delta second stage fired its engine and was guided on a stabilized path while the satellite actively manoeuvred on a collision course. From an initial separation of almost 200 kilometers, the vehicles collided at a combined speed of almost 3 kilometers per second. At impact, the vehicles were within 15 to 30 centimeters of the anticipated trajectories. The experiment has been described as probably the most complex communications exercise ever mounted in the United States involving 38 radar installations worldwide, 31 satellite communications links and six Boeing EC-18B tracking aircraft. More than one million lines of new computer code also worked first time.

Although not part of the SDI, mention should also be made of a test in September 1985 of an air-launched anti-satellite (ASAT) weapon. This test resulted in the destruction of a satellite and was the first test of this device against a realistic target. The United States Congress placed a one year moratorium on such tests shortly afterwards. In late September 1986, a further test of the ASAT weapon took place to allow experiments with its guidance system. The "target" was a star, not a satellite, so the test complied with the Congressional ban.

Battle Management and Systems Support

These programmes cover a wide variety of areas including command, control, and communications, systems architecture, launch vehicles, power generation, and systems survivability. The battle management aspect poses probably one of the most formidable tasks faced by the SDI. It would entail the design and construction of communications and data processing systems with speeds and capacities well beyond those offered by present technology, and there has been considerable debate about whether such systems could ever function sufficiently well to cope with large-scale, defensive engagements. Certainly, even the most enthusiastic supporters of strategic defence acknowledge that the information technology elements of the SDI are likely to be among the most demanding of the whole programme but, feasible or not, the SDI has made progress in this area with the design, for instance, of radiation-hardened microchips and data collection techniques. In addition advances have been made in simulating defensive engagements in order to develop the necessary hardware and software.

As regards other aspects of these programmes, work is progressing on the design of a small, space-based nuclear reactor, and funds for a transatmospheric vehicle are also coming, in part, from the SDI. Indeed, one of the goals of the SDI is to investigate space launcher technologies with a view to cutting launch costs by 90 per cent.

SOVIET STRATEGIC DEFENCE TECHNOLOGY

As noted in previous reports, the Soviet Union is conducting a research programme which is broadly similar to the United States' SDI. Naturally, however, it is not possible to catalogue this programme in the same detail.

Directed Energy Weapons

The Soviet Union's laser programme is believed to be on a larger scale than its American counterpart. At least six major research and development facilities have been identified, with at least two facilities at the Sary Shagan Missile Test Centre which has long been associated with Soviet anti-ballistic missile work. Programmes are believed to include air defence lasers, anti-satellite lasers and ballistic missile defence lasers. A wide variety of lasers is under investigation including excimer, free-electron, X-ray, gas-dynamic, electric discharge, and chemical lasers. Research is also being conducted into components for laser weapons such as advanced optical systems and power supplies. A significant development in this latter area is a rocket-driven magnetohydrodynamic generator which produces over 15 megawatts of electrical power and which has no counterpart in the West. In some cases, ground-based lasers are sufficiently powerful to interfere with, though not destroy, satellites, and by the end of the decade a prototype space-based anti-satellite weapon may be tested. It is believed that a ground-based ballistic missile defence laser may also be tested at about the same time, though an operational capability is not foreseen before the late 1990s. Space-based lasers for ballistic missile defence are not envisaged until after the year 2000.

The Soviet Union is believed to have been investigating particle beam weapons since the late 1960s and in the late 1970s publications on some aspects of particle beam research ceased, presumably as its weapons potential was realized. Prototype particle beam weapons designed to disrupt satellite electronics may be tested in the 1990s, though such weapons for ballistic missile defence purposes would require several additional years of research and development. It is worth noting that much recent progress in American particle beam research is based on Soviet work conducted in the late 1960s and early 1970s. The Soviet Union has also conducted research into strong radio frequency signals with the potential to disrupt electronic components on satellites or ballistic missile warheads.

In late May or early June 1986 Soviet laser research suffered a severe setback when an airborne laser weapon laboratory was destroyed by fire. The aircraft was an Ilyushin IL-76, heavily modified to incorporate a rotating turret on top of its fuselage. The aircraft's primary purpose was probably to have investigated laser propagation in the upper atmosphere but air defence applications may also have been studied. It is estimated that a replacement will take at least two years to construct.

New evidence of progress in Soviet laser weapons emerged when an American reconnaissance satellite discovered two new, large facilities under construction on mountains near the Soviet-Afghan border. American intelligence agencies agree that the facilities involve laser weapons but do not agree on their precise nature. The facilities, located near Dushanbe, could be intended to be operational anti-satellite laser sites, laser development facilities or simply laser research facilities. The sites, which apparently dwarf American laser facilities, are in an advanced state of construction. One site is believed to house two laser systems and the other, one laser and one microwave system.

It is also worth noting that between Spring 1981 and Autumn 1982, French counter-intelligence services obtained a series of Soviet documents on technological espionage which clearly showed that the Soviet Union was vigorously seeking Western technology to advance its own ground-, air-, and space-based lasers.

Kinetic Energy Weapons

The simple truth about this is that next to nothing is known about Soviet kinetic energy weapons research. Devices such as electromagnetic rail guns, sensors and other related hardware can be investigated in closed facilities with few external clues as to their purpose. It is known that in the 1960s the Soviet Union developed an experimental "gun" that could shoot streams of particles of a heavy metal such as tungsten or mobyldenum at speeds of nearly 25 kilometers per second in air and over 60 kilometers per second in a vacuum, and that Soviet capabilities in guidance and control systems are adequate for use against some objects in space. However, definitive appraisals of the state of some key aspects of kinetic energy weapons are simply not available in the open literature.

Much more is known about defensive missiles which have progressed beyond the research stage into advanced development or deployment. The best known of these is the GALOSH anti-ballistic missile system intended to defend Moscow. GALOSH missiles were first deployed in the late 1960s and were armed with a relatively large nuclear warhead which would be detonated in the vicinity of incoming warheads before they re-entered the atmosphere. The 1972 ABM Treaty permits deployment of up to 100 defensive missiles to protect a national capital but the maximum number of GALOSH missiles deployed was 64. Several years ago, however, modernization of Moscow's defences began and it now appears that 32 GALOSH are in place and are supplemented by a new system designated ABM-X-3. ABM-X-3 consists of the SH-04 long-range, exoatmospheric interceptor and the SH-08 short-range, endoatmospheric interceptor plus associated radars known as the Flat Twin and the Pawn Shop. The SH-04 is a three-stage missile, somewhat smaller than the GALOSH, armed with a nuclear warhead and with a range of 300-400 kilometers. This missile can reportedly stop and re-start its engines several times in order to "loiter" before making its final approach to an interception. The SH-08 is a two-stage missile armed with a nuclear warhead and has a range of less than 100 kilometers. The Flat Twin radar, which will replace older steerable radars, is a hybrid of mechanically steered and phased-array radars and will be used to track incoming warheads. The Pawn Shop radar is mechanically steered and will be used to guide interceptors. These missile systems will operate in conjunction with the Pushkino battle-management phased-array radar under construction near Moscow which provides 360° coverage. This in turn is supplemented by other old and new radars of various types.

As regards the status of the modernization of Moscow's missile defences, some sources state that the system will contain 100 operational interceptors by 1987, though towards the end of 1985, the authoritative "Jane's

Defence Weekly" reported that this number had recently been reached. It is also unclear as to whether the GALOSH missiles will be phased out or will remain in service.

In addition to interceptors intended solely for anti-ballistic missile purposes, some types of Soviet air defence missiles have an anti-ballistic missile capability. The most capable of these, the SA-12 "Gladiator", has been tested against a ballistic missile roughly similar to the Pershing II and, again according to "Jane's Defence Weekly", may be used in conjunction with the Krasnoyarsk radar - when completed - to protect SS-18 silos from submarine-launched ballistic missiles. Other surface-to-air missiles believed to possess some anti-ballistic missile capability are the SA-5 and the SA-10.

STRATEGIC DEFENCE AND THE ANTI-BALLISTIC MISSILE TREATY[1]

In 1972, after several years of negotiations, the United States and the Soviet Union signed the Anti-Ballistic Missile Treaty. This Treaty placed strict limits on deployment of defensive missiles and a subsequent protocol restricted them still further. The Anti-Ballistic Missile (ABM) Treaty was profoundly important because, along with the SALT I agreement on offensive strategic systems, it formalized a strategic balance guaranteed by offensive forces. Strategic deterrence was assured by the fact that the United States and the Soviet Union possessed nuclear arsenals capable of inflicting massive damage on each other. Neither party possessed, or was permitted to possess, missile defences capable of significantly limiting the damage the other party could inflict, and each party's offensive forces were structured such that even after suffering a nuclear attack, they could still retaliate with devastating effect.

The term used to describe this deterrence doctrine was "Mutual Assured Destruction" (MAD) and, essentially, this principle remains as valid now as it has in the past. That is not to say that the doctrine has remained unquestioned: there have been, and indeed still are, frequent debates about the vulnerability and effectiveness of elements of nuclear arsenals and the consequent temptation for an adversary to attempt to strike first, thereby gaining some strategic advantage. There have also been debates about the morality and efficacy of deterrence based on holding nations hostage to the threat of nuclear devastation. Nevertheless, the underlying basis for deterrence is still the vulnerability of the superpowers and their allies to the offensive nuclear arsenals of their potential adversaries. This situation is preserved by a strategic arms agreement - SALT II - which established the "ground rules" for offensive arsenals, and by the ABM Treaty which does the same thing for defensive systems. There is, however, the prospect that these "ground rules" may eventually be altered, either by the establishment of new, agreed arms control regimes or by an uncontrolled breakdown of the existing regimes. Both possibilities give rise to concern, though to different degrees. In the former case, even an agreed shift in strategic deterrence could meet with opposition if the shift were to mark a radical departure from a formula which seems to have worked well, and the latter case would naturally be even more disturbing.

Many complex issues have coalesced to create the prospect of a change in the strategic status quo. Doubts have been expressed, for instance, about the Soviet Union's adherence to existing arms control agreements including SALT II and the ABM Treaty. These developments alone could sufficiently erode confidence in these regimes for the United States eventually to adopt force structures outside these treaties to counter perceived Soviet advantages. This would be a regrettable state of affairs but an understandable one if the United States felt that compliance with the treaties were one-sided and jeopardized its national security.

Another factor leading to reappraisals of the MAD doctrine is technological progress. New possibilities for defensive systems are emerging which were not available when the ABM Treaty was negotiated, and though there is debate about the feasibility of these possibilities, the feasibility of defensive systems is certainly greater now than in the early 1970s. Thus, there are technical grounds for re-assessing the foundations of deterrence and for questioning whether overwhelming reliance on offensive systems, the sole technically feasible possibility in the late 1960s and 1970s, remains the only possibility for the 1990s and beyond.

The United States and the Soviet Union are both conducting research programmes in strategic defence technologies, and the Soviet Union actually possesses some operational defensive systems. In the West, at least, there is concern about the effect of these programmes on the ABM Treaty. It is feared that the decision may be taken to proceed to a stage where programmes will infringe the terms of the ABM Treaty which, once broken, may be irretrievable, leading to an expensive and potentially destabilizing competition in strategic defences. Concern also arises from American - and, no doubt, Soviet - interest in examining the prospect of moving towards defensive deployments if technology provides the means, and if strategy and politics suggest that a more acceptable form of deterrence should be sought. The problem at the moment is that there is no agreement that technology will in fact provide the means, nor is there agreement that a more acceptable form of deterrence can be found. Consequently, there is reluctance to jeopardize the ABM Treaty regime at least until it becomes clear that the benefits of doing so outweigh the costs. This reluctance, it should be noted, is shared by the American Administration which has gone to great pains to ensure that strategic defence programmes are fully compliant with the ABM Treaty. Current plans call for the feasibility of strategic defences to be appraised by Treaty compliant research, so that decisions about a shift in deterrence posture and modifications to the ABM Treaty (or the establishment of a new form of defensive arms agreement) could then be made. As a result, American strategic defence research is fully compliant with the ABM Treaty, and it will be several years before programmes reach a point where to progress further would entail modifying the Treaty, infringing the Treaty, or curtailing programmes. Soviet programmes, however, are already raising questions about compliance and the lack of information about the state of strategic defence research makes it difficult to assess when further questions might arise.

This chapter will not explore the issues surrounding a prospective change in strategic deterrence, controlled or otherwise. Suffice it to say that alternative strategic equations placing heavier emphasis on defensive systems, can be envisaged, some of which would be stable, and some of which would be unstable. At present, however, it is simply not possible to foresee what options will be technically feasible and which of these - if any - will be deemed strategically and politically desirable or necessary. This chapter will explore the specific concerns generated by the strategic defence programmes of the superpowers with respect to the ABM Treaty.[2]

The ABM Treaty: a Summary

The ABM Treaty begins with a short preamble which, among other things, declares the desirability of limiting offensive and defensive systems. Following this preamble are 16 agreed articles which form the main body of the Treaty. These articles are summarized below.

Article I bans the deployment of ABM systems except for those permitted under Article III.

Article II defines an ABM system as one intended to counter strategic ballistic missiles. This article defines current ABM components as interceptor missiles, their launchers, and their radars.

Article III states that the only permitted exceptions to a ban on ABM deployments are:

(a) one system centred on a national capital, consisting of no more than 100 interceptors, and six radars and launch complexes;
(b) one system centred on an ICBM basing area, consisting of no more than 100 interceptors, two large phased-array radars, and eighteen smaller ABM radars.

Article IV allows ABM systems or their components used for development or testing to be located at mutually agreed test sites. These sites may not include more than fifteen ABM launchers.

Article V prohibits the development, testing and deployment of sea-based, air-based, space-based or land-mobile ABM systems or components. This article also prohibits the development, testing and deployment of ABM launchers for multiple launch or rapid reloading.

Article VI prohibits (a) the modification of "non-ABM" systems to perform ABM functions and (b) the deployment in the future of early warning radars except on the periphery of national territory and oriented outward.

Article VII permits the modification and replacement of ABM systems and components subject to the provisions of the Treaty.

Article VIII directs that ABM systems and components in excess of the provisions of the Treaty be destroyed, or dismantled.

Article IX prohibits the transfer of ABM systems or components to other states, and prohibits the deployment of ABM systems and components outside national territory.

Article X forbids the assumption of any international obligations which would conflict with the Treaty.

Article XI is an undertaking to continue negotiations on strategic offensive arms.

Article XII specifies that Treaty verification shall be conducted by national technical means and that these will not be interfered with, nor will concealment measures be taken to impede verification.

Article XIII establishes the Standing Consultative Commission (SCC) to deal with compliance questions and possible ambiguities. The SCC will also be the forum for voluntary exchanges of information to ensure compliance, will consider questions of unintentional interference with national technical means of verification and possible changes in the strategic situation relevant to the Treaty, will agree upon procedures for destroying or dismantling ABM systems as required by the Treaty, will consider (as appropriate) possible proposals for increasing the viability of the Treaty (including proposals for amendments), and will consider (as appropriate) proposals for further measures aimed at limiting strategic arms.

Article XIV establishes that each Party may propose amendments to the Treaty and that the Treaty will be reviewed at five-year intervals.

Article XV establishes that the Treaty is of unlimited duration, unless a Party considers that extraordinary events have jeopardized its supreme interests whereupon the Party will give six months notice of withdrawal and will specify the relevant extraordinary events.

Article XVI is concerned with the ratification of the Treaty.

When the ABM Treaty was signed on 26 May 1972, the United States and the Soviet Union also initialled several agreed statements, common understandings and unilateral statements pertinent to the Treaty. These are summarized below.

Agreed Statement A permits the retention of existing non-phased array ABM radars already operational within the ABM system deployment area for a national capital.

Agreed Statement B defines the parameters for the smaller of the two large phased-array ABM radars referred to in Article III of the Treaty.

Agreed Statement C states that the centres of the two ABM sites permitted by the Treaty shall be at least 1300 kilometers apart.

Agreed Statement D states that if ABM systems based on other physical principles, including components capable of substituting for ABM interceptors, launchers, and radars, were created in the future, specific limitations on such systems and their components would be subject to discussion in accordance with Article XIII and agreement in accordance with Article XIV of the Treaty.

Agreed Statement E prohibits the development, testing, and deployment of ABM interceptor missiles capable of carrying more than one guided warhead.

Agreed Statement F prohibits the deployment of phased array radars with certain characteristics except as provided for in Articles III, IV and VI of the Treaty, or except for space tracking purposes or for national technical means of verification.

Agreed Statement G explains that Article IX of the Treaty is taken to prohibit the provision of other states with blueprints or technical descriptions used for the construction of ABM systems and components.

Common Understandings A and B were statements by the American Delegation which specified the locations of American ABM deployment areas, and the locations of American and Soviet test ranges. Understanding B also states that non-phased array radars of types used for range safety or instrumentation may be located outside ABM test ranges and this was agreed by the Soviet Union.

Common Understanding C pointed out that in the view of the United States Delegation, Article V of the Treaty, prohibiting work on mobile land-based ABM systems and components, would rule out the deployment of mobile ABM launchers and radars which were not permanent fixed types. The Soviet Delegation indicated that there is a general common understanding on this matter.

Other Common Understandings related to the relationship between the SCC and other consultation bodies and negotiating forums, and also established the adherence to the ABM Treaty after signature. Various unilateral statements were made including one by the United States Delegation stating that if more complete agreements on strategic offensive arms limitations were not achieved within five years, American supreme interests could be jeopardized. The American Delegation also stated that Soviet "Hen House" early warning radars have significant ABM potential so that any increases in the defences around these radars would be inconsistent with an agreement.

In 1974, the United States and the Soviet Union limited ABM deployments still further and signed a protocol to that effect.

Article I limits ABM deployments to only one of the two sites provided for in Article III of the ABM Treaty. The United States chose to centre its site on an ICBM deployment area, and the Soviet Union chose to centre its site on its national capital.

Article II specified that the centre of an ABM deployment area can be changed only once and after prior notification. This article also specified how procedures for this would be effected.

Article III reaffirmed the rights and obligations of the ABM Treaty as modified by the protocol.

Article IV dealt with ratification procedures.

In addition, the Standing Consultative Commission arrived at agreed procedures for replacment and dismantling of ABM systems and defined criteria for the term "tested in an ABM mode".

The various agreements, statements and protocols - conveniently referred to as the ABM Treaty - relating to strategic defences place strict limits on the deployment of defensive systems. If one or both superpowers decides in the future to move to a deterrent posture more reliant upon defences, the Treaty will have to be modified, replaced or simply abrogated. As mentioned above, there is reluctance to see the Treaty eroded by current strategic defence programmes but there is concern that this may be occurring. The purpose of this section is to examine these programmes to see how they comply with the Treaty.

United States Strategic Defence Programmes

The United States has not deployed any missile defences since the early 1970s, when an ABM system was briefly put into service and subsequently decommissioned after doubts were raised about its utility. As a result, there is only one area where the Soviet Union has suggested American non-compliance with regard to operational systems. The Soviet accusation concerns the modernization of early warning radars at Thule in Greenland, and Fylingdales in the United Kingdom. The former is now complete and the latter should be complete by the end of the decade. The ABM Treaty is not actually specific on this point: existing early warning radars were certainly permitted to remain operational and Article VII permits the modification and replacement of ABM systems and components subject to the other provisions of the Treaty and, during ratification hearings, it was pointed out that Article VI did not affect existing ballistic early warning radars. Consequently, American Administration claims that these modernizations do not infringe the Treaty seem well founded.

Most concern regarding American compliance relates to the SDI. President Reagan directed that this programme be formulated in a fully compliant manner and the Department of Defense continually reviews the programme to ensure that compliance is maintained. Since the ABM Treaty places no restrictions on research, and the overwhelming emphasis of the SDI is on research, compliance for the time being remains relatively unproblematical. Those aspects of the SDI which relate to "field testing" could raise compliance questions if they were not conducted within the limits laid down by the Treaty, but in fact these tests can be, and are being, conducted in a fully compliant manner.

The activities in the SDI which qualify as "research" fall into two categories: Category 1, conceptual design or laboratory testing, and Category 2, field testing of devices that are not ABM components or prototypes of ABM components. Examples of Category 1 research include ground-based electromagnetic rail gun experiments which will not produce devices capable of being integrated into ABM systems. The rail guns in question will demonstrate the capability to launch projectiles at high speeds but they will be at least a generation away from devices which might qualify as ABM components. Many laser experiments fall into the same category. Existing laser capabilities are well short of those needed for ABM use and even if fitted with aiming mirrors the combination could not be construed as an ABM component. Category 2 experiments will include programmes such as the Boost Surveillance and Tracking System (BSTS) Experiment which is essentially an experimental device to detect and track missiles shortly after launch. The device itself will not be a prototype of an ABM component, but to ensure compliance, will not have a "real-time" tracking capability. Other sensor experiments such as the Airborne Optical Adjunct and the Space Surveillance and Tracking System (SSTS) Experiment will not be capable of acting as ABM components but will facilitate a decision regarding the applicability of more advanced technology to ABM purposes. A laser experiment which also falls into Category 2 will involve attempts to destroy sounding rockets with a laser beam. In this case, the beam will be below a useful ABM level, and the target rocket will not have the characteristics of a strategic ballistic missile so Treaty compliance will be assured. In total, 13 experiments fall into Categories 1 and 2: these involve six DEW related experiments and seven SATKA and KEW experiments.

SDI activities beyond research fall into Category 3, "field testing" of fixed land-based components. These will involve tests of launchers, interceptors, and radars which probably qualify as components under development or perhaps even as prototypes. Tests of HEDI and ERIS interceptors are planned, as are tests of a ground-based radar, and a ground-launched sensor probe. These devices are more sophisticated than older ABM components operating on similar principles and their development and testing is permitted by the ABM Treaty provided certain conditions are met. These include the use of agreed test ranges, the absence of concealment measures, the use of fixed launchers incapable of rapid re-loading, and the use of only one independently targetable warhead per interceptor. All the required restrictions will be met so there is no compliance ambiguity.

It should be pointed out that not all observers are convinced that the SDI is fully compliant with the ABM Treaty though, in general, doubts are raised regarding future rather than current activities. Indeed, as the SDI moves forward, compliance will become more difficult to assess because of differing interpretations placed on some Treaty provisions which are indeed unclear. For example, regarding the definition of a "component", an Office of Technology Assessment report points out the difficulty of distinguishing between an ABM component, the testing and deployment of which is prohibited, and a subcomponent or adjunct, the testing and deployment of which is permitted. The report also points out that it is difficult to determine whether a system, component, or subcomponent is capable of substituting for a missile, a launcher, or a radar. For instance, a laser with a power output compatible with ABM purposes poses definition problems: is it a "component", or a "subcomponent" if it does not have an aiming capability?

In fact, the Treaty is lamentably vague regarding defensive systems operating on principles different from those used in the early 1970s, to the extent that widely differing interpretations are placed on the Treaty's provisions. In reviews of the Treaty conducted by legal experts in the Departments of Defense and State, for example, significant differences in interpretation emerged, but both assessments concluded that the Treaty permitted much more advanced work on "exotic" defensive technologies than was hitherto accepted. It is believed that these reviews interpreted Agreed Statement D as essentially giving the United States and the Soviet Union the right to conduct research, development and testing with respect to systems based on "other physical principles" essentially without restriction. Following these reviews, there was a great deal of debate within the American Administration about whether to abide with the more restrictive interpretation or the more liberal one. The decision reached - and formally announced by Secretary of State, George Schultz, at the meeting of the North Atlantic Assembly in October 1985 - was that the "new" interpretation was accepted as a matter of law, but the "old" interpretation was accepted as a matter of policy. In other words, the SDI would be conducted in accordance with the more restrictive interpretation of the Treaty.

Undoubtedly, experiments and tests can be conducted such that new defensive technologies can be quite thoroughly investigated (though not thoroughly integrated) in full accordance with the letter of the restrictive interpretation of the Treaty. Experiments can, for instance, use simulated anti-satellite devices instead of missile warheads as targets, and hardware can be tailored to avoid impinging on the specific provisions of the Treaty. On that basis, there is no reason to doubt the American Administration's claim that the SDI will remain compliant with the Treaty. However, the purpose of the SDI is to provide information about whether it is feasible to move towards a deterrent strategy placing heavier emphasis on defensive systems, while the purpose of the ABM Treaty is to preserve a deterrent strategy precluding emphasis on defensive systems. At present, the two are not incompatible, but within the next few years an extremely difficult choice will have to be made. If it is decided to depart from the ABM Treaty, it is to be hoped that it will be replaced by a regime which is both practical and more stable than the regime which by then will have served well for more than two decades.

Soviet Strategic Defence Programmes

Soviet actions will be a major factor in the American decision to depart from or remain within the ABM Treaty. If, for instance, the Soviet Union unambiguously "breaks out" of the Treaty by deploying defences beyond Treaty limits, this would provide considerable incentive for the United States to follow suit. Barring such large-scale infractions, the United States may decide to retain the political advantage of adherence . The situation is complex though; it could for instance be argued that the SDI provides the Soviet Union with the incentive to remain within Treaty limits because the Soviet Union may fear that the United States' superior technological capacity would yield an American advantage in an unrestrained defensive arms competition.

The Soviet Union's record regarding ABM Treaty compliance is certainly highly questionable. The best known compliance infraction is the Krasnoyarsk radar. The United States maintains that this radar is a clear violation of the Treaty because it is not sited on the periphery of national territory facing outwards. In fact it is situated almost centrally and provides coverage of approximately 4000 kilometers of Soviet territory. The Soviet Union maintains that the radar is intended for space tracking purposes and is therefore permitted by the Treaty. Admittedly, there is an overlap between early warning and space tracking radars, and American early warning radars, for instance, play a major role in space tracking; but Soviet claims that the distinction will become clear once the radar becomes operational are highly dubious. The radar's face is directed towards the horizon rather than angled upwards as on existing space tracking radars, its location would enable it to track only 10 per cent of the satellites currently in orbit, and its coverage would largely duplicate that provided by existing systems. Consequently, the issue is not whether the Krasnoyarsk radar is a violation of the ABM Treaty, but what type of violation it represents. If the radar has little ABM battle management capability but is best suited to early warning, it is in technical violation of Article VI; if however, it does have a battle management capability, which is altogether more ominous, it is in violation of Article III.

Other questions raised about Soviet compliance with the ABM Treaty are rather more ambiguous due to a lack of clarity in the Treaty's wording. These grey areas involve mobile ABM components, the rapid reload of ABM launchers, and the use of non-ABM systems for ABM testing and possible deployments.

In the first case, involving mobile ABM components, the components in question are the Flat Twin and Pawn Shop radars used in the ABM-X-3 system. These radars are mobile in the sense that the Flat Twin can be erected on a prepared site in six to eight weeks, and the Pawn Shop is housed in a van-sized container without wheels. Common Understanding C of the ABM Treaty, as noted earlier, constituted an American statement to the effect that "a prohibition on deployment of mobile ABM systems and components would rule out the deployment of ABM launchers and radars which were not permanent fixed types". When asked if they agreed with that interpretation, "the Soviet Delegation said there is a general common understanding on this matter". At first sight, it appears that the Flat Twin could be construed as a fixed radar depending on whether "mobile" is interpreted as movable within six or eight weeks, but the Pawn Shop seems to be clearly mobile. However, the United States has declared that the evidence on Soviet actions with respect to ABM component mobility is ambiguous. Perhaps this ambiguity resides in the fact that the ABM-X-3 system needs both the Flat Twin and the Pawn Shop radars and only jointly do they fit the definition of a "component".

In the second case, the rapid reload of ABM launchers, two SH-08 interceptors have reportedly been fired from a single launcher within two hours. Again there is ambiguity about a possible Treaty violation because there is no definition of the term "rapid".

In the third case, the use of non-ABM systems for ABM testing and deployments, two compliance questions have been raised. Firstly, air defence radars have been used at the Sary Shagan test site during ABM tests. Ambiguity arises because the radars could have been legitimately used for range instrumentation or illegally for developing air defence radars with ABM capabilities. The matter has been discussed several times in the Standing Consultative

Commission with an agreement reached in 1978, and a further agreement reached in June 1985. Even so, the American Administration remains concerned about the issue. The second type of violation falling into this category is the testing of the SA-X-12 air defence missile against a ballistic missile. Ambiguity arises from the fact that there is no agreement on the precise meaning of the relevant Treaty provision which includes in the definition of an ABM interceptor missile those types "tested in an ABM mode". The American Delegation's Unilateral Statement B attempts to clarify this phrase by stating that "tested in an ABM mode" would include testing an interceptor against a vehicle "which has a flight trajectory with characteristics of a strategic ballistic flight trajectory", but this is itself open to interpretation.

The actual target vehicle used appears to have been an SS-12 medium-range ballistic missile, but the trajectory followed may have exhibited characteristics in common with the trajectory of a strategic missile because the altitude of the missile apparently exceeded 40 kilometers. However, there is no agreement about what characteristics represent a "strategic ballistic flight trajectory", and, for example, submarine-launched ballistic missiles which are considered "strategic", in some cases have flight trajectories similar to land-based missiles which are considered of "intermediate range".

The above compliance issues relate to deployed systems; Soviet compliance with respect to strategic defence research is fortunately more straightforward. As discussed previously, the Soviet Union is conducting strategic defence research programmes broadly similar to those in the SDI. Comparatively little is known about them though, and it is not possible to give a case-by-case analysis of where compliance issues are likely to arise. For the moment there appear to be none. As with the SDI, Soviet programmes can no doubt be structured such that compliance is assured while the feasibility of new defensive technologies is studied. According to American estimates, the first defences employing "exotic" technologies such as lasers may reach the prototype phase by the end of the decade, and component testing might begin in the early 1990s. Presumably then, the Soviet Union is already assessing the problem of how these new technologies are limited by the ABM Treaty and will soon face the decision whether to move towards a deterrent strategy with more reliance on defensive systems than the ABM Treaty permits.

Preserving the ABM Treaty

There are obvious parallels between the situations faced by the United States and the Soviet Union. Both nations are pursuing research programmes which have relevance for the ABM Treaty, and both will soon be in a position to decide whether "defence dominated" strategies are feasible and so will have to decide whether such strategies are desirable. There are also important differences: the United States is conducting its strategic defence programmes essentially in the open as far as security permits, while the Soviet Union enjoys the luxury of not having to worry about domestic public opinion. The Soviet Union also has a poor track record regarding compliance with the ABM Treaty. Even if a question mark were to be placed over American radar modernizations at Thule and Fylingdales, the Soviet Union has one clear violation against it and at least four other cases to answer. That said, it is now clearly established that the Soviet Union traditionally exploits grey areas of treaties so the West can claim disappointment over Soviet compliance with the ABM Treaty, but not surprise. As Soviet research progresses it is to be expected that further compliance questions will arise. Action should now be taken to limit the opportunities to exploit the ambiguities and emerging "loopholes" in the ABM Treaty. The forum for this exists - the Standing Consultative Commission - and this should be used to tighten definitions and to clarify precisely which activities will and will not be permitted. In recent years, the SCC may not have been fully exploited so that accusations about compliance have emerged in other forums before attempts to resolve them have been given sufficient attention in the SCC. This criticism, incidentally, is not one-sided: both superpowers seem to have avoided raising issues at the SCC at one time or another. The superpowers may eventually decide to consign the ABM Treaty to history: on the other hand, they may decide to maintain the regime. In order to preserve this latter option, the Soviet Union should bear in mind that its compliance record jeopardizes the maintenance of the regime; and both superpowers should ensure that they exploit the Treaty's consultative framework to preserve the Treaty as a viable option in the future.

THE SDI AND ALLIANCE PARTICIPATION[3]

In May 1985, the United States formally invited the NATO nations plus Japan, Australia, and Israel to participate in the SDI and this section of the Report examines the reactions to this invitation. Before embarking on this examination, however, it is worth discussing some of the general issues involved in international participation in the SDI.

The SDI is undoubtedly a contentious issue throughout the Alliance. Debate takes place at all levels and despite the broad NATO support for the SDI expressed, for instance, at the Nuclear Planning Group meeting in Luxembourg in March 1985, formal acceptance of the offer to participate could be divisive in some nations which have substantial factions with strong reservations about the SDI. On the other hand, in Europe at least, there is considerable concern about the technology "gap" between the United States and Europe and the SDI is generally perceived - rightly or wrongly - as a programme which will contribute to the United States' technological advantage, regardless of whether or not it ultimately succeeds in producing viable ballistic missile defence technologies. As a result, there is a feeling that participation in the SDI could help Europe to close the technology gap, or at least prevent it from becoming any wider.

For participation to yield this benefit, however, involvement must be relatively substantial and must enable participants to work in areas which are technically both demanding and promising: participation should not be of a "metal bending" sort. Reservations arise on this matter because the United States has been less than forthcoming about sharing advanced technology for fear that the technologies in question might leak to the Eastern bloc. While Allies are naturally sympathetic, there are grounds for caution in that American technology transfer controls may inhibit either access to key technological areas, or the exploitation of advanced technologies derived from SDI participation. In other words, one of the motives for participation is the prospect of developing technologies which can be widely exploited but this could be undermined by restrictions placed on the use of these technologies.

Another factor in deciding whether to participate is that a governmental refusal to participate need not prevent the involvement of industry and non-governmental research institutions. Indeed, no government has forbidden this form of participation so that non-governmental bodies can negotiate SDI contracts at their discretion, assessing for themselves the pros and cons of conducting SDI research. In this way, assuming that participants would not negotiate disadvantageous terms, the technical and economic benefits of participation could be realized without the risk of incurring domestic political costs. Also, as the award of an SDI contract will depend upon merit, a government agreement should not make the difference between winning or losing it. That said, a formal governmental agreement could possibly facilitate the achievement of more favourable terms, or save time in negotiating a specific contract.

Given the complexity of all the factors which governments must presumably consider in deciding whether or not to participate in the SDI, it is not surprising that reactions have been mixed. Each nation must appraise these technical, economic, and political aspects of participation and these will no doubt differ considerably from nation to nation.

The United Kingdom became the first nation to agree formally to participate in the SDI when on 6 December 1985, the United Kingdom and the United States signed a Memorandum of Understanding (MoU) on SDI participation. This 20-page MoU, the result of months of negotiations, is classified though some of its provisions have emerged. The MoU defines 18 technological areas in which the United Kingdom can participate, these being:

- Studies for a Western European system against short-range and theatre ballistic missiles.
- Electro-magnetic ("rail") guns and their effects.
- Ion sources for use in particle beam weapons systems.
- Laser-based computers, switches and limiters to control SDI systems.
- Advanced thyratons (gas-filled tubes) for use as switches.
- Radar research.
- Thermal sensors.
- Research into laser radars, imaging and vibrometry.
- Research into short-range missile interceptors.
- Countermeasures research, focussing upon non-missile systems including non-physical destruction.
- Research into particle beam, laser and radio frequency lethality, vulnerability and hardening.

- Ballistic missile C^3 systems.
- Software security.
- Signal processing.
- Phase conjugation.
- Electronic materials.
- Non-electronic materials such as coating for space platforms or weapon housings.
- Unspecified space experiments.

The MoU is also believed to ensure that British research bodies will get non-discriminatory access to the right to tender for SDI contracts and it establishes a mechanism for potential participants to complain if they believe themselves to be victims of discrimination. To facilitate non-discriminatory contract awards, the areas covered by the MoU are exempted from the United States' "Buy American Act" and the "Balance of Payments Program" so that British contractors are placed on an equal footing with their American counterparts. The agreement also contains provisions on technology transfer and intellectual property rights. Although no details on these provisions have emerged, the British Ministry of Defence claims that the MoU is much better than previous MoUs with the United States on defence procurement, intelligence, nuclear matters, and Trident.

Both the United States and the United Kingdom have taken steps to facilitate British participation. British officials and industrialists have visited Washington D.C. to explore opportunities, and SDI officials have held briefings in the United Kingdom. The British Embassy in Washington D.C. has expanded its Defence Attaché's office to assist British companies interested in participation, and the Ministry of Defence in conjunction with the Departments of Trade and Industry, and Education and Science, has established an SDI Office to co-ordinate and stimulate British participation.

Naturally, there is a great deal of interest about the value of SDI contracts which the United Kingdom will obtain. During the MoU negotiations, it was reported that the United Kingdom was seeking an assurance that it would receive approximately 1.5 billion dollars of SDI funds over the next five years, though this was denied in both London and Washington. Estimates of the value of contracts vary from about 60 million dollars to "several hundred million dollars". The simple fact is that it is not possible to produce a definitive figure because contracts will be competed for and the SDI budget does not have a specific sum allocated for foreign participation. In testimony before a sub-committee of the House of Representatives' Committee on Banking, Finance and Urban Affairs, Gerald Yonas, the SDI Organization's chief scientist stated that there is no preconceived notion of how much will be spent abroad. He also stated that "the purpose of dealing with our allies is to provide a way of solving these problems better, faster, and cheaper than if we did not go outside our borders" and that there is "considerable scientific and technical expertise amongst our allies...(that) could reduce both the schedule and cost of the SDI research programme". The SDI Organization has also stated that contracts will be awarded purely on their merits and competitiveness.

That being the case, and given the strength of the British defence research base (and the particularly close relationship with the United States) the United Kingdom is extremely well placed to compete for SDI contracts. As yet, only a few contracts have been signed and these probably only total a few million dollars but, since the participation agreement is less than 12 months old and it takes time to prepare proposals which must then be appraised, it is too early to determine the scale of funding that the United Kingdom will eventually receive. Many companies expect to, or already have, put forward proposals and these include Barr and Stroud, British Aerospace, GEC Avionics, Hunting Engineering, Hymatic, Logica, Marconi, Pilkingtons, Plessey, Racal, Scicon, Shorts, Systems Designers Scientific, and Westland. Research institutions may also seek contracts and the British SDI office has written to many universities to solicit interest in SDI participation. Ten contracts are being negotiated through the Ministry of Defence and contracts have already been won by the Ministry of Defence, Heriot-Watt University, Ferranti, the General Electric Company, Ford Aerospace, the Culham Laboratory and the Rutherford Appleton Laboratory. Contracts won so far are worth over $30 million and the director general of the Ministry of Defence's SDI participation office has said that he would be disappointed if contracts gained in 1987 were worth less than $75 million.

There is a multi-faceted debate in the United Kingdom about the implications of SDI participation. One of the key aspects of this debate is the extent to which the United Kingdom will be able to capitalize on the research it performs. There are fears that ideas and technologies once developed in the United Kingdom will be passed on to American enterprises for further, more lucrative, larger-scale development in subsequent "rounds" of contract awards or that exploitation of technologies developed will be restricted by security controls. As the MoU is classified, and as participation is for the present embryonic, it is too early to assess the validity of these fears. Certainly, in some areas, contracts are being awarded for essentially basic, unclassified research, the results and applications of which will not be constrained by security considerations. The Ministry of Defence's letter to universities, for instance, states that "The inter-governmental arrangements that have now been concluded make adequate provision for the protection of information that may be contributed by UK organizations and for the free use by the UK of information that is generated in the UK with the aid of US funds." The letter also states that projects will be funded from the SDI's Innovative Science and Technology Programme under which research will not be classified, and scientists can publish their results in the usual way.

Consequently, it appears that the research contracted out to British universities will not have unacceptable "strings" attached. The situation regarding research conducted by industrial concerns is less clear. Undoubtedly some contracts will be classified, as are many defence-related research projects, but it is not possible to assess whether commercial exploitation will be unduly inhibited or not, nor is it possible to predict the scale of "follow-on" contracts. It is perhaps worth noting, however, that participating companies will be aware of their contract conditions and presumably would not enter into disadvantageous agreements.

Essentially, given past Alliance disagreements over technology transfer, conjecture about possible difficulties arising from SDI contracts is understandable. However, in recent months, the technology transfer "climate" appears to have improved. On the basis of governmental assurances, British SDI participation should not give rise to new technology transfer disputes, but the situation merits close attention to see if specific accusations about unfair treatment and contract conditions do emerge. It will be interesting to see whether the eventual degree of participation will be large enough to contribute significantly to Britain's technological capacity and whether fears about inhibitions on exploiting SDI-generated technologies prove justified. Definitive judgements are not yet possible, but cautious optimism certainly seems appropriate.

The Federal Republic of Germany signed an SDI participation agreement at the end of March 1986. This agreement was negotiated by the Economics Ministry, not the Defence Ministry as in Britain's case, and the agreement also included broader provisions relating to other aspects of technological co-operation. German concerns about intellectual property rights and technology transfer are essentially similar to those of the United Kingdom but the ruling coalition had to contend with the additional considerations of West Berlin's demilitarized status and the possible consequences of SDI participation on relations with East Germany and the Soviet Union. The views of the ruling coalition were divided as there were varying degrees of enthusiasm for participation, with the FDP having the strongest reservations and the CSU urging a strong commitment. A compromise was eventually reached in the cabinet and conditions for participation were then negotiated with the United States. It appears that German demands to allow firms in West Berlin to participate and to maintain civilian (i.e. not Defence Ministry) supervision over German participation were agreed to in return for a separate accord whereby West Germany would impose tighter control over exports of advanced technology to the Eastern bloc.

The tests of the accords were published in full by a West German newpspaper as were letters exchanged between Mr. Richard Perle, US Assistant Secretary of Defense and Dr. Lorenz Schomerus, the divisional department head for economic policy in the West German Economics Ministry. Mr. Perle's letter asked for details about how German law would be changed to strengthen technology export controls and suggested bilateral consultations to harmonize approaches at COCOM meetings. Dr. Schomerus' reply described some of the measures to be taken to strengthen export controls, pointed out that these would require parliamentary approval, and made no commitment to consult with Washington before COCOM meetings.

Concern about the West German participation accord was expressed on the grounds that the United States would have too much control of the technology and security relating to SDI work and that the trade relationship with East Germany would be adversely affected. There was also concern elsewhere that the leaking of the participation accords would jeopardize industry's chances of gaining SDI contracts.

In fact, several West German companies have since won SDI contracts. MBB has gained a $4 million study contract for a space platform to conduct a survey of infra-red background signatures. If the study is acceptable, MBB expects a $40 million contract to build the platform. Dornier has won a $21 million contract to conduct SDI research in conjunction with an American company, and several other German companies have won contracts from the SDIO, or subcontracts from American companies working on the SDI.

The success of MBB and Dornier in obtaining SDI contracts is not surprising and, indeed, there is potential for obtaining still more. MBB is already working on a ground-based, air-defence laser which involves technologies relevant to some aspects of the SDI, and the company also has a wide range of capabilities in aerospace technology. Dornier developed the Instrument Pointing System designed for shuttle astronomy experiments, and as a result gained considerable expertise in compensating for spacecraft vibration and aiming instruments with remarkable precision. Dornier also has experience in other SDI-relevant technologies in aerospace and free electron lasers. These and other companies are well placed to compete for SDI contracts and many other companies such as Zeiss and MAN have shown interest in the programme. As in the United Kingdom, however, it is too early to judge the level of SDI participation that the Federal Republic will achieve and whether fears about restrictions on exploiting SDI-generated technologies will prove justified.

In May 1986, Israel became the third nation to sign an SDI participation agreement. Details of the agreement are assumed to be similar to the British and German agreements, and Israel is known to be particularly interested in the threat from short-range ballistic missiles. Israeli firms and research establishments are already working on space-based sensors, kinetic-kill vehicles and defence against tactical missiles and such projects could be promising candidates for SDI contracts.

On 19 September 1986, Italy signed an SDI participation agreement which, it is believed, essentially formalizes government approval for Italian companies to tender for SDI contracts. Before the agreement was signed, more than 10 Italian companies had already submitted contract proposals, and Fiat, Aeritalia, Selenia, and a consortium of seven companies led by Agusta were known to have been actively seeking contracts. After the participation agreement was signed, it was reported that Italian companies had submitted about 70 projects of which about one third were being considered. Rocket propulsion, electronic sensors, radar, and "tethered" satellites are areas where Italian firms seem particularly well placed to compete for contracts.

Japan also announced in September that it will allow participation in the SDI, and a formal agreement is expected to be signed before the end of 1986. The agreement will probably permit Japanese companies to negotiate SDI contracts but government institutions are unlikely to participate: a resolution adopted in by the Science Council of Japan (and based on the Japanese constitution) precludes engaging in scientific research for military purposes. The Japanese private sector, however, seems keen to seek SDI contracts and, indeed, a report compiled by 21 Japanese companies, after a tour of laboratories working on SDI projects, was a major factor in the government's decision to permit SDI participation. The report maintained that SDI participation could have a "very favourable impact on the improvement of Japan's technical standards" and that there would be "numerous technological spin-offs". The report also cautioned that participation would have to be arranged such that Japan could "use the results in a proper manner", an indication that Japanese industry also fears that restrictions may placed on the exploitation of SDI-generated technology. Japan's participation could be in areas such as artificial intelligence, parallel processing, and gallium arsenide chips. There are doubts, however, about the willingness of Japanese companies to contribute their most advanced technologies for fear of revealing too much to potential American competitors.

Australia, Canada, Denmark, France, Greece, Norway and the Netherlands have declined the invitation to sign a participation agreement, but industrial concerns in these nations are not prohibited from seeking SDI contracts except in Norway where parliament has not yet resolved this issue. French industry has certainly shown considerable interest. Indeed, the French position regarding participation has changed in recent months. The Defence Minister M. Paul Quiles declared that it would be "regrettable" if French industry did not participate and more recently M. Jacques Chirac, the Prime Minister, stated that "France cannot afford not to be associated with this great research programme". Although the French Government remains opposed to the strategic concepts underlying the SDI and is unlikely to sign a participation agreement, it appears that France now sees private sector SDI participation as one means of keeping abreast of developments in high technology. Aerospatiale, CGE, Matra, REOSC and Thomson are known to be interested in obtaining SDI contracts, as are smaller companies such as Sesa and Cap Gemini Sogeti. The French defence industry has an extremely good reputation in high technology and industrialists are optimistic about winning SDI contracts now that the only government condition on participation is that it does not prevent companies from conducting work for the French defence effort.

The position of Allies such as Belgium, Luxembourg, Spain, Portugal and Turkey remains unclear. Belgian industry seems enthusiastic about gaining SDI contracts but, despite occasional rumours to the contrary, the government does not seem to have determined whether to participate formally. Other remaining nations are possibly assessing their potential to benefit from seeking SDI contracts in the face of competition from other Allies with more substantial defence research infrastructures.

It is less than one year since the first SDI participation agreement was signed and the pattern of Alliance involvement in the SDI is still indistinct. Certainly, there is concern about the consequences of Alliance SDI participation but whether these concerns will prove to be well founded remains to be seen. Setting aside objections to SDI participation arising from reservations about the programme's strategic consequences, doubts about the merits and demerits of involvement are still present. These doubts are that American technology transfer controls may inhibit exploitation of SDI-generated technology, that technologies may be produced in Alliance countries only to be further developed (more lucratively) by the United States, that the value of SDI contracts may be relatively small (and possibly in less interesting fields) thereby contributing little to the Allies' drive to close the technology gap, and that SDI participation will deprive other promising research areas of resources and talent. Another, relatively recent, concern is that legislation before the United States' Senate could curtail the scope for awarding SDI contracts to non-US bodies.

Some of these doubts are inconsistent with each other; for instance, if the ultimate value of "foreign" SDI contracts is small then there is little to fear from exploitation restrictions or American access to Allies' technology. For the moment, though, all these fears are at least plausible but the actual validity or otherwise of each of them will only become evident as Alliance participation evolves. That such fears have arisen is due to past experiences with, for example, technology transfer problems and competition for American defence-related contracts where in some cases the Allies have had cause for complaint. However, the United States has gone to great pains to point out that competition for contracts will be open and that contracts will be awarded on merit.

By October 1986, the Allies had won SDI contracts amounting to one or two per cent of the SDI's funding for the current fiscal year. As already noted, the contract process is time consuming and participation agreements are relatively recent so such a low figure need not be cause for disappointment, but nor is it cause for elation. Clearly, it will be interesting and worthwhile to follow the progress of SDI participation very closely.

In conclusion, your Rapporteur feels it appropriate to recall the four sentiments regarding the strategic future expressed by President Reagan and the British Prime Minister, Margaret Thatcher, in December 1984 at Camp David. These were that:

- the United States' and the West's aim is not to achieve superiority but to maintain balance, taking account of Soviet developments;
- SDI-related deployment would, in view of Treaty obligations, have to be a matter for negotiation;
- the overall aim is to enhance, not undercut, deterrence; and
- East/West negotiations should aim to achieve security with reduced levels of offensive systems on both sides.

NOTES

1. For broader discussion of the political and strategic debate surrounding strategic defence programmes see the Report of the Political and Special Committees.

2. This subject is also addressed in the Interim Report of the Special Committee.

3. This subject is also addressed in the Interim Report of the Sub-Committee on Defence Co-operation. The General Report of the Military Committee and the Interim Report of the Sub-Committee on Conventional Defence: New Strategies and Concepts also examine tactical ballistic missile defences.

6

Nuclear Strategy and Arms Control

John Cartwright

THE GENEVA ARMS CONTROL NEGOTIATIONS

The End of Round 4

The fourth round of the Geneva negotiations ended inconclusively in all areas on 4 March 1986. The prospect for a separate deal on the INF question, which had been a topic of some speculation for a number of weeks, was therefore left unclear. In the final days of the negotiations it was reported that compromise proposals were under discussion, yet outside the talks the Soviets were sending out ambiguous and, at times, contradictory signals.

A flurry of serious diplomatic activity had taken place in February following Soviet indications of flexibility in two key areas which it was thought might help pave the way for a separate agreement on INF. The first of these arose out of the 15 January 1986 comprehensive arms control proposal of General Secretary Gorbachev in which he seemed to reverse previous Soviet demands for compensation for the British and French nuclear forces. The new Soviet position merely called for a freeze at existing levels.

The second major impediment to an INF deal - Soviet insistence that progress on INF was hostage to progress in the other two "baskets" of the negotiations - appeared to be removed when General Secretary Gorbachev informed US Senator Edward Kennedy in Moscow on 6 February that an agreement on INF was possible regardless of whether there was any movement on strategic or space weapons. A week later the Special Committee met the US negotiators in

Geneva about the time the negotiated implementation of the "zero option" on INF seemed to be a realistic prospect. This was discussed in some detail with the negotiators, and Members were struck by the underlying sense of optimism which they encountered.

The zero option, which had been first formally proposed in 1981 by President Reagan, in fact contradicts the original rationale for NATO's dual-track decision.[1] The doctrine of flexible response emphasizes that the US nuclear arsenal must be clearly coupled to the defence of Western Europe and that the Soviet Union will be deterred from aggression so long as there is a substantial risk of conventional war leading to nuclear strikes. The theory has it that the American commitment will be reinforced by the deployment of missiles with sufficient range to strike the Soviet Union from Western Europe.

Ironically, representatives of several Western European governments who had originally supported the zero option began to express their reservations as it became clear that it might, this time, become a reality. European concerns about decoupling and increased vulnerability were the principal pretexts cited, and these were supported by statements made by NATO Supreme Allied Commander General Bernard Rogers in Brussels and Paris in February.

In response to the unexpectedly strong voices of concern emanating from America's European and Asian allies about "discriminatory" treatment, President Reagan retreated significantly from the zero option and proposed instead a steady elimination of INF over three years. He suggested two different approaches to this end.

There was an air of anti-climax surrounding the INF issue as round four came to an end, but this seemed to be accompanied by a degree of genuine optimism that some sort of an interim INF agreement was now possible.

In the areas of space and strategic weapons no such optimism could be discerned at the end of the fourth round, despite the fact that both sides had agreed on the necessity for radical reductions in their strategic arsenals. The critical issue, and the chief stumbling block to meaningful progress in the space and strategic categories, remained the US Strategic Defense Initiative (SDI). Through the multitude of proposals and counter-proposals which characterized rounds three and four of these talks, one element had stood out above all others: there would be no strategic arms control deal unless or until the United States clearly showed a willingness to make concessions on the SDI issue.

The framework for a major, far-reaching deal on strategic weapons was becoming apparent as each side attempted to upstage the other with dramatic and sweeping arms control proposals designed to appeal to public opinion. The "grand compromise" objective observers had in mind involved deep cuts in offensive weapons coupled with a long postponement of any deployment of strategic defences.

Round 5

INF Strategy

Developments in round 5 of the negotiations did not follow the consistent pattern of the previous round and there was little apparent progress made on the INF question. The United States began laying out its verification criteria for any future INF agreement almost from the first day. It proposed more data, on-site inspection, as well as some monitoring of critical installations such as production facilities. These were formally proposed at the beginning of the fifth round. The Soviets made clear that they were less interested in working out detailed verification procedures than in agreeing on a framework for reductions.

The two sides had agreed to pursue further a compromise on INF at a scheduled meeting in May between US Secretary of State Shultz and Soviet Foreign Minister Shevardnadze - it was hoped that such a meeting would accelerate the progress which had been made - but in the event the meeting was cancelled by the Soviet Union on 18 April following the US bombing of Libya.

Nevertheless the Soviet Union fulfilled its undertaking to table a draft INF agreement in Geneva on 15 May. The proposal called for the setting of equal limits on Soviet and American medium-range missiles and their eventual elimination. The draft did not deal with missiles in Asia but did call for a freeze on French and British missile technology, and an agreement that the United States would not transfer missile technology to other countries. However it received a cool response: the chief American negotiator, Max Kampelman, describing it as "merely a formal treaty carrying out statements previously made to the United States."

On 23 June General Secretary Gorbachev sent President Reagan a letter outlining new proposals in the area of INF which he indicated would be formally proposed during the sixth round. According to press reports Gorbachev made allusions to a formula in which the Soviet Union would be permitted to retain some limited levels of INF in Europe and Asia, and the United States would be allowed to keep an equal number in Europe and elsewhere.

Although the fifth round of talks concluded on 26 June the diplomacy continued outside the negotiating forum for some weeks. When President Mitterand of France visited Moscow on 7 July, French Government officials detected a slight softening of the Soviet attitude towards French nuclear forces. According to a report in the Washington Post, a Soviet Foreign Ministry spokesman said:

> "The Soviet Union fully respects the right of France to be free to decide its own nuclear force. Our position is that US and Soviet missiles should be removed from Europe."

This was followed by the visit of Soviet Foreign Minister Shevardnadze to Britain on July 16, during which he indicated that the proposed freeze on British and French forces did not rule out modernization.

Strategic and Space Weapons

For several months Soviet officials and negotiators hinted that their original insistence on a complete ban on SDI research embodied a measure of flexibility, but they had consistently shown a reluctance to spell out what this meant in practical terms.

On 29 May the Soviet Union tabled a new proposal for restricting the development of defensive technologies and for reducing strategic offensive weapons. The proposal appeared to offer the critical compromise on the SDI which had been hinted at for some months.

On the space and defensive side the Soviets proposed -

-- that each side agree not to invoke the (six month) withdrawal clause of the 1972 ABM Treaty for 15-20 years;

-- to permit laboratory research on space-based systems, the "threshold" already reached by the United States;

-- to ban space weapons such as ASAT and "space strike" weapons;

-- to define ABM terms such as "components" and "research".

On the offensive side the Soviets also appeared to make some significant compromises and proposed -

-- to limit each side to 8000 nuclear "charges" (warheads and bombs);

-- to limit each side to 1600 strategic nuclear delivery vehicles;

-- to limit nuclear charges to no more than 60% in any one based mode. This would allow each side up to 4800 ICBM warheads;

-- to include long-range air-launched cruise missiles and submarine-launched cruise missiles within the 8000 nuclear charges ceiling. Sea-launched cruise missiles would be banned;

-- to drop inclusion of US forward-based systems (the intermediate-range missiles, medium-range bombers and carrier-based aircraft) from the US strategic totals if their numbers are not increased and if systems are not redeployed.

Many leading experts saw in the Soviet proposal the basis for a general framework for the control of strategic weapons and one which appeared to move both sides closer to the "grand compromise" envisaged between offensive and defensive limitations. Nevertheless some within the Reagan Administration immediately poured scorn on the Soviet initiative.

The US Defense Secretary, Caspar Weinberger, for example, described the proposal as "terribly wrong ... and against our national interest." He added that "extending the ABM Treaty or doing anything which would prevent our doing all the things we need to do to develop a Strategic Defense Initiative is something obviously we would be very much opposed to." Secretary Weinberger and other hardliners in the US Administration characterized the proposal as an attempt to kill the SDI on the grounds that if the system was not to be deployed for 10-20 years

Congress would refuse even to fund the research. As Secretary Weinberger described it in an interview on 4 June, "The Soviets know you can't get funding for a programme you've said you're not going to use for 10 years."

Notwithstanding this negative response from some members of his Administration, President Reagan appeared to take an optimistic tone in a speech at Glassboro, New Jersey on June 19 when he said "we believe that possibly an atmosphere does indeed exist that will allow for serious discussion."

As the most productive round of the Geneva negotiations to date drew to a close the United States decided against a Soviet suggestion to prolong the round on the grounds that it needed time to develop a response to the Soviet proposals.

The Current Situation

Space and Strategic Weapons

In late July the United States responded to the Soviet June proposal in a letter sent by President Reagan to General Secretary Gorbachev. This contained a broad statement of new proposals. The critical issue concerned the SDI. Reportedly President Reagan proposed a delay in the deployment of space-based missile defences for 7 1/2 years in exchange for an agreement by the Soviet Union to allow research, development and testing of defensive technologies and components during this time.

In addition, President Reagan guaranteed that the United States would continue to adhere for 5 to 7 years to the ABM Treaty. The proposal envisaged that the Soviet Union and the United States would agree to wait 5 years after giving notice, plus 2 more years if they agreed to discuss the possibilities of sharing missile defence technologies. Research on new systems could be conducted throughout this period and deployment could begin in the last 2 years by mutual consent.

The letter was described by one US official as a supreme exercise in "creative ambiguity" which appeared to give something to the hawks in the Pentagon as well as to arms control proponents in the State Department. For the arms-controllers there was the positive sign that President Reagan had, for the first time, shown a willingness to bargain over the SDI. For the hardliners there was the satisfaction of knowing that the Reagan letter had apparently supported once more the "broader" interpretation of the ABM Treaty which had caused such a controversy when it was announced in late 1985. During the 7 1/2 years before deployment is to be allowed the United States would reserve the right to proceed with the research, development and testing of the SDI "which is permitted" by the ABM Treaty.

A long process of bargaining can be expected to take place in the coming months. As we recently saw at the Reykjavik mini-summit between Gorbachev and Reagan, a spectacular "grand compromise" on offensive and defensive systems cannot be ruled out, though it would take substantial concessions from both sides. Moreover, it would probably need to be preceded by a renegotiation of the ABM Treaty, since the differing interpretations of what this agreement prohibits and permits seems to be at the heart of the disagreement.

Some independent American experts have suggested in recent months compromises between the hardliners in the US Administration and many of its sternest critics outside. Some stress that since the President's vision of a near-perfect shield involves technology which will not be available until well into the next century, the SDI is relatively easy to reconcile with, say, a 10-year reaffirmation of the ABM Treaty and laboratory-based research programmes. It is therefore argued that a negotiated arms control agreement which would allow the President to protect his long-term vision would be possible "but only if he pulls his Administration together and refuses to allow the proponents of partial defence to use his vision as a stalking-horse for a short-term programme that would inevitably erode or break the ABM Treaty."[2]

Others, such as former US Secretaries of Defense Melvin Laird, James Schlesinger and Harold Brown, former US Secretary of State Cyrus Vance and former US National Security Advisor Brent Scowcroft, favour a US arms control strategy which centres on a sharply limited SDI research programme, continued compliance with the SALT II and ABM Treaties and the introduction of sophisticated strategic weapons. The five former officials let their collective views be known in a memorandum presented to Secretary of State George Shultz on 4 August.

The memorandum proposes that SDI research should be continued within the limits of the "restrictive" interpretation of the ABM Treaty and at a "measured technological pace". It stresses that the near-term SDI work should emphasize ground-based terminal defence of the US missile silos rather than the more ambitious Reagan vision.

In the negotiations with the Soviets the former officials advise that the United States should be prepared to accept limitations on testing of exotic kinetic-energy or directed energy anti-missile weapons in space for 10 years "as part of a meaningful agreement on strategic offensive force reductions."[3] They also propose that the superpowers agree not to withdraw from the ABM Treaty on grounds of "supreme national interest" except after 5 years' notice.

INF Weapons

At the beginning of the sixth round of the Geneva negotiations on 18 September the United States announced that it was prepared to accept a Soviet suggestion that only token INF forces on both sides be kept in Europe. The idea of radical cuts in missile warheads had apparently been advanced by the Soviets during two days of special arms control consultations which took place in Washington on 5 and 6 September.

Both sides seem to agree that 100 warheads would be a suitable limit for an "interim" INF agreement in Europe. It is envisaged that the Soviet Union would retain 100 warheads on SS-20s targeted against Asia, with the United States having the option of retaining an equivalent number in the United States.

Senior Soviet officials, including General Secretary Gorbachev and Foreign Minister Shevardnadze, continued to emphasize a desire for an interim INF accord during much of September, even at the height of the difficulties over Nicholas Daniloff (the US reporter arrested by the Soviets on spying charges on 23 August but released on 29 September). The Soviets appeared to be interested in a politically useful framework agreement which might form the centrepiece of a Gorbachev-Reagan Summit. Such an agreement would be consistent with Secretary Gorbachev's carefully orchestrated campaign to present a better image of the Soviet Union in Western Europe, which may have been intended to compensate for the wave of negative European opinion caused by the Chernobyl disaster.

If agreement were reached at the level of 100 missiles it would require the elimination of about 136 US warheads and more than 1200 Soviet warheads in the European theatre.

At the time of writing, however, several key issues require resolution before agreement can be guaranteed. As in the space and strategic categories there remain significant differences within the American Administration as well as between the United States and the Soviet Union. Three can be summarized as follows:

(a) The two sides must agree on the permissible numbers of Soviet intermediate-range SS-20 missiles targeted on Asia and of short-range missiles on both sides based in Europe, as well as the mix of US intermediate-range weapons in Europe.

The Soviets now have approximately 200 SS-20s east of the Urals targeted on China Japan and Alaska giving a combined total warhead capacity on those systems of about 600.

(b) There is also the problem of verifying compliance with the agreement, and of its duration. Several members of the US Administration, including Defense Secretary Weinberger, continue to insist that verification will remain a major impediment to a successful agreement on medium-range missiles and have expressed dissatisfaction with the Soviet unwillingness to be forthcoming on this issue. On 28 September, for example, Secretary Weinberger laid out a series of very stringent conditions which would appear to have little hope of being accepted by the Soviet Union:

> You have to have the ability to go on each other's soil ... you have to have the ability to look at the factories and look at the gun sights. You have to have the ability to do what bank examiners do.[4]

(c) Thirdly, there is the difficult issue of Soviet short-range missiles (SS-21, SS-22, SS-23) which the United States would like to see cut back. In the absence of some regulation covering this category of missile system, there is a fear that a "grey area"

> will be created capable of being exploited by the Soviet Union.
>
> Some analysts have even suggested that the Soviet Union has offered to cut back drastically on its SS-20 force in the knowledge that these other systems, if left unconstrained, could fulfill the same objectives as the SS-20s.
>
> This issue is very important for the Europeans and particularly for the West Germans since the SS-21, SS-22 and SS-23 are capable of covering all targets in the Federal Republic and those in many other parts of Europe. The concern is growing that Soviet short-range missiles may become as volatile a political issue as the SS-20s were in the 1970s. There is already a major debate in NATO, and within expert circles in the West, about the wisdom of developing an anti-tactical missile or anti-theatre missile (ATM) capability to counter such systems. It will not be long before this debate spills over into the public realm.

Allied Reactions

On 22 September President Reagan made a major speech to the UN General Assembly in which he suggested "the ice of the negotiating stalemate could break" during the sixth round of the Geneva negotiations. In a sweeping assessment of the entire arms control scene President Reagan made public his response to the proposal by Mr. Gorbachev to abide by the ABM Treaty for 15 more years in return for an agreed 30% reduction in offensive systems. President Reagan offered to observe the treaty for a further 7 years and in the meantime limit SDI efforts to research and testing. He reiterated his willingness to discuss with the Soviets the "ground rules" for the transition towards greater reliance on defensive weapons and, once more, offered to share with the Soviet Union the fruits of the SDI research efforts.

In the speech Mr. Reagan expressed optimism about reaching an understanding with the Soviet Union over intermediate-range missiles. The announcement a week later that President Reagan and General Secretary Gorbachev had agreed to stage an unprepared meeting - at the suggestion of the Soviet leader - in

Iceland on 11-12 October added to the speculation that an accommodation on INF missiles was close at hand. The simultaneous resolution of the Daniloff case contributed to the sense that a breakthrough might be imminent.

European Governments have in recent months been generally supportive of an interim agreement to reduce INF forces in Europe, especially the Federal Republic of Germany.[5] President Reagan, in fact, met NATO Foreign Ministers immediately after his UN speech in New York and discussed this proposition with them. The NATO Foreign Ministers expressed a desire to see concurrent restraints on short-range nuclear weapons as well as conventional weapons in Europe, but it is understood that the Europeans did not make their support for an interim INF deal conditional on an achievement of these aspirations.

The Kohl Government in the Federal Republic of Germany no doubt regarded the prospect of an INF deal as a potential boost to its fortunes in the January 1987 election. The prospect of Pershing IIs and SS-20s leaving Central Europe in considerable numbers would be electorally popular in the Federal Republic of Germany. It would also vindicate the Government's consistent argument that the deployment of these missiles was essential to persuade the Soviets to negotiate seriously.

Although the next general election is further away in the United Kingdom, a similar set of motivations may lie behind the Thatcher Administration's strong support for an interim agreement. The recent dispute between British Labour Party leaders and key Pentagon officials over Labour's defence policies might provide the US Administration with a further reason to move towards an agreement.

The SALT II Controversy

On May 27 President Reagan announced that future decisions on the structure of the US strategic nuclear forces would be based on the "nature and magnitude of the threat posed by Soviet strategic forces and not on standards contained in the SALT structure." In the statement the President declared that the SALT arms control regime had been undermined by Soviet non-compliance. In addition he repeated his belief that the unratified SALT II treaty was "fatally flawed".

The President's decision was the latest element of a controversy which has dogged the SALT II treaty since it was signed by the United States and the USSR in Vienna in 1979. The treaty, although never ratified or voted on by the US Senate, would have expired at the end of 1988 if it had been ratified. Nevertheless the treaty has been fairly closely observed by both the United States and Soviet Union for the last six years.

The treaty has been criticized by President Reagan for codifying arms build-ups rather than arms reductions. As evidence of this he has pointed out that the 1979 agreement allowed each side a total of 820 MIRVed ICBM launchers, whereas at the time the treaty was signed the United States had plans for only 550 such launchers and the USSR only possessed 600. Similarly SALT II permitted 1200 MIRVed ballistic launchers (ICBMs and SLBMs) when the US had 1050 and the Soviet Union 750. Equally important for the President was the fact that SALT II placed limits on launchers only, with no constraints on missiles or warheads.

During the Carter Administration debate on the treaty within the Senate Foreign Relations Committee was heated, and only 9 of 15 members voted to send it to the full Senate for ratification. The Committee's recommendation was accompanied by a number of reservations. In addition, although it was under no requirement to do so, the Senate Armed Services Committee also held hearings on the treaty and issued a critical report.

In fact, the treaty never reached the Senate Floor. Following the Soviet invasion of Afghanistan, President Carter asked that it be removed temporarily from the Senate calendar. As the situation in Afghanistan deteriorated and the US presidential elections approached, it became politically unfeasible to bring the treaty to a vote. After the election of Ronald Reagan, who had actively campaigned against the treaty, it was clear that SALT II would never be submitted for ratification.

The Interim Restraint Policy

Many American conservatives had hoped that President Reagan would scrap the treaty altogether. However, in a Memorial Day address at Arlington Cemetery in May 1982, the President stated that the United States would refrain from actions that would "undercut existing agreements" so long as the Soviet Union showed equal restraint. The USSR, while insisting that the United States should still ratify the treaty, indicated that if the United States were to observe SALT I and SALT II then the Soviet Union would abide by the provisions of these agreements to the same degree. This informal agreement to respect the limits of SALT II became known as the policy of "interim restraint".

The President's decision to abide by SALT II was motivated by both political and military considerations. Politically it was felt that by retaining the SALT II restraints, the Administration demonstrated to both the USSR and the NATO Allies its serious interest in arms control. This was particularly important at a time when President Reagan's harsh anti-Soviet statements were causing concern among the NATO Allies. In addition, the United States sought to improve the East-West climate as part of its efforts to begin negotiating with the USSR in the START and INF talks in Geneva.

Militarily, the provisions of SALT II did not have any effect on the US strategic build-up. All the major weapons programmes planned by the United States, including MX, Trident II, and the B-1 bomber, could be carried forward within the limits laid down in the accord. The dismantling of several new Polaris submarines undertaken as the new Tridents came into service was an obligation resulting from the SALT I treaty. In addition the Polaris boats were approaching the end of their service lives.

It has also been argued that the commitment not to undercut the treaty has restrained Soviet strategic programmes. While the USSR may have increased the number of its MIRVed ICBMs, for example, it has remained within the numerical limits established by SALT II, when it had the capability to exceed them. Soviet missile production lines remain open and according to unclassified CIA data they could more than double the size of their force (by 1992) should they decide to break out. In addition, to comply with both SALT I and SALT II more than 1,000 Soviet land-based missiles, 250 sea-launched missiles and 14 SLBMs have been removed from operation as new systems have been deployed.

Interim Restraint Re-Assessment

Compliance with the terms of SALT II during the 1981-1985 period would appear to have served US strategic interests. Beginning in 1985, however, new factors emerged which called into question a continuation of the policy of interim restraint. First, the US strategic programme was beginning to push at the SALT II limits. Sea trials of the seventh Trident submarine, the USS Alaska, in October 1985 would put the United States over the SALT ceiling of 1200 MIRVed launchers. To remain in compliance with the agreement, 14 MIRVed launchers would have to be eliminated. The systems that would have to be dismantled were not at the end of their service lives and would still be effective weapons. In addition, as each successive Trident submarine entered service an additional 24 MIRVed launchers would have to be eliminated, probably in mid-1985. Furthermore, the SALT II limit of 1320 on the total number of MIRVed launchers and heavy bombers equipped with air-launched cruise missiles (ALCMs) would be reached by mid-1986, and any subsequent increase in the numbers of ALCMs carrying bombers would require the elimination of Poseidon and/or Minuteman III launchers on a one-for-one basis.

The second factor which influenced US policy towards SALT II was evidence that the Soviet Union was violating the agreement. In February 1985, the Administration released a report to Congress which cited three areas of Soviet non-compliance: (i) encryption of telemetry during Soviet ballistic missile test flights (ii) testing and deployment of a second new type of ICBM, the SS-X-25, and (iii) deployment of the SS-16 ICBM. In addition the United States accused the Soviet Union of violating the 1972 ABM treaty by deploying a large phased array radar in Central Siberia.

In addition to these two considerations, the fact that the SALT II treaty was to expire in December 1985 raised questions as to the future attitude of the United States following that date. If a change in policy were to be implemented, it was only logical that it be announced as the expiration date approached. In any case the United States would have had to make known its intentions towards the agreement once it had expired.

President Reagan had been instructed by Congress to report by June 1, 1985, on the consequence of continuing adherence to SALT II. After delaying his decision, the President announced as of June 10 that the United States "would continue to refrain from undercutting existing strategic arms agreements to the extent that the Soviet Union exercises comparable restraint and provided that the Soviet Union actively pursues arms reductions agreements in the currently... ongoing talks in Geneva." As a direct consequence of this decision, the United States de-activated and dismantled one Poseidon submarine when the seventh Trident submarine entered service later that year.

In his statement President Reagan described his decision as going the "extra mile" towards establishing a framework of mutual restraint with the Soviet Union, and he urged the USSR to co-operate in this endeavour. He also stressed that this was a policy of interim restraint and stressed once again Soviet violations of the treaty. He clearly indicated that if the Soviet Union were to continue to violate the treaty the United States would undertake appropriate and proportionate responses. Specifically he referred to the Midgetman ICBM programme as one possible response to the Soviet SS-X-25. The President also instructed the Department of Defense to conduct a comprehensive review of the consequences of Soviet violations and to identify specific actions the United States could take to accelerate or increase its strategic modernization programme in response to Soviet violations.

Finally, the President's statement emphasized that this decision was an interim one; future decisions on US strategic modernization would be made "in light of Soviet actions correcting their non-compliance and promoting progress in Geneva."

The decision to go the extra mile and continue a policy of interim restraint continued to be implemented during 1985 and the first half of 1986, even though the SALT II agreement expired in December 1985 and despite evidence of continuing Soviet non-compliance. In his report to Congress in December 1985 on Soviet violations, the President noted that the pattern of Soviet non-compliance increasingly affected US national security and "raised fundamental questions about the integrity of the arms control process itself." Nonetheless, no new action on SALT II was taken until May 1986.

Abandoning the Salt II Limits

President Reagan's 27 May 1986 statement marked a change in US policy in that he decided to abandon the policy of interim restraint. In short the United States is no longer bound by the provisions of SALT II, and in the absence of an agreement to reduce strategic nuclear weapons, decisions on the modernization of US forces will be made solely in response to the threat posed by Soviet strategic forces and not by the limits established by

SALT II. This decision has had no direct practical consequences yet on US strategic programmes. Even as the President announced that the United States would no longer abide by SALT II, the United States dismantled two Poseidon submarines for military and economic reasons, leaving the United States in technical compliance with SALT II for the present. In addition the Pentagon announced that it had fallen behind schedule in deploying cruise missiles on bombers.

This delay is likely to relieve pressure on the Reagan Administration; when the 131st strategic bomber is equipped with ALCMs the United States will be in violation of SALT II unless MIRVed ICBMs or SLBMs are dismantled. Originally, the equipment of the 131st bomber was scheduled for the fall of 1986; the delay will most probably postpone this critical decision until sometime in early 1987.

Nevertheless, the political implications of the President's May 27 1986 decision remain; the United States has announced that it no longer considers itself bound by the SALT II guidelines. Unless this decision is reversed or an agreement is reached in Geneva on strategic nuclear arms, it seems inevitable that at some point the United States will be in violation of the treaty as its strategic modernization programme progresses. This prospect has raised concern over the implications for the US-Soviet strategic balance, the arms control negotiations in Geneva, and the relationship between the United States and its NATO Allies.

Possible Impact on the US-Soviet Strategic Balance

The Soviet Union has stated publicly that as soon as the United States violates the SALT II agreements it would consider itself to be freed from its SALT obligations as well. Critics of the Administration's decision argue therefore that abandoning SALT II will lead to an acceleration of the arms race. They believe that the Soviets are in a much better position than the United States to increase their nuclear arsenal. Senator Albert Gore has stated for example that the USSR now has four "hot" production lines for making ICBMs and can also rapidly expand the number of warheads deployed on the SS-18 missile, whereas the United States has only one "lukewarm" production line and no real ability to increase the number of deployed warheads. A report by the Chairman of the House Armed Services Committee, Congressman Les Aspin, also states that the greater throw-weight of Soviet ICBMs could allow them to increase the number of warheads per missile by as much as 2.2 times current levels.

In a study undertaken by the Congressional Research Service (CRS) in July 1986 on projected growth of the US and Soviet strategic forces, four case studies are presented, one with SALT restrictions and three without. In case one, it is assumed that both sides would continue to observe their political commitments to SALT II, i.e., that each side would retire old systems with the deployment of new ones. However, it is also assumed that each side would deploy two new types of ICBMs although the agreement only permits one. For the Soviet Union the new ICBM is considered to be the SS-25; for the United States it is the single warhead Midgetman, deployed as a proportionate response to the SS-25. According to this scenario, by the year 2000 the United States would have 2308 delivery vehicles (DV) as opposed to 1931 on December 31, 1985 and the Soviet Union would have 2504 DVs as opposed to 2492. In terms of warheads, US deployed warheads would increase from 11,639 at present to 11,884 by the year 2000, and the Soviet Union would increase the number of its warheads from the current level of 10,024 to 15,724 during the same period.

The other three case studies contained in the CRS report all presume that the SALT II guidelines are abandoned by both the United States and the Soviet Union. The political, military, and economic assumptions in each case vary, and each case involves a certain amount of speculation as to each nation's intentions about the modernization of its force structure and its industrial capacity to produce the quantities of weapons predicted. It is not possible here to detail each scenario. However, the table below provides the results in terms of aggregate warheads deployed on offensive nuclear delivery systems.

	1985	Case 2	Case 3	Case 4
US	11,639	13,060	20,326	36,406
USSR	9,924	20,934	25,794	48,908

The US Administration does not agree with these and other assessments. In President Reagan's July 1986 report to Congress on US interim restraint policy and on representative Soviet and US forces with and without SALT I and II, the Administration indicates that the

Soviet Union now has approximately 10,000 strategic nuclear weapons (missile warheads and bombs). The report projects that the Soviet Union will increase the number of its weapons to over 12,000 in the next five years, assuming it were to remain in compliance with SALT II. The report also states that in the absence of the SALT II constraints the USSR would not necessarily expand its forces significantly beyond the above figure of 12,000. In addition, if the Soviets were not to dismantle their older systems in the absence of SALT II as rapidly as they would otherwise, the overall threat to US security would remain the same in light of the Soviets' current strategic modernization programme. The report's worst case scenario assumes that in the absence of all SALT II constraints the USSR would expand its nuclear forces to at most 15,000 weapons by 1991.

These assessments, although based on the known production capability of the Soviet Union, necessarily involve a certain amount of guesswork. The multitude of factors which influence decisions on strategic modernization make it extremely difficult to predict future patterns of behaviour with a high degree of certainty. While most critics of the Administration contend that the Soviet Union would be in a far better position than the United States to upgrade its strategic nuclear forces without the SALT II constraints, the Administration's argument that the current level of the Soviet strategic forces is sufficient to meet "reasonable military requirements" cannot be rejected out of hand.

Implications for the Allies and the Geneva Negotiations

The political consequences of the US decision no longer to be constrained by the numerical limits of the SALT II agreement are more immediate. The NATO Allies see the SALT treaties as important milestones in US-Soviet efforts to manage superpower relations. In addition the SALT agreements are seen as part of the broader arms control process, stepping stones to future agreements. A move away from SALT is seen as potentially destabilizing and could lead to a period of unrestrained superpower competition. In addition, the Allies, aware that the decision may be seen among sectors of their publics as a sign that the United States is not interested in arms control, fear the Soviet Union could use it as an opportunity to exploit differences within the Alliance.

Finally, concern has been expressed over the implications of the decision for the arms control negotiations in Geneva.

At the spring meeting of NATO Foreign Ministers in Halifax, Nova Scotia, these concerns were clearly expressed. Brian Mulroney, the Canadian Prime Minister, stated publicly that the decision "will not be endorsed by NATO and certainly not by the Canadian Government." The British Government expressed "regret" over the move.

The impact of the President's decision on the Geneva negotiations is less clear. It has been argued that the decision is a bargaining strategy designed to increase pressure on the Soviets to negotiate a compromise by threatening to break out of the SALT limitations. Although the Soviets have declared publicly that the President's May 27 announcement calls into question the future of the Geneva talks, they have taken no action to date to jeopardize them.

On the other hand, it is argued that if deep reductions in strategic arms forces are to be achieved - a goal to which General Secretary Gorbachev and President Reagan committed themselves at the November 1985 summit - an agreed ceiling from which to reduce is needed. SALT II would appear to provide such a ceiling; removing those limitations would greatly complicate the negotiators' task.

Developments since May 27

US compliance with SALT II appears more possible now than at the time the President announced his decision. First, as indicated earlier, the United States remains in technical compliance with SALT II, and is likely to do so until at least the end of this year, given the dismantling of two older Poseidon submarines and the delays in the air force's programme to equip the 131st bomber with air-launched cruise missiles.

Secondly, the United States agreed, at the Soviet Union's request, to meet in an extraordinary session of the Special Consultative Commission (SCC) in July 1986. Set up in 1972, the SCC is mandated to oversee implementation of US-Soviet strategic arms agreements. Although no progress was made in resolving the disagreements over SALT II, the United States made clear that President Reagan's offer, contained in his May 27 statement, to establish with the USSR an interim framework of mutual restraint remained open, pending a verifiable agreement on deep reductions in nuclear offensive arms.

Finally, in a letter sent to Congress in August, the President stated that although he has decided no longer to abide by the numerical limits of SALT II, he would continue to retire older nuclear systems as the US strategic modernization programme progressed, assuming "no significant change" in the nature of the Soviet threat.

In conclusion, it would appear that the President is leaving the door open for compromise with the Soviet Union over continued compliance with SALT II. In particular, efforts by the USSR to address directly US charges of non-compliance, especially in the field of encryption of telemetry, could lead to an agreement by the United States not to undercut SALT II. Such a compromise could perhaps be worked out within the context of broader discussions currently taking place between the United States and the Soviet Union. If not, the next opportunity to do so would be at the regular autumn meeing of the SCC scheduled for this year.

THE STRATEGIC DEFENSE INITIATIVE

The US SDI Programme

The American Strategic Defense programme, which, according to the latest Defense Guidance issued by the US Secretary of Defense on 31 December 1985, now occupies a position of equal programme priority with that of the Administration's strategic force modernization goals, is divided into five project groups:

-- Surveillance, Acquisition, Tracking and Kill Assessment
-- Directed Energy Weapons
-- Kinetic Energy Weapons
-- Systems Analysis and Battle Management
-- Support Programmes.

As an illustration of the priority the Reagan Administration attaches to the SDI programme, the President, in submitting his FY87 budget proposal to Congress on 5 February, unsuccessfully requested that it be exempt from the general budget cuts associated with the Gramm-Rudman-Hollings Amendment.

Solving the complex problems of surveillance and acquisition, and battle management issues, is the key to developing an effective ballistic defence. A comprehensive system must be able to warn of attacks; detect and track missiles, post-boost vehicles, and re-entry vehicles throughout their trajectories; distinguish targets from decoys; and pass target location information to the defending weapons systems - and all in a matter of seconds.

Directed systems concepts offer the possibility of space-based defensive weapons effective over thousands of miles, at or near the speed of light, and able to attack missiles in their boost or post-boost phases. The directed energy development programme will determine the feasibility of these laser and particle beam weapons.

Kinetic energy weapon systems, which destroy their targets by direct impact, are potentially effective at any stage from boost to re-entry and can be fired either from the ground or from space. Boost phase interception would be carried out by low-orbit satellites firing rockets out of pods. Scientists have pointed out, however, that kinetic energy weapon systems have considerable potential for intercepting re-entry vehicles during the mid-course and terminal portions of their flight. In the latter case, the warheads are heated and slowed by friction with the atmosphere, thus rendering themselves vulnerable to tracking by airborne or ground-based radars. Kinetic energy weapons are reported to be well enough advanced to be available by the 1990s, much earlier than directed energy weapons.

The system analysis, battle management and support programmes are designed to provide overall SDI system integration, communication technologies and general supporting technologies.

Purpose and Scope

The President and a dwindling, but totally committed, group in the Administration - including Defense Secretary Weinberger - continue to insist that a foolproof population defence is the objective of the SDI and can be achieved. As recently as July 1 Mr. Weinberger repeated that "it's not our missiles that we seek to protect but our people .... And we must never lose sight of that goal." He criticized the Senate Armed Services Committee for warning about air-breathing systems, saying that the goal of SDI was "total defence".

Others in the Administration, however, are openly sceptical - and occasionally openly scornful - of the vision of "rendering nuclear weapons impotent and obsolete", although they continue to support President Reagan's programme for a variety of other reasons. Some see the role of strategic defences as one of defending missile silos, thus depriving the Soviet Union of the first-strike capability they allege it now has.[6] This school of thinking is concerned with reinforcing deterrence, as opposed to moving beyond deterrence, which is President Reagan's stated intent. For example, Mr. Weinberger's deputy, Mr. Richard Perle, declared in June that the leak-proof defence concept "is not a short-term proposition and it may not even be possible in the long-term." He added that the immediate goal of the SDI was "not the defence of the nation as a whole but the defence of America's capacity to retaliate".[7]

The contradictory statements from Reagan Administration officials on the purpose and scope of the SDI programme continued throughout 1986 and have undoubtedly contributed to the confused nature of the debate in the Alliance. It is difficult to take seriously President Reagan's frequent offers to share both the technology and any system it eventually produces with the Soviets, most recently repeated in his speech to the UN in late September. As the Chairman of this Committee has recently stated:

> "Sheerly on the basis of logic, sharing a star wars defensive system would be unsound, because to know the technology is to know how to defeat it. And on a practical level it is preposterous, because such a system would embody <u>all</u> of our most advanced technology - defensive, offensive and otherwise."[8]

Some of Mr. Reagan's senior officials have issued statements at variance with the President on the question of sharing SDI technology. For example, Mr. Perle in December 1985 informed the House Foreign Affairs Committee that such a proposition envisaged a quite different USSR, including the elimination of the Soviet threat.

The Cost Effective Criterion

Recent statements from senior members of the Reagan Administration about the cost-effectiveness of any future SDI system have caused some concerns among the NATO Allies. In February 1985 Ambassador Paul Nitze had delivered an important policy address to the Philadelphia World Affairs Council which set out a number of criteria which he said needed to be met before the United States would proceed to deploy a comprehensive system. In this address Mr. Nitze highlighted two key elements:

(1) The technology would need to produce defensive systems which would be survivable "against pre-emptive attack".

(2) The systems would need to be "cost-effective at the margin, that is, they must be cheap enough to add additional defensive capability so that the other side has no incentive to add additional offensive capability to overcome defence".

Since these comments were made there has been a substantial body of independent technical evidence suggesting that space-based defences will not meet the two tests laid down for it.[9]

However, in May 1986 the US Department of Defense seemed to drop the "cost-effective at the margin" criterion in its unclassified report to Congress. General Abrahamson, the Director of the SDIO, merely stated in the report that the United States should deploy SDI if it -

-- has a "potential role in US strategy";

-- would "serve as a deterrent to surprise attack and enemy escalation";

-- would make a "contribution to our arms control objectives"; and

-- is technically possible.

According to a report in the New York Times of 14 May, Secretary of State Shultz delivered a "stinging memo" to National Security Advisor Admiral Poindexter complaining about the report before it was released but was evidently not successful in preventing its publication in this form.

For some months before the release of the report, Pentagon officials had privately conceded that they wished to see the criterion dropped, despite the fact that it had been formally adopted as an Administration policy in National Security Council Directive Number 172. Their rationale was that ballistic missile defences might at some point assume such a critical importance that the

United States should be prepared to deploy them despite the fact that they might initially be more costly than Soviet countermeasures.

However, in early June, Ambassador Nitze reiterated that cost-effectiveness remained part of the US SDI policy in a speech delivered to the Time magazine conference on the SDI.

Foreign Policy Institute Study of SDI Costs

The controversy which had erupted over the criterion of cost-effectiveness was given a new dimension when in late July a major study was released under the auspices of the Foreign Policy Institute of Johns Hopkins University. This attempted to calculate the future cost of a space-based defence against nuclear missiles.

According to Dr. Barry Blechman and Dr. Victor A. Urgoff, the authors of the study, such a system if technically practical would cost $770 billion to build and operate for 10 years or "roughly comparable to what the Navy or Air Force currently invests in all weapons development and procurement." It adds that the Western Alliance would need to spend another $160 billion to improve non-nuclear weapons if the Soviet Union also decided to build an SDI shield to negate the usefulness of NATO's nuclear arsenal.

The report makes some very optimistic assumptions about technical progress in space weaponry, such as the assumption that satellites can be made resistant to attack without much added cost - an immense technical challenge. It also assumes only 90% effectiveness for the system - a lower success rate would increase the costs further. It was dismissed by the US Department of Defense as "an exercise in absurdity to try to estimate the cost of a system which hasn't been defined."

The controversy which erupted around the Nitze criterion of cost-effectiveness reflects deeper divisions inside the Reagan Administration on the future direction and scope of the SDI programme. These divisions have their roots more in differences over existing and future arms control regimes and the management of relations with the Soviet Union than in the intrinsic merits of the technical programme itself. It is therefore natural that the United States' NATO Allies have shown, and continue to show, a healthy interest in the outcome of this internal debate.

Technical Progress

In the year since Lt. Gen. Abrahamson appeared before the Committees of the North Atlantic Assembly in San Francisco in October 1985 - during which he stated that great progress was being made in the technical work necessary for a successful SDI system - there has been a consistent stream of comments and quotations from officials in the White House, the Pentagon and the SDIO confirming the seemingly inexorable advances which are being made in the programme.

For example, one month after his San Francisco appearance, General Abrahamson appeared before reporters at the Pentagon on 26 November to claim that the programme "is at its most inventive stage" and that "we're seeing invention and innovation coming along at just an incredible pace."[10] At this same press briefing the SDI programme's chief scientist Dr. Gerold Yonas singled out four high points:-

-- the technique for compensating for aberrations in the atmosphere;

-- advances in the development of the free electron laser;

-- lethality experiments undertaken at White Sands Paving Grounds;

-- mid-course discrimination.

Less than three months later on 7 February 1986, and just over a week after the Challenger disaster, President Reagan himself declared that "the technology to create a high-tech shield against nuclear missiles is advancing far more rapidly than we even dared hope three years ago" in a speech he delivered at the Thomas Jefferson High School in Annandale, Virginia.

A month later on 4 March General Abrahamson, in testimony before the House Armed Services Sub-Committee on Research and Development, continued the up-beat tone and stated that research on the SDI was moving from technology development into "major experiments". General Abrahamson told the Congressmen that "we've already demonstrated the technical feasibility" of the SDI, and that "our challenge is now to bring costs down and demonstrate how we can make it more affordable."

The series of so-called breakthroughs and declarations of "amazing progress" have been cited as evidence that the SDI is on track, technically feasible and therefore fully justifies its unprecedented level of funding. Films and photographs have been regularly released to demonstrate such claims, and officials have denied that any serious damage was inflicted on the programme by the series of aerospace disasters which began with the Challenger explosion of 28 January.

The Challenger shuttle plane, which had cost $1.2 billion, exploded 74 seconds after lift-off, killing seven astronauts and destroying a $100 million satellite. Experts believe that the United States' shuttle fleet will now be grounded until the beginning of 1988. This was followed by another aerospace accident which occurred on 18 April when a Titan 34D rocket exploded after lift-off from the Vandenberg Air Force Base in California, destroying a secret military payload; the second Titan failure in a row. The third rocket failure occurred on 3 May when a Delta satellite launcher exploded 71 seconds into flight.

These setbacks to the American space programme led some analysts to suggest that the SDI programme would be much more damagingly affected than the Administration's officials had admitted. The triple crisis, for example, meant that the ability of the United States to lift major satellites into orbit was immediately halted, as were scientific tests in space.

Launcher or rocket power is an integral part of the anti-missile vision. According to a recent official statement[11], an initial SDI deployment in the late 1990s might require about 600 space launches during a three-year period, or more than one rocket lift-off every two days. The official added that a first line anti-missile system might include 3200 rocket-carrying battle stations in 40 different orbits and additional satellites. This is considered an optimistic assumption by some analysts.

The first anti-missile experiment which had been carried out by the US shuttle occurred in June 1985, during which a beam from an earth-based laser was bounced off a special mirror aboard the shuttle Discovery. Subsequently six other shuttle flights undertook minor SDI experiments.

According to the NASA authorities the pace of testing was expected to accelerate considerably from the beginning of 1986. It is believed that six major SDI shuttle tests were planned between 1986 and 1988.

On 26 June the SDIO Report to Congress was released and appeared to acknowledge, for the first time, the monumental challenge facing the SDI in the area of space transportation. It notes that:

> "success in nearly every element of the program is dependent on major advances in ... space transportation and logistics ... It is clear that there is not now an adequate knowledge of the supply requirements and logistics infrastructure to support a space force of the magnitude and complexity envisaged for a multitiered ballistic missile defence."

If the series of aerospace disasters subsequently increases the costs of future space transportation[12] it will have a direct impact on the cost-effectiveness criterion. This is especially the case if one considers that for defensive weapons in space to be "survivable", heavy shielding will be required to protect battle stations from attack, and powerful jets will need to be developed in order to move them during space wars. Each different precautionary measure dictates that defensive weapons will have to become heavier - and thus more costly to lift into orbit. This may explain why the cost-effectiveness criterion did not appear in the latest SDIO Report to Congress.

There is little doubt that some significant progress has been achieved in the SDI programme over the last 3 1/2 years - and the great strides which have been made in the development of many key technologies such as the free-electron laser, for example, are a testimony to this. But there is nonetheless profound scepticism in the US scientific community on whether such progress merits descriptions like "amazing" and "incredible".

Indeed, these doubts are not confined to experts outside the programme. Some SDI scientists have let it be known over the past year that results have been exaggerated by Administration spokesmen and they worry that the credibility of the programme - and their own reputations - risk being undermined by such inflated claims.

Proxmire, Johnston and Chiles Report on SDI

It was partly in response to claims of great progress

by SDIO officials and demands that projected funding levels for the programme therefore should be maintained that three senior members of the Senate Defense Appropriations Sub-Committee - Senators William Proxmire, J. Bennett Johnston and Lawton Chiles - requested an intensive staff review of the SDI at the beginning of 1986. The mandate they set the staff was to report on actual progress and changes made in SDI research, and to comment on the challenges and problems which lay ahead. The findings of the report, released on 17 March[13], was based on information the staff authors had gleaned from 40 top scientists, engineers and managers deeply involved with, and supportive of, SDI research.

The Report's findings represent a comprehensive critique of several important aspects of the management, prioritization, and presentation of the SDI to date. It has had a powerful impact on legislators in the United States Congress. For these reasons the Rapporteur believed it appropriate to cite, verbatim, a number of its key findings for the information of the Committee:

- "While some significant progress has been achieved in each of the five major programmes of the SDI, none of it could be described as 'amazing'. Interviews with key SDI scientists involved in the research revealed that there have been <u>no major breakthroughs</u> which make a mid- to late-1990s deployment of comprehensive missile defences more feasible than it was three years ago.

- In fact, the 'schedule-driven' nature of the current research program, which requires that a development decision be made by the early 1990s, has aroused significant concern among scientists at the national weapons laboratories. The concern is twofold. First, promising long-term research will be compromised to reach an arbitrary schedule. Second, in an effort to maintain public support for high funding levels and an early development decision, SDI experiments will degenerate, in the words of a senior scientist at the Livermore National Laboratory, into 'a series of sleazy stunts'.

- Much of the progress that has been achieved has resulted in a greater understanding of program difficulties, which are much more severe than previously considered. Briefly, they are:

- The high-leverage, boost-phase defence faces considerable difficulties with survivability, which are greater than the obvious technical difficulties of developing operational weapons systems. A senior SDI researcher at the Sandia National Laboratory suggested that the technical problem of survivability was so intractable that the solution might well be a joint US-Soviet space station to co-ordinate space-based defence efforts.

- If the boost-phase defence proves more challenging than expected, then the problems of midcourse discrimination of Soviet warheads from decoys will be both geometrically and qualitatively multiplied. The threat scenarios posed by the weapons labs are ten times as great and far more complicated than those generated by the SDIO in the summer of 1985.

- Passive discrimination of the midcourse threat may have little utility. Possible Soviet countermeasures make passive discrimination by itself ineffective. Some progress has been made in research of a new type of discrimination - interactive discrimination. At this point, however, interactive discrimination is little more than an interesting and promising concept.

- The shuttle tragedy pointed out current logistical difficulties with the deployment of space-based payloads. Unless fairly dramatic advances are made in US space transportation, logistics and support capabilities, it may be impossible to begin deploying any SDI system until after the year 2000. This raises serious questions about the current schedules and emphasis of the program.

- After three years, the SDI budget has nearly tripled. SDIO has slowed the pace of some of its research efforts; however, this has not been done primarily as a result of Congressional budget cuts, as efforts seem to be driven as much by their lack of technical promise (as was the case with chemical lasers), and by SDIO's insistence on keeping to an unrealistic "technology-limited" research schedule.

- Public debate on the SDI has often centred on the desirability of performing a robust research programme. The authors of this report consider that question moot. Public support for research is broad and bipartisan. The more relevant question involves the pace and direction of this programme.

- SDI funding levels are as large as the combined services' technology-based research and development programmes. The FY1987 budget request would more than quadruple the SDI budget in just four years. Despite the magnitude of this request, SDIO has yet to produce a definite set of systems architectures, which can be tested against a generated and realistic set of threat scenarios. In fact, there appears to have been no consensus reached on the range of threat scenarios these deployment options might be expected to face."

The Report also came to some important conclusions for the US Congress which bear repeating:

1. It advocates "a certain degree of scepticism over claims of tremendous advances in SDI research" and suggests "hard questions should be asked about what any so-called 'spectacular breakthroughs' really accomplished and how far the research was actually advanced compared to the task at hand."

2. It proposes "a closer look at whether boost-phase intercept can ever be made to work and whether space-based assets can ever be made survivable. If the evidence shows that boost-phase intercept cannot work and space-based assets cannot be made survivable, with or without arms control, serious questions should be raised about the feasibility of implementing the President's vision of a comprehensive strategic defence."

3. It claims that "the problem of discriminating warheads from decoys in the midcourse phase of defence is much larger than Congress has been led to believe. SDIO is just scratching the surface in addressing this problem. Furthermore, it appears

that there is no clear consensus on what kind of realistic threat strategic defence would face in the future."

4. It addresses "the priority shifts SDIO has made in its program" which "appear to indicate that, contrary to public pronouncements, SDIO still does not have a firm idea of how a strategic defence system might be implemented."

5. It questions "why SDIO is rushing to arrive at a development decision by the early 1990s since comprehensive ballistic missile defences would not become fully operational until nearly two decades from now." It notes "the serious risks involved in making a premature decision on whether to develop strategic defences."

6. It notes that the "Congressional debate over SDI has centred largely on its national security implications and on whether strategic defences are militarily feasible. Much more scrutiny, however, must be given to whether it is feasible to produce, deploy and maintain such a system. It may well be that the production, transportation, support, logistics, and administrative requirements of a strategic defence system are as tremendous as the military and technical requirements."

7. It suggests that "a closer look should be taken at current and future US-Soviet arms control regimes and their relationship with SDI. Proposals to dismantle SALT, if implemented, would only make SDI's task more difficult. Abandoning the ABM Treaty now would only leave the Soviet Union with an advantage for the near term in the deployment of hard-point defenses. The evidence indicates that further arms control constraints on the Soviet Union are necessary in order to make strategic defences feasible. The question remains, however, whether an arms control regime can be established to make strategic defences feasible."

8. Finally, it concludes that "after completing this review of the SDI research and the defensive systems being envisioned, we are struck by myriad uncertainties and unknowns at every turn in the

> programme - uncertainties and unknowns that bear directly on the effectiveness of a comprehensive ballistic missile defence we might deploy in the future. And much of that uncertainty will likely remain, for even with strategic defences in place, the United States would never be able to adequately test the system under realistic conditions."

The Role of the US Congress

The release of such critical reports on the SDI and the growing dissatisfaction with conflicting accounts of the objectives and scope of the programme by government officials, have resulted in the flurry of Congressional activity which has been a key feature of the debate over the last year.

On 19 December 1985 the Congress, in passing the Defense Department FY86 Appropriations Bill, agreed to a ban on ASAT testing so long as the Soviet Union respected its self-imposed moratorium. The legislation also further restricted the Pentagon from using money appropriated in FY85 for ASAT tests, stating that:

> "None of the funds appropriated by this Act may be obligated or extended to carry out a test of the Space Defence System (anti-satellite weapon) against an object in space until the President certifies to Congress that the Soviet Union has conducted, after 3 October 1985, a test against an object in space of a dedicated anti-satellite weapon."

The Congressional action was designed to encourage the Reagan Administration to pursue seriously an ASAT arms control agreement. Development money was, however, appropriated as a hedge against the Soviet Union breaking its own testing moratorium. In addition $5 million was appropriated "to carry out a research programme to develop new and improved verification techniques (to monitor compliance with any ASAT agreement) that may be entered into by the United States and the Soviet Union."

There is little doubt that the ASAT ban has an inhibiting effect on SDI development and this is openly conceded by Administration officials. For this reason a recent report by Undersecretary of Defense for Research and Engineering Donald Hicks said that the Pentagon would seek "corrective action" to "promptly restore our ability to conduct" tests against targets in space.

Congressional action has been targeted in the opposite direction. Representative Lee Aucoin, one of the chief sponsors of the legislation, let it be known in February this year that he and others in the Congress regarded the ASAT testing ban as permanent unless Congress declared otherwise. Aucoin wrote to Secretary Weinberger asking him to describe the negotiating position on ASAT and explain how it differed from one "designed to induce the Soviets to abandon all ASAT restraints and to deploy the maximum possible threat against essential US satellites."

On 26 March, the Chairman of the House Armed Services Committee Les Aspin, together with a Democratic colleague Representative George Brown, issued a statement proposing that - on grounds of cost, lack of technical progress and arms control considerations - the US Congress kill the ASAT programme outright. They cited three reasons for this conclusion:

(a) The cost had grown 51% in 3 years, while the schedule had slipped by 5 years;

(b) The F15 engine might need to be improved to gain the necessary velocity to launch the missile into space, and to do so would increase costs further;

(c) To cut costs the USAF had suggested basing the system on the East Coast and cutting two-thirds of the planned missiles (from 112 to 34), "thus leaving too few missiles to engage all the targets the Air Force told the United States in 1983 it needed to engage."

Through much of 1986 Administration officials pressured Congress vigorously to lift the ban on ASAT development and testing, arguing (as the Director of the Arms Control and Disarmament Agency did in June) that the Soviets were pursuing better ASATs using high-energy lasers in disregard of the US test halt.

In July, reports surfaced in the professional literature and the major American newspapers about internal USAF disagreements over capabilities, direction and opportunity-cost considerations of any future ASAT development programme. Congressional and Pentagon sources declared that the Pentagon would probably abandon the existing ASAT programme (utilizing F15s) if the

Congressional testing ban were continued. Another system, using technology under development in the SDI programme, was being suggested by some officials as worthy of serious consideration.

In August, the House of Representatives, as part of a series of limitations on the SDI programme, passed an amendment to the defence authorization bill extending the US ASAT testing moratorium until 1 October 1987. The proponents pointed out that the ASAT testing ban, which had been proposed by the Soviet Union and agreed to by the US Congress, represented the only arms control measure put into effect during the Reagan Administration. It was also pointed out during the debate that the existing Soviet ASAT weapon had functioned only 11 out of 20 times, with the advanced heat-seeking version failing in all six tests. A similar amendment, proposed by John Kerry in the Senate, was narrowly set aside. However, in October the Conference Committee agreed to extend the ASAT ban for a further year.

Since the early part of 1986 there has been a steady erosion of Congressional support for the levels of funding the US Department of Defense has requested for the SDI. Critics of the programme have been active in highlighting the programmatic incoherence, arms control dangers and potentially damaging economic implications of the SDI. Thus on 10 April two former Defense Secretaries Harold Brown and Robert McNamara advised the Senate Appropriations Defense Sub-Committee that SDI spending should be cut and the pace of the research slowed down.

There is little doubt that the series of aerospace disasters starting with Challenger has also had a negative impact on funding requests for the SDI programme.

The Administration, in response to this growing trend, has attempted to apply pressure of its own. For example, in May, the 1986 Arms Control Impact Statement, issued annually by the Arms Control and Disarmament Agency (ACDA), suggested that the Administration would continue to abide by the restrictive interpretation of the ABM Treaty only as long as the SDI "receives the support needed to implement its plan". It said that if the support were not forthcoming the SDIO might restructure the programme and adopt the broader interpretation.

Key Administration officials such as Assistant Secretary of Defense Perle and SDIO Director Abrahamson have made periodic statements about the new opportunities to save time and money which result from a less restrictive interpretation of the ABM Treaty. Perle, in early June, predicted this would happen during "the lifetime of the Administration"; and Abrahamson said he foresaw problems relating to the narrow interpretation of the treaty somewhere in 1989 - two years earlier than previously estimated.

In the event it was the Senate Armed Services Committee, in completing its markup of the 1987 Defense Authorization Bill, that proposed a series of measures which would make it difficult to apply the broader interpretation. It also proposed concrete measures to redefine the objectives of the SDI, rejecting the notion that its primary purpose is to shield the population.

The Armed Services Committee report, which was written by two influential Senators - Sam Nunn and William S. Cohen - states that the "major emphasis" of the SDI should be on protecting US strategic forces and not on "comprehensive, nationwide population defence". In doing so the Committee also voted to cut the President's budget request of $4.8 billion for 1987 to $3.6 billion.

Senator Nunn had declared that US Administration officials were in "total disagreement" and "total disarray" regarding SDI goals. However, Secretary of Defense Weinberger severely attacked the report of the Committee and declared that "it's not our missiles that we seek to protect but our people. And we must never lose sight of that goal."

In August, the full Senate for the most part supported the Committee report and voted to scale back the 1987 SDI budget to $3.96 billion. Meanwhile the House of Representatives voted to cut the SDI expenditure to $3.12 billion. The obvious compromise figure of $3.5 billion was eventually agreed in October - a considerable setback for the President's programme.

The Senate also passed some additional amendments to the authorization bill, two of which call for the Administration to provide reports on (a) projected total cost of SDI and (b) technologies to be developed or adopted within the next 5-10 years, by 15 March 1987.

In another amendment, of some considerable relevance to America's Allies, the bill contains language forbidding funds to foreign contractors unless American contractors could not do the work. This amendment was tabled by Senator John Glenn.

The substantial cutback in Congressional funding for the SDI in the fiscal year budget from a requested $5.3 billion to an authorized $3.5 billion, together with other related Congressional action (such as the extension of the

ASAT ban, through 1987), will certainly dictate major changes in the direction of the SDI programme in the next four years. The relatively free hand to determine priority and pace which the Administration enjoyed in the first three years of the SDI programme appears to be at an end.

As we have noted earlier the future progress of US-Soviet arms control negotiations also feeds into this process into a major way. The SDI remains the centrepiece of any "grand compromise" which might bring about drastic reductions in levels of offensive systems. The future of the ABM Treaty, due for renewal in 1987, is also an integral aspect which it now appears is being addressed in a serious way by the superpowers.

It is in the context of this complex, but fluid situation that experts are grappling with how best to design and implement a workable strategy for the SDI that, in the words of one authority:

> "recognizes that the programme will neither be strangled in its crib nor attain instant success. Such a plan should permit us all to consider, in a responsible way, whether there is, as claimed, a useful future role for missile defences in Western nuclear strategy without in the meantime destroying confidence in deterrence, starving other technological initiatives and defence programmes, or forcing us to forego attainable and useful agreements on offensive forces before we know the result of the research".[14]

This is really the essence of the problem. The US Congress clearly has an important role to play in this regard, as indeed do the NATO Allies. However, it is President Reagan himself who is the decisive player and it is he who ultimately must decide - soon in the opinion of this Rapporteur - whether he is prepared to use the SDI to obtain a drastic cutback in Soviet offensive forces. Early analysis of the outcome of the Reykjavik mini-summit meeting in October suggests that the unique bargaining position which he currently enjoys may not be with him for very much longer.

The Soviet Strategic Defence Programme

As General Abrahamson reminded the Committees of the

Assembly last October, the Soviet ballistic missile defence programme is a formidable one. It is graphically laid out in annual reports, released around budget time, by the US Department of Defense called Soviet Military Power. The Department of Defense has also recently released a special report, Soviet Strategic Defense Programs. The latter cites important recent Soviet activities in ballistic missile defence as the following:

-- Upgrading and expansion of the world's only operational anti-ballistic missile (ABM) system around Moscow;

-- Construction of the Krasnoyarsk ballistic missile detection and tracking radar, violating the 1972 ABM Treaty;

-- Extensive research into advanced technologies for defence against ballistic missiles, including laser weapons, particle beam weapons and kinetic energy weapons;

-- Maintenance of their strategic air defence forces; and

-- Improvements in their passive defences by maintaining deep bunkers and blast shelters for key personnel and enhancing the survivability of some offensive systems through mobility and hardening.

Although the Department of Defense publications clearly take a worst-case view of the Soviet BMD efforts, even organizations which have traditionally taken a critical stance against the US SDI programme concede that Soviet efforts in this area are not insignificant. Thus, the London-based International Institute for Strategic Studies remarks that

> "regardless of the actual dimensions of the Soviet Union's exotic BMD programme, the overall thrust of the BMD effort suggests that the ability to begin widespread deployment will not be the sole prerogative of the United States."[15]

Similarly the US Congressional Office of Technology Assessment in a 1985 study acknowledges that the Soviets are "vigorously developing advanced technologies potentially applicable to BMD."[16] Such comments, and a careful scrutiny of Soviet programmes, place in perspective Soviet charges about US "militarization of space". That said, it seems difficult to justify the frequent utterances from US Administration officials - including the President himself - that a major rationale of the US SDI programme is to "catch up".

It is true that the Soviets possess the only operational ABM system around Moscow, and this is permitted under the terms of the ABM Treaty. However, experts concede that it is of vintage quality similar to the US technologies of the late 1960s. The United States voluntarily decommissioned as ineffective its own system - surrounding a Minuteman missile site at Grand Forks, South Dakota - based on that technology.

It is also true that the Soviet Union maintains an operational ASAT system, but this is an extremely modest capacity to blind US satellites only if they are directly overhead. Such a system is a long way from an effective, versatile ASAT capability, much less a viable missile defence system. Indeed the more sophisticated Soviet infrared-guided anti-satellite system, which might take them closer to their goal, has failed in all six of its tests. Such a performance record has all but forced the Soviet Union to abandon this programme.

Of more legitimate concern perhaps is the heavy investment the Soviets have placed in the maintenance of a large air defence system, designed primarily to intercept and destroy enemy aircraft before they can attack targets inside Soviet territory. This air defence system includes over 1000 sites and 12,000 launchers for the various types of interceptor surface-to-air (SAM) missiles the Soviets keep in their inventory.

The SAM technology has been progressively upgraded over the years and is similar in some respects to that required to intercept ballistic missiles - particularly tactical and theatre systems. It may also be capable against some older SLBMs. Concern has been expressed in the US intelligence community that Soviet air defences and radars - such as that at Krasnoyarsk - could provide the basis for a nationwide ballistic missile defence system.

Special Committee Visit to MIT

In order to obtain a better perspective on the range and scope of Soviet BMD efforts, the Special Committee visited, in May of this year, the Massachussetts Institute of Technology (MIT), where it met several leading technical experts in this field.

They confirmed that, although the main public concern in the West has tended to focus on kill mechanisms - like lasers, particle beams and homing projectiles - the keys to the success or failure of the SDI programmes on both sides are the technologies of target acquisition, tracking and pointing and command and control. One leading MIT authority on Soviet BMD efforts with whom the Committee met, Professor Stephen Meyer, has described it thus:

> "Sensors, computers and highly-engineered electro-mechanical systems - products of electronics and miniaturization - are the linch-pin of SDI. Even the lasers (or other kill mechanisms) will depend heavily on micro-miniaturization of sub-components. All of these technologies play to the overwhelming advantage of the United States."[17]

In the computing technology it is common knowledge that the Soviet Union is only now learning to master third generation computers while the United States and Japan are marching towards prototype fifth-generation systems.

The Committee was told that the lag in Soviet software development is perhaps even worse, particularly in the area of sensors. Professor Meyer's conclusion from this analysis is as follows:

> Given the Soviet lag in these areas, it must be painfully obvious to the Soviet leaders that they must begin to reallocate research and development resources now if the USSR is going to be a serious contender in the 'new type of arms race'. This in turn will require a major overhaul of the scientific and engineering sectors of the Soviet military economy, not to mention its production sectors. This is a very long lead-time endeavour, as the Soviet leaders acknowledge, and one that calls for an early decision on investment priorities.[18]

It seems clear that the Soviet leadership realizes that they are at a watershed point in their defensive arms race with the United States, and this would seem to explain much of their current obsession with the US SDI programme.

This may in part explain why Soviet spokesmen in recent months have been discussing possible Soviet countermeasures to the SDI (referred to by Professor Meyer as "off-setting responses"). Hence, General Secretary Gorbachev on 18 August said that the Soviet response to the SDI "will not be what the United States expects. But it will be an answer that will devalue the Star Wars programme ... It would be wrong to hope to intimidate the United States or to prompt the United States to needless expenditure."[19]

The most obvious Soviet countermeasure to the SDI would be to upgrade the offensive missile force to guarantee that it can penetrate, evade or overwhelm the defence. Increasing the number of warheads, spinning boosters to dissipate laser energy or shielding launchers with reflective or ablative materials are all programmes which might be started and put in place in a relatively short period of time. The Soviets could also shorten the boost phase by developing fast-burn boosters to foil the boost phase intercept capability of the SDI.

Other changes to the Soviet strategic force - such as putting greater reliance on invulnerable long-range cruise missiles - might also be considered.

The Soviets might also invest in active countermeasures against the defence if they believed that vital components of a US BMD system were vulnerable to attack. In this context some experts have suggested that the Soviets might develop space mines, anti-satellite weapons and ground-based lasers to attack space-based components such as satellites. The acquisition of weapons such as these - though requiring a significant research and development effort on the part of the Soviet Union - would also serve to increase the offensive options for the Soviets.

The ABM Treaty

Since October 1985 the interpretation of the 1972 Anti-Ballistic Missile (ABM) treaty has aroused a great deal of public controversy. At that time, the Reagan Administration changed the official US interpretation of the treaty and announced that it permitted the development and testing of strategic defence technologies, which had previously been considered to be prohibited. This reinterpretation, made public by then National Security Advisor Robert McFarlane, sparked much debate within the Administration and caused deep concern among the NATO Allies.

While maintaining that this broader interpretation of the treaty was legally correct, the Administration also stated that it would continue to abide by the earlier narrow interpretation. In a speech to the North Atlantic Assembly in San Francisco on 14 October, Secretary of State George Shultz declared that the "Strategic Defense Initiative will be conducted in accordance with the restrictive interpretation of the treaty's obligations." The position of the Administration appears therefore to be somewhat ambiguous. Nonetheless, the declared policy is that the broader interpretation is valid, even though it will not be applied at present.

This is a source of much disquiet for America's Allies. The ABM treaty reflects Western strategic doctrine of the last two decades, that the appropriate relationship between the United States and the Soviet Union is one of mutual vulnerability. As such the treaty is seen as the cornerstone of the US-Soviet relationship. In addition, the ABM treaty is linked to the SALT I limits on offensive nuclear systems. Fears have been expressed that a loosening of the ABM regime could also erode the restraints established in the SALT framework, thereby provoking an acceleration of the arms race.

Legal Arguments Behind the Reinterpretation

The treaty itself bans the deployment of ABM systems by the United States and the Soviet Union with two exceptions: one system centred on a national capital and another centred on an ICBM basing area. Limits are established on the size, composition, and modernization of the two permitted systems. In 1974, the two sides agreed to limit ABM deployments even further and signed a Protocol to that effect. Article I of the protocol limits ABM deployments to only one of the two sites mentioned above. The United States chose to centre its site on ICBMs in South Dakota (the now dismantled Sentinel), the Soviet Union around Moscow (still operational).

In article II, the treaty defines an ABM system as one intended to counter strategic ballistic missiles and defines current ABM components as interceptor missiles, their launchers and their radars. Article V prohibits the development, testing and deployment of sea-based, air-based, space-based, or land-mobile ABM systems or components and bans the development, testing, and deployment of ABM launchers for multiple launch or rapid reloading.

In its review of the treaty, the State Department concluded that these articles applied only to defensive systems operating on technologies used in the 1970s, but not to work on advanced or "futuristic" technologies that were unknown at the time. To support this argument US officials point to agreed statement D which was initialled by both sides at the time the treaty was signed.

Agreed statement D states that if ABM systems based on other physical principles, including components capable of substituting for ABM interceptors, launchers and radars were created in the future, specific limitations on such systems and their components would be subject to discussion within the Special Consultative Commission (SCC) established by the treaty to deal with compliance questions and possible ambiguities. It is believed that the State Department Review concluded that agreed statement D permits both the United States and the Soviet Union to conduct research development and testing on systems based on "other physical principles" essentially without limitation. Of course, much of the SDI programme would fall into this category. In addition, the Administration argues that article II of the treaty, which defines an ABM system and its components, limits the ban to those elements described in the article. In other words, it believes the components enumerated in the article are not simply examples of technologies covered by the ABM treaty but describe only those technologies whose development and testing is banned by the treaty.

Finally, the Administration bases its case on the negotiating record of the treaty. This record is secret, but Judge Abraham Sofaer, the State Department legal advisor and one of the chief architects of the new interpretation, has argued that the record shows no agreement between the United States and the Soviet Union on limitations of advanced technologies. He has also stated that the record indicates that the United States offered wording that would have included advanced systems in the prohibitions contained in article V but that the Soviet Union rejected this proposal.

The Debate Over the New Interpretation

Members of the SALT I negotiating team have contested the new interpretation. John Rhinelander, who had been the legal advisor to the SALT I delegation, testified that the Reagan Administration's approach was

> "absurd as a matter of policy, intent and rationale. If the Administration sticks with it as the best legal interpretation of the treaty, then the Administration has effectively repudiated the ABM treaty as a legal instrument. If the truncated treaty remains in effect, both the United States and the Soviet Union can develop and test, without quantitative or geographic limits, any sea-based or mobile land-based ABM system or component provided they utilize exotic technology such as lasers."

The chief negotiator of the treaty, Gerard Smith, echoed these statements when he spoke of the ABM treaty being rendered a "dead letter" in the current reinterpretation.

The public record also confirms that the Nixon Administration, which negotiated the treaty, intended that futuristic defences would be limited under the provisions. The treaty was defended in Senate ratification hearings by Nixon Administration officials largely on these grounds. Indeed, the record shows that former Senator James Buckley of New York finally voted <u>against</u> the ABM treaty (he was one of only two) on the floor of the Senate because the scope of article V prohibited the possibility for futuristic defences.

Others argue that the situation of the time was not so clear-cut. In a letter accompanying the treaty's submission to the Senate, then Secretary of State William Rogers stated: "a potential problem dealt with by the treaty is that which would be created if an ABM systems were developed in the future which did not consist of interceptor missiles, launchers and radars. The treaty would not permit the deployment of such a system." In his letter Secretary Rogers did not, however, refer to testing and development of such a system. In addition in testimony during the ratification hearings Gerard Smith stated:

> "...one of the Agreed Understandings says that if ABM technology is created based on different physical principles, ABM systems or components based on them can only be deployed if the Treaty is amended. Work in that direction, development work, research, is not prohibited, but deployment of systems using those new

principles in substitution for radars, launchers, or interceptors, would not be permitted unless both parties agree by amending the treaty."

This statement would also appear to support those who argue that only deployment of systems using new technologies would be prohibited, and that testing and development could take place.

Broader Policy Considerations

Despite the conflicting evidence, what does emerge from the controversy is the fact that the reinterpretation of the treaty is based as much on political considerations as legal ones. Those who believe that the SDI is crucial to the security of the United States and its Allies would argue that the restrictive interpretation places an unacceptable limitations on the programme. Others who place a higher value on arms control believe that whatever the legal justification of the new interpretation, its unilateral application by the United States would severely undermine the ABM treaty, thereby sending shock waves through the existing arms control regime which could irreparably damage the current negotiations in Geneva.

The Soviet Compliance Record

The United States has expressed concern that the Soviet Union has been violating the ABM treaty. The best known example of these allegations is the Krasnoyask radar. Article VI of the treaty prohibits the deployment of early warning radars except on the periphery of national territory and oriented outward. The Krasnoyarsk radar is centrally located and covers almost 4000 kilometres of Soviet territory.

The Soviet Union maintains that the radar is for space tracking purposes only and is therefore permitted by the treaty. However, the radar is not angled upwards as on current space tracking radars, and its location would prohibit it from tracking the vast majority of the satellites currently in orbit. Alliance Governments have therefore generally supported the US accusation that the radar constitutes a violation of the treaty. There is less agreement, however, on the radar's military utility.

Other accusations about Soviet non-compliance are less clear. Commmon Understanding C stated the American view that article V of the treaty which prohibits work on mobile land-based ABM systems and components also rules out the deployment of mobile ABM launchers and radars which were not permanently fixed types. The Soviet delegation said there was common understanding on this matter. The United States believes that the Soviets have violated this understanding because two of its radars used in the ABMX-3 system around Moscow are mobile. The Flat-Twin radar can be erected on a prepared site in six to eight weeks and the Pawn Shop radar is housed in a van-sized container without wheels. The ambiguity here is obvious, and depends on whether or not mobile is interpreted as meaning movable in six to eight weeks, although the potential mobility of the Pawn Shop radar is harder to dispute.

The third area of violation concerns the testing of an SA-X-12 air defence missile against a ballistic missile. This would appear to be a violation of article VI of the treaty, which prohibits the modification of "non-ABM systems to perform ABM functions". However, there is a certain amount of ambiguity here, since there is no agreement of the precise meaning of the treaty provisions which refer to "tested in an ABM mode". Although the United States maintains that this includes testing an interceptor against a vehicle which has a flight trajectory with the characteristics of a strategic ballistic flight trajectory (US Delegation Unilateral Statement B), there is no agreement on this point between the two sides.

Conclusion

The preceding discussion has highlighted the growing interpretative difficulties which are arising from the ABM treaty. Much of these problems arise from the fact that both the United States and the Soviet Union are undertaking research on defensive programmes which are directly relevant to the treaty. As their respective research progresses, there is every reason to believe new controversies will emerge.

In addition, the Soviet tendency to exploit the so-called "grey areas" of arms control agreements has aroused suspicions about the Soviet commitment to arms control. This is particularly the case of the ABM treaty, which is ambiguous in many of its provisions.

Yet this cannot justify scrapping the ABM treaty altogether. The treaty itself was designed to stand the test of time with established mechanisms for the introduction of modifications permitting it to remain relevant to future developments. First and foremost the treaty established the Special Consultative Commission as a forum specifically created to discuss ambiguities arising from the treaty. This should be used to tighten definitions and to determine which activities are permitted by the treaty. It is the view of the Rapporteur that the potential of the SCC has not yet been fully exploited. Accusations about compliance have been made publicly in other forums before any attempts have been made to solve them within the SCC. This approach runs counter to the spirit of the treaty.

Secondly, article XIV of the treaty establishes that each side may propose amendments to the treaty and that it will be reviewed at five-year intervals. The treaty is next up for re-examination in 1987. This provides one opportunity to amend it under the provisions of article XIV in order to take into account future technologies and strategic options.

Finally, signs are emerging that continued compliance with the ABM treaty may form part of a broader agreement on strategic arms reductions. Such an approach would be consistent with the spirit of the ABM treaty itself, which forms an integral part of the SALT arms limitation process. In addition, this type of agreement certainly would not preclude, and could even perhaps facilitate President Reagan's desire to see a transition from offensive strategies to defensive ones, should SDI technologies prove feasible.

NATO'S NUCLEAR STRATEGY - PROBLEMS AND PROSPECTS

Current NATO Strategy

Background

When American nuclear weapons were first deployed in Europe in 1954, the United States enjoyed unquestioned strategic superiority over the Soviet Union. It was considered at this point that the doctrine of massive retaliation was a credible deterrence posture for NATO and would remain so until the point at which the Soviet Union could create the perception of a significant nuclear threat to the United States as well as to Europe. Only in this eventuality could the credibility of the American deterrent be realistically called into question. This point was duly reached around the time President Kennedy took office in the early part of the 1960s.

Because US nuclear strength was, from an early point, integral to NATO's posture, any apparent alteration in American nuclear strategy or system deployments touched directly upon West European sensitivities. This has been an enduring feature of Alliance politics for almost 40 years. A pointed example came in the aftermath of the 1962 Cuban Missile Crisis when the withdrawal of Soviet-targeted US missiles from Italy and Turkey was, despite US denials, generally understood by Europeans to be a trade-off for Soviet withdrawals from Cuba. It was in part to provide a clear assurance that the US nuclear commitment remained firm that the US subsequently undertook to maintain a certain number of Polaris submarines in the Mediterranean, and later supplemented this with the allocation of a substantial number of Poseidon SLBMs to SACEUR, for targeting purposes. Placing such systems under SACEUR helped to sharpen the perception between "tactical" and "strategic" systems.

It was also in the early 1960s that the United States, responding to the growing Soviet capability for nuclear retaliation, became concerned with the escalation implications of a doctrine which relied too heavily upon nuclear weapons. In an effort to raise the nuclear threshold, the United States, prompted by Defense Secretary Robert McNamara, began to place greater emphasis on conventional defence. There followed an intensive and protracted debate in NATO between 1961 and 1967 on the nature and purpose of flexible response. This culminated in the revised NATO doctrine (MC-14/3), which embodied the concept of a continuing and balanced deterrent. At the end of this period, however, though flexible response appeared to denote a somewhat more judicious use of tactical nuclear weapons than hitherto, it scarcely placed an increased reliance on conventional forces. Under the revised doctrine, theatre nuclear forces (TNF) became the central leg of a "NATO triad" tying together NATO's conventional and strategic forces, while leaving purposely vague the circumstances under which nuclear weapons, either theatre or strategic, would be employed.

In Europe the actual use of theatre nuclear forces in anything resembling classic military combat has naturally remained a horrifying notion. Thus while constantly opposed to any lessening of US nuclear deployments in Europe, West Europeans have remained concerned that NATO's INF posture should not have the perverse effect of "decoupling" America from Western Europe by permitting the possibility of a devastating war on European soil without danger to, and hence strategic commitment by, the United States. To overcome this "decoupling" paradox American and European officials have generally sought to emphasize the deterrent aspects of INF deployments, stressing the escalatory linkage to US strategic forces rather than the war-fighting capabilities of specific INF systems.

Nonetheless - and almost inevitably - European confidence in the "coupling" of America and Western Europe for defensive purposes has fluctuated over time under the influence of such factors as the internal European political climate, the state of East-West relations, recurrent debates on arms control and NATO strategy, the presence and visibility of US INF in Europe and perceived trends in American and Soviet military strength.

Long-Range Intermediate Nuclear Force (LRINF) Modernization

The adoption of the strategy of flexible response in 1967 put to rest, temporarily, many of the doubts which had dominated Alliance discussion in the 1960s. However, in the mid-1970s public attention was drawn again to the adequacy of the Alliance nuclear strategy as a result of the coincidence of developments. The outcome of this was the 12 December 1979 NATO ministerial decision to modernize NATO LRINF through the deployment of 572 single warhead nuclear missiles (464 ground-launched cruise missiles and 108 Pershing II missiles) in five European countries.

Alliance officials presented the rationale for LRINF modernization as resulting from the coincidence of three separate but related developments: strategic parity; the obsolescence of existing NATO LRINF; and Soviet modernization of this category of nuclear weapons. It was argued that the development of strategic parity, as codified by the SALT process, had raised doubts about the credibility of the American strategic nuclear guarantee to Europe. These had been further diminished by the declining effectiveness of existing NATO long-range nuclear assets in Europe, notably American F-111 and British Vulcan aircraft, whose penetration capability had been put in doubt by both their own obsolescence and Soviet improvements in air defences. It was further maintained that since the 400 Poseidon warheads allocated to NATO were part of America's strategic forces, they were not sufficiently identified with, or linked to, the defence of Europe. Neither did their characteristics facilitate their use for the selective response that NATO strategy required. These deficiencies in NATO's forces contrasted with the very substantial improvements in Soviet LRINF capabilities targeted on Europe, notably the introduction of the SS-20 and the Backfire bomber.

As a result of these related developments, Alliance officials maintained that NATO's strategy of flexible response had become deficient. A gap existed in the area of long-range theatre nuclear systems which the Soviet Union might exploit. During a crisis, Soviet LRINF could provide the Soviet Union with the means to escalate to a level at which NATO had no credible response, because both NATO's existing LRINF and the threat of American strategic retaliation lacked credibility.

Breakdown in Consensus

The events of the last seven years have proved the determination of NATO Governments to carry through the 1979 December decision by modernizing intermediate-range nuclear forces in Europe while simultaneously seeking to negotiate with the Soviet Union to reduce the numbers of such systems or obviate them altogether.

Despite vocal and well organized internal opposition in Western Europe, NATO Governments continue to believe that the deployments of US cruise and Pershing II missiles guarantee improved deterrence, "couple" the United States to the defence of Western Europe and open a route to serious arms control negotiations.

The capability of the Alliance to take a difficult and controversial multilateral nuclear decision in the face of sustained and powerful Soviet opposition was a major concern among NATO planners in the late 1970s, especially after the 1978 "neutron bomb" episode. The successful implementation of the 1979 decision is, in the opinion of many, testimony to the continuing strength and cohesion of the Alliance in the most testing circumstances.

This success has not been achieved without cost. The controversy surrounding the cruise and pershing II deployments has greatly contributed to a destruction of the traditional post-war consensus on defence issues in at least two key countries: the United Kingdom and the Federal Republic of Germany. The main opposition party in each country is now firmly committed against both the missiles and several key tenets of NATO's nuclear strategy.. The election of either to Government could, therefore, threaten the whole thrust of NATO's current strategy.

The SDI and the Dangers of Decoupling

Some argue that flexible response is also under threat from a different source and point to the perennial European fear of decoupling which has been rekindled as a result of the debate about strategic defences. It is on this issue that some analysts see a potential conflict of nuclear philosophies across the Atlantic which would undermine flexible response.

Despite American assurances that the SDI programme is designed to offer protection for both the United States and its Allies, many remain sceptical. There is an underlying fear that should the two superpowers successfully achieve strategic defence, Europe would be much more exposed to a Soviet conventional attack.

There has been a great deal of discussion over the last year about the early application of SDI technology to the European theatre, and even to the development of a separate European Defence Initiative incorporating ATBMs (anti-tactical ballistic missiles). However, even assuming that defences against medium- and short-range Soviet missiles could be successfully developed (and SDIO officials have been expressing increasing confidence on this issue), this may have important implications for a NATO strategy relying for its credibility on the flexible and graduated use of nuclear weapons.

Current Status of INF and SS-20 Deployments

According to NATO's Special Consultative Group (SCG) the Soviet Union has maintained its deployment of SS-20 launchers at 441 (1,323 warheads). The Soviets continue to insist that only 243 SS-20s are targeted at Europe and that some of these missiles have been taken off stand-by alert. They remain vague about the precise number of missiles deployed in Asia. For NATO, the alert status of the SS-20s is irrelevant. Given the mobile characteristic of the SS-20s, so long as there is no evidence of destruction or dismantlement of launchers or missiles, the Allies assume that there are 441 missiles deployed and available in time of crisis.

The SCG has noted that the Soviet Union is modernizing its INF arsenal. These developments include testing of an improved, more accurate version of the SS-20 and two new types of sea-launched cruise missile (SLCM) capable of operating in a ground-launched mode. It should be said that the United States also has a modernization plan which entails increasing its own arsenal of SLCMs.

In the absence of any INF agreement the deployment of cruise and Pershing II missiles is proceeding on schedule. As of 31 December 1985, NATO had announced that it had deployed 108 Pershing II missiles, the full complement in the Federal Republic of Germany, and 128 cruise missiles in Belgium, the United Kingdom, Italy and the Federal Republic. More than one half of the full 572 Cruise and Pershing missiles called for in NATO's 1979 dual-track decision are therefore in place.

In November 1985 the Dutch Government decided it would accept deployment of 48 cruise missiles as provided for by the 1979 NATO decision and signed an agreement with the United States authorizing this deployment. The agreement was ratified by the Dutch Parliament in February 1986. At the same time the Dutch Government announced its intention of discontinuing certain nuclear tasks.

Continuing Implementation of the 1983 Montebello Decision

At the Nuclear Planning Group (NPG), meeting in Montebello, Canada, in October 1983, NATO made a decision to reduce its stockpile of battlefield nuclear weapons by 1400. This reduction was over and above the withdrawal of 1,000 LRINF agreed upon in the context of the 1979 dual-track decision. In March 1986 the NPG received an update on the implementation of the Montebello decision. Under a detailed plan drawn up by General Rogers, SACEUR, NATO will have withdrawn 1400 nuclear weapons by 1988, bringing the number of nuclear bombs, missiles and shells stationed in Europe to below 4,800. This will mean that NATO will have fewer nuclear weapons in Europe than at any time over the last 20 years.

In addition, regarding the numbers of these nuclear systems, the Montebello decision also called upon SACEUR to draw up a modernization plan for NATO's battlefield nuclear weapons. The second phase of General Rogers' plan, involving improvements in such nuclear weapons stationed in Central Europe, was shelved by the NPG on grounds of cost and political sensitivity, since it called for the introduction of new systems into the European theatre. This was of particular concern for the Federal Republic and Great Britain.

In August NATO officials confirmed that a new 8" nuclear artillery shell had been deployed in the Federal Republic. The new W79 warhead has a range of 18 miles and replaces the W33. Sources indicated other countries in possession of the W33 would also receive the W79.

At the end of August General Rogers in an interview in Amsterdam suggested that to decrease the vulnerability of its nuclear weapons stockpile NATO should re-distribute more nuclear warheads to its southern flank and to the Netherlands. This suggestion does not appear to have been discussed in the NPG.

Revision of Formal Guidelines for Nuclear Escalation

In late September it was reported that NATO nuclear planners were working on the first major revision of the Alliance's formal political guidelines on nuclear escalation since 1969. The new guidelines, which are far more comprehensive than the provisional political guidelines agreed in 1969, are expected to be adopted at the next NPG meeting on 20-21 October in Gleneagles, Scotland.

Some press reports suggest that the new guidelines contain a more sophisticated view of the relationship between political and military objectives of nuclear escalation. In a departure from the 1969 provisional guidelines the new agreement will cover nuclear weapons at sea as well as the follow-on use of nuclear weapons. The current guidelines on consultation within NATO before the release of nuclear weapons are not affected, and NATO officials have been at pains to point out that the new draft guidelines do not indicate a basic shift in strategy.

The Role of the UK and French Nuclear Forces

The well publicized modernization of British and French nuclear forces brought these independent national deterrents out from beneath the shadow of the "superpower" arsenals and focussed renewed attention on their impact on Alliance and East-West relations.

Many of the questions raised in the present discussion are not particularly novel but relate, in fact, to recurring themes and unresolved debates given new prominence by the imminent growth of British and French nuclear forces. Debate has long centred on the degree of their independence, their contribution to Alliance security and the possibility that they could form the basis of a common European deterrent.

Other questions have become salient much more recently. For example, with parliamentary elections due to occur shortly in the United Kingdom and the national consensus on nuclear weapons in tatters, the future of the Trident modernization program and of NATO nuclear weapons in Britain is uncertain. In addition, the increased capabilities of the modernized British and French nuclear deterrents may bring changes in the way these forces might be used and the tasks they might be required to perform. With these and other related issues pending, it is an especially appropriate time to review the role of British and French nuclear forces.

Strategies: The Credibility of Deterrence

Although the development of British and French nuclear forces differs substantially their respective strategies stem from the same fundamental assumptions and necessities. Both are comparatively small forces with limited targeting flexibility compared to Soviet and US arsenals. As a result, they have both had to meet the requirements of deterrence with considerably more modest strategic objectives. The resulting strategies are forms of proportional deterrent which rely on sufficiency criteria well below that of the United States'.

The "sufficiency" of any deterrent relies upon a number of interactive and, in some cases, highly subjective judgments, of which three are deemed essential. These judgments can vary considerably from one country to the next and may alter according to changing circumstances. The first of these criteria is an assesment of the value a potential aggressor places on attacking. The second is that it must represent a sufficient counter-threat to a potential aggressor to convince him not to attack.

The third criterion is an estimation of the probability that the threatened response will occur. In other words, the defending state must appear to have the means and the will to carry out its deterrent threat, and the potential aggressor must believe that the defender has the will as well as the means.

Both Britain and France recognized very early on that they would not be able to field forces even approximating the size of those opposing them in the Soviet Union. However, both felt that equality was not a prerequisite of adequate deterrence. It was not necessary to be able to obliterate the Soviet Union, but rather to make the costs of attacking outweigh the potential gains. Obviously, neither country felt, in itself, that it posed sufficient threat or constituted sufficient prize to the Soviets to warrant a deterrent force the size of the United States'. Accordingly, both countries adopted national deterrent strategies which threatened to inflict severe but somewhat less than mortal damage on the Soviet Union if it should attack, and both assembled forces which they believed capable of accomplishing that mission. The fundamental rationale behind these strategies remains valid today for both Britain and France, although the specific requirements for meeting them have changed somewhat over time.

Early British and French strategies were exclusively countervalue. British V-bombers were aimed at destroying urban-industrial targets, while the first French strategies were specifically "anti-cities". During that time (the late 1950s to mid-60s for Britain and the late 1960s to mid-70s for France), it is likely that sufficiency was determined according to probable civilian casualties, but there is evidence to indicate that both nations' strategies have evolved since then towards more demanding strategic objectives.

In 1962, Prime Minister Macmillan and President Kennedy signed the Nassau Agreement, which committed the United Kingdom to an increased role in NATO and the purchase of Polaris SLBMs from the United States. The former meant that British nuclear forces would thenceforth be consigned to SACEUR, they would receive their targets from the US Joint Strategic Target Planning Staff, and their operational plans would be formulated at SHAPE. The latter meant that as the V-bombers approached obsolescence in the late '60s Britain would have to make do with far fewer warheads.

In essence, Britain's nuclear weapons had taken on a dual role. While they were technically assigned to SACEUR, Whitehall continued to produce operational plans for their use as a national deterrent. In this latter role, given the sharp reduction in target coverage, British officials were forced to choose between threatening a fairly small number of Soviet cities with possible destruction or concentrating their efforts on ensuring the destruction of one very important city. The target objective which appears to have emerged is now commonly known as the "Moscow criterion".

Had the objective been to maximize civilian casualties, striking one city, even one the size of Moscow, would clearly not have been the best way of achieving it. However, there are other important reasons for threatening Moscow; most prominent among them, that it is the seat of Soviet government. The option of targeting population per se was not foreclosed by adoption of the Moscow criterion, but there are several reasons for believing that it has been voluntarily abandoned.

By the late 1970s, British nuclear weapons began to reflect the change. In 1982, the United Kingdom began refitting Polaris SLBMs with a new warhead system called Chevaline. The Chevaline program was specifically designed as a countermeasure to improvements being made in the Soviet ABM system deployed around Moscow. The result was a reduction in warhead numbers and size on each missile from three 200 kiloton warheads to two 40 kiloton warheads, thus, if anything, reducing the British force's ability to cause civilian casualties while enhancing its ability to strike Moscow.

The most recent indication of a shift in British objectives can be found in the Ministry of Defence "Statement of the Defence Estimates 1985," which contends that a British national deterrent must "be capable of posing a credible threat to key aspects of Soviet state power." With the increased capabilities of Trident in prospect, this phrase has been interpreted liberally to indicate even more demanding targeting options. Whether or not such options are being contemplated, this statement suggests that the British are concentrating on the Moscow criterion rather than on civilian targets.

French strategy has undergone a similar evolution. Early French strategy was very much a prisoner of technical limitations. In 1966, when the force de frappe became operational, it consisted of only 42 Mirage IV bombers, which required aerial refueling in order to reach the Soviet Union. And, unlike the British, the French military did not have the benefit of targeting information from US satellite reconnaissance. Without that information, they were restricted to targets whose location was already established with certainty, namely cities.

By the 1970s, improved French intelligence and a significantly more capable force made the change to a more demanding targeting strategy conceivable. Concurrent with these growing capabilities was an increasing unease about the credibility of French targeting doctrine. Specifically, several officials of Giscard d'Estaing's Administration questioned the threat to kill millions of Soviet civilians in the face of a wide range of options open to the USSR. In the words of d'Estaing's Prime Minister, Jacques Chirac, "where deterrence is concerned, to promise without convincing is to sign one's own death warrant."[20] No.Obviously, the French could not afford to match Soviet targeting flexibility. Calls for such flexibility were apparently rejected in 1980. However, they could reduce the all-or-nothing character of the French deterrent by threatening more discriminating use; and this they appear to have done.

In 1980, official French statements moved away from the notion of targeting the Soviet population and in the direction of political and industrial targets. The term used to describe this new objective was oeuvres vives, or "vital works." The change was not seen as a shift away from fundamental French strategy but, rather, a shift in the method of calculating proportionality. It was a simple matter of replacing the old quantitative measure with a qualitative, albeit technically more demanding, one.

These shifts in strategic objectives demonstrate the difficulty a "medium" nuclear power has in maintaining the credibility of its deterrent.

To maintain technical credibility, Britain and France must ensure the survivability of their delivery systems and their ability to strike the targets at which they are aiming. An evolving Soviet preemptive threat and increasingly capable strategic defences including ABM, anti-submarine warfare (ASW), air defence and civil defence have made this a continuing challenge. Their success at meeting this challenge is debatable.

Both Britain and France have reduced their airborne strategic nuclear forces (to the point of virtual elimination in the case of the United Kingdom) in favour of survivable submarine-based systems. If modernization proceeds as planned, a greater percentage of these forces will be on station at any given time, thus reducing the number of SSBNs in port, where they are extremely vulnerable to attack. They will also be less vulnerable to Soviet ASW due to the increased area of operations made possible by the longer-range SLBMs they will be carrying (the French M-4 and Britain's Trident II).

Assuming the available missiles were ever launched, they would still have to contend with the uncertainty caused by Soviet ballistic missile defence. The Moscow ABM system is of obvious concern to the United Kingdom in view of its apparent preference for a Moscow-specific strategy. To date, the ABM Treaty has helped to manage this problem by defining and limiting the extent of Soviet defences. Nevertheless, both countries' modernization programs call for substantial increases in the number of deliverable warheads carried on their SLBMs. Both Governments believe that this additional capability will allow them to cope with near-term Soviet improvements to the Moscow system. However, with the Treaty's future increasingly in doubt and rumours of a possible rapidly-deployable nationwide Soviet defence under development, there is concern in both Britain and France that even planned improvements will not be sufficient.

As mentioned above, technical credibility is only one aspect of the overall credibility of a nuclear deterrent. Establishing in the mind of a potential aggressor that one also has the will to carry out the threat of retaliation is arguably even more important than the actual ability to do so.

One important aspect of this equation is the value the defender places on the object of aggression. For example, a direct attack on national territory would be considered the most credible reason for threatening the use of nuclear weapons. After that might follow contiguous territories, allies, important resources and, finally, peripheral interest. Clearly, this is all highly theoretical, especially with regard to a quantity as unknown as nuclear weapons. It has, nevertheless, served as a basis for British and French nuclear deterrents and an equal basis for debate.

French and British Nuclear Forces as Independent Deterrents

The relative independence of British and French national deterrents is very much a function of the historical development of their respective nuclear forces. Both nations invested a considerable amount of national pride in their early achievements of their nuclear capabilities. But the differential treatment they received by the United States in the immediate post-war period had a significant influence on the subsequent development of their respective strategies and co-operative arrangements.

Conventional wisdom following World War II held that failure to develop a nuclear weapons capability was tantamount to inviting military obsolescence. France and Great Britain had seen their prestige as world powers, their colonial empires, and their economic solvency severely weakened. France in particular had suffered a prolonged and demoralizing occupation for the greater part of the war. When it was over, nuclear research for both peaceful and military uses held perhaps the greatest promise for recouping at least some of their perceived losses.

However, passage of the McMahon Act by the United States in 1946 prohibited the sharing of atomic secrets with <u>any</u> foreign government and ensured that progress by the British and, in particular, the French would be slow at best. Britain, with the benefit of its wartime participation in the Manhattan Project, managed its first atomic explosion in 1952. French nuclear research, on the other hand, had remained in a state of suspended animation during the war, and it was not until 1960 that they were able to develop their first nuclear device. These were but the first indications of differences between the two countries' nuclear programs which would widen with time.

As the Cold War began to heat up, US co-operation with Britain on nuclear issues underwent a warming trend. The eventual existence of a British nuclear force was taken more or less for granted. The French, on the other hand, were actively discouraged by the United States from seeking atomic weapons. In 1955, for example, France and the United Kingdom were in the midst of negotiations which would have sent certain British "technological know-how" on isotope separation to France when the United States intervened to prevent the transfer. In 1958 the McMahon Act was amended to allow assistance to countries which had made "substantial progress" toward developing a nuclear weapons capability. In 1962 the French, having already demonstrated a nuclear capability two years earlier, requested the right to purchase some related technologies from the United States under the revised McMahon guidelines. Even with support of a number of knowledgeable officials inside the US Government, the request was refused.

In sum, both countries had considerable prestige wrapped up in their nuclear weapons programs. They saw them as the "great equalizers", the vehicles responsible for their return to great power status. At the same time, each moved in a very different direction vis-à-vis the United States.

Britain accepted that the United States would play the dominant role in Western defence planning after World War II, and used the influence it had gained by joining the nuclear club to ensure that British interests were represented in that planning. The "special relationship" also brought with it a number of other significant advantages. For instance, Britain continues to test its nuclear warheads under US auspices in Nevada. The United Kingdom received valuable targeting data as a result of its direct co-operation with the US JSTPS. In addition, the British have purchased US SLBMs and benefited from US technological co-operation to help build quieter, more effective nuclear submarines.

Still, the "special relationship" has been a mixed blessing. The Nassau Agreement increased - albeit marginally - the value of a Soviet strike on the United Kingdom while it diminished the British ability to deter attack. The Agreement came simultaneously with a US announcement that the Skybolt program had been cancelled. Skybolt was meant to extend the useful life of Britain's V-bombers by giving them a standoff capability, and its cancellation hastened their demise. The result was a British deterrent force dependent on a capability to strike sixteen or, at most, thirty-two targets instead of the 180 which the V-bomber force represented. Although consignment to SACEUR of British weapons meant only nominally more attention as a Soviet target (the United Kingdom had long been a launching platform for NATO/US nuclear and conventional weapons), the association of the independent deterrent with NATO and, more precisely, the United States may have contributed to the erosion of the United Kingdom's consensus on the value of nuclear weapons.

The independence of the British nuclear deterrent is therefore open to doubt. To the extent that independence means having ownership of weapons, having one's own strategy, and having the ability to use those weapons if desired, Britain's is an independent force. But to the extent that Britain has depended on the United States for new technology, for updates of targeting data, and general support, it is less than independent. This lack of independence has an impact on public opinion which may be crucial. On the other hand, the British public may have little appreciation of Britain's nuclear role within NATO.

In contrast, the French nuclear program evolved in the opposite direction. Nuclear weapons became the symbol of French independence, which in turn became the symbol of resurgent national pride in the post-war years. As General de Gaulle said in 1959 on seeing a model of the first French atomic bomb: "...you see, the most important thing about what we have done is that we have accomplished it all by ourselves, I say entirely on our own."[21] The French requirement for independence of action with respect to their military forces reached a peak in 1966 when they withdrew from NATO's integrated military command. Since that time, consensus on French nuclear policy has remained consistently strong (the strongest in the Atlantic Alliance), due in no small part to the perceived independence it represents.

The question has already been raised whether that independence - real or perceived - will continue. Rumours abound that secret agreements exist between France and the NATO Allies to co-ordinate efforts in the event of war. There is little doubt that a co-ordinated strategy would be most beneficial to the Alliance, but all indications point to the political impossibility of such a move being made publicly by France. One French general put the situation rather succinctly: "co-operation only involves conventional forces, and therefore excludes all nuclear force employment planning."

While this statement makes current French policy on nuclear co-operation quite clear, it does provide an interesting opening. The tacit acceptance of overt conventional co-operation would have been anathema to French declared policy not long ago. It is possible to construe from this admission the possibility of nuclear co-operation sometime in the future. If nothing else, it appears that French officials have discussed their nuclear plans with NATO. This is a long way from integration, but it may make for fewer surprises in a crisis.

Even so, the French deterrent force appears, for the moment, to be quite independent. It still produces its own systems, target lists, and maintains ultimate control over the political and military use of its nuclear forces. How long this will remain the case is an open question. However, as long as public support for the force hinges on at least the appearance of independence, it is hard to see how the situation is likely to change in the near future.

The Contribution of the Independent Nuclear Forces to NATO

At Ottawa on 19 June 1974 the North Atlantic Council declared that independent nuclear forces were "capable of playing a deterrent role of their own, contributing to the overall strengthening of the deterrence of the Alliance...". This was the first time official recognition had been given by NATO to the contribution of British and French independent nuclear forces. However, the Ottawa declaration did not settle the issue in either official or unofficial circles.

Arguments offered in support of a positive contribution are several. Probably the most oft quoted is the argument that multiple decision making centers complicate any Soviet decision to launch an attack against the Atlantic Alliance, in much the same way a mine field induces caution in anyone who attempts to cross it. The British Statement of the Defence Estimates 1985 said, "[n]uclear weapons in the possession of the United Kingdom greatly complicate the calculations of the Soviet leadership in assessing whether they could undertake [aggression against Western European democracies] without risking a nuclear conflict." The assumption is that more than one decision making center increases the probability that a Soviet decision will be taken in the negative.

The perceived necessity to "complicate" Soviet calculations stems from a loss of credibility in the US guarantee to use nuclear weapons on behalf of Europe. The French have always been very straightforward about their doubts. The British, on the other hand, have given at least the semblance of confidence as indicated in the 1985 Defence White Paper. "The key factor is the Soviet perception of the United States willingness to hazard its own territory and citizens for the sake of its Allies. In certain circumstances, the Soviet leadership might doubt this commitment and miscalculate the consequences of aggressive action...". (emphasis added)

Unlike the United States, France and Britain have a direct stake in European security by virtue of their location, if nothing else. This vested interest theoretically makes British or French use of nuclear weapons on behalf of themselves and other European states more credible to the Soviets. This credibility, in turn, enhances deterrence.

It might be argued that, even granting the validity of the multiple decision making centers, the independent forces are too small to make a difference. However, according to a second argument, the independent forces can affect Soviet actions by acting as a sort of reducing agent. By launching initial attacks against the USSR they might alter the strategic balance between the superpowers. The Soviet Union could thus face a situation in which it would find the destruction of a "non-negligible part of its cities, of its industrial and administrative means, and of its communications, when the other great nuclear powers would retain their economic and military potential intact".[22]

Independent nuclear forces might also add to NATO's ability to conduct conventional operations in the course of a European conflict. Britain and, to a much lesser extent, France would probably serve as essential staging areas for major conventional troop movements. In World War II, Britain, "the unsinkable air craft carrier", served not only as the launching point for strategic bombing and the Normandy invasion, but also as a central command center for European operations. If British nuclear weapons could help to "sanctuarize" Britain for this purpose it would be a significant contribution to Alliance conventional staying power.

It is worth noting that this role requires an extremely robust deterrent as, during the course of an ongoing war, the value of the sanctuary would be likely to appreciate well beyond pre-war levels. Thus, pre-war deterrents which were on a minimum scale before conflict began might be severely taxed by altered Soviet assessments of the necessity to strike.

Several arguments contend that the contribution of independent deterrent forces is a negative one. The original argument offered by Robert McNamara in the 1960s raised two issues. He felt that the money being spent on independent forces would be more profitably spent on bolstering conventional capabilities. Until recently, this argument was belied by the low cost of nuclear forces compared to conventional ones. However, with military budgets tightening in nearly every corner of NATO, there has been a revival of this argument.

One of the most salient criticisms being leveled at both French and British modernization programs is the strain they are placing on conventional military budgets. Both opposition parties in Britain have used increasing cost estimates of the Trident program and the possible opportunity costs in conventional capabilities to attack the Conservative Administration's support for the program.

Secretary McNamara's second point was that a "minefield" in Europe may not necessarily be conducive to greater security. In his view, the proliferation of decision making centers was a serious breakdown in NATO command and control structures. Carried to its logical extreme, the multiple decision making centers argument suggested that all West European states should "go nuclear". This, of course, has never been NATO policy. Officials in the United States still echo this complaint arguing that the nuclear thresholds of independent nuclear states may be significantly lower than that of the United States. They fear that early resort to nuclear weapons would undercut NATO conventional operations and drag the United States into an unwanted and perhaps unnecessary nuclear exchange. These concerns are aggravated by elements of independent strategies. A premature attack on the Moscow criterion could undermine attempts to control the escalation of a conflict.

Prospects for a European Deterrent

It is widely accepted within the Alliance that nuclear weapons are necessary to deter the Soviet Union from launching an attack against Western Europe. Deployment of NATO nuclear weapons in Europe underlines the belief that this goal cannot be accomplished by nuclear weapons based in the United States alone. However, there is now revived interest in the concepts of a specifically nuclear deterrent as a supplement to US forces and as an insurance against any failure of the US nuclear guarantee.

The Federal Republic of Germany and France have discussed nuclear co-operation in one form or another since the 1950s. Yet, discussions have never produced anything more than agreement to consult - when possible - on the use of French tactical nuclear weapons on German territory. Reactions to the prospect of a significant

German nuclear capability would be highly unpredictable in Europe and especially in the Soviet Union. Many in the Federal Republic itself are likely to show resistance. In 1963, Konrad Adenauer rejected the idea of a German nuclear role in the context of the Franco-German friendship treaty on the basis that it would be inconsistent with NATO policy. Strong support for this position remains today. These feelings may eventually change, but they show no sign of doing so in the near future.

Anglo-French co-operation based on existing nuclear forces but respecting the political structure of both nations offers better prospects. Nonetheless, here too, historical differences must first be overcome.

Britain and France would also face the problem of maintaining public support for nuclear weapons which were to be used to defend more than purely national interests. This problem is especially acute in France where the public view of nuclear weapons is so closely linked to the issue of French independence. However, there are some signs that French attitudes are changing and that there is a willingness to explore the possibilities of practical collaboration with the British on the operation of existing nuclear forces. An Anglo-French arrangement is liable to put at risk the United Kingdom's longstanding nuclear co-operation with the United States. The United States has always been reluctant to share weapons technology with France, and it seems unlikely they would countenance doing so through the British.

Britain and France would both face the problem of maintaining national consensus on nuclear weapons while trying to extend their guarantee beyond national borders. This problem is especially acute in France, where the public image of their national deterrent is so tightly intertwined with the question of French independence. While the vested interest of Britain and France would add credibility to the notion of a European nuclear umbrella, it might also place severe strains on the requirements of the force which supplies it. Ostensibly, British and French forces have been sized to preserve national sanctuaries. Should they decide to extend that deterrent, they may find that comfortable margins for error translate into significantly larger and more capable forces - a position to which the United States has by now grown accustomed. Where doubt exists, credibility can only be reestablished in one of three ways: reduce "vital interests", increase capabilities, or alter threat assessments. The first is politically inconsistent with a European deterrent. The second is economically incompatible.

Alternatives to NATO's Nuclear Strategy

Nuclear-Free Zones

NATO is faced with an unsettling and by now familiar dilemma. On the one hand, it must present a sufficient nuclear threat to the Soviet Union to dissuade it from aggression. On the other hand, it must not set the threshold for use of nuclear weapons so low that early use becomes automatic if deterrence fails. The concept of nuclear-free zones has been advanced as one way of addressing these inherent dangers.

Two different types of nuclear-free zones have been proposed. The first proposes a nuclear-free corridor along the line separating NATO and Warsaw Pact states. The best known proposal of this kind is the Palme Commission recommendation that an area extending 150 kilometres in each direction from the border be cleared of nuclear weapons and storage sites. The principal objective of creating such a zone would be to minimize pressures on either side to resort to early use of nuclear weapons. It would accomplish this by battlefield systems which, because of their vulnerability, might need to be either withdrawn, used or lost in the early stages of a conflict.

Nuclear-free zones of the corridor type do not really constitute alternatives to current strategy but offer, instead, methods of mitigating the effects of NATO's flexible response dilemma. The Alliance has already taken unilateral steps in this direction by approving removal of some 3000 battlefield nuclear weapons from the European theatre. However, a nuclear-free zone, requiring as it does bilateral negotiations, has the additional advantage of addressing the concern for East-West dialogue expressed in the Harmel Report and reaffirmed in its 1984 review.

The second type of nuclear-free zone would eliminate flexible response as an option. Proposals of this kind encompass a much larger area, extending "from the Atlantic to the Urals", and would rely for deterrence on conventional and central strategic forces. This European nuclear-free zone resembles nuclear exclusion zones such as Latin America and, more recently, the South Pacific. The main difference is that existing zones are preventive in nature, while a European zone would have to be created in an environment in which large quantities of nuclear weapons are already in place and have been an essential element of military doctrine for some forty years.

Critics argue that both nuclear-free concepts would accentuate the conventional disparities between NATO and Warsaw Pact which prompted the Alliance to introduce nuclear weapons into Europe in the first place. In the case of the corridor proposal, the deficiencies would be less pronounced. However, if the option of forward defence were to be kept open, NATO nuclear forces would have to be restructured to accomodate more longer-range weapons (a requirement the Soviets have already met), or much more serious attention would have to be given to the conventional balance either through increases in NATO strength or negotiated reductions to parity on the part of the Soviets. Such objectives are not necessarily undesirable, but even if they were achieved, opponents claim, geographic asymmetries would still favour the Warsaw Pact to a dangerous degree.

A European nuclear-free zone would not only highlight the conventional imbalance, but would also further reduce NATO's nuclear options. By removing the intermediate steps of flexible response, Alliance nuclear strategy would return the ultimate concept of a massive retaliation.

Opposition Parties and Nuclear Strategy

A number of opposition parties in Alliance member countries have adopted defence policies - several of which incorporate nuclear-free zone concepts - which, if realized in their present form, could have profound effects on NATO strategy in general and nuclear strategy in particular. Individual member states are responsible for formulating their own defence policies according to their individual needs as they perceive them. Still, since the resultant policies affect NATO to a greater or lesser extent, it is appropriate that these impending changes should be examined as part of the alternatives to NATO's nuclear strategy.

The Alliance between Social Democrats and Liberals in the United Kingdom has set a course for Britain's own nuclear policy that might alter relationships among NATO members significantly in the years to come. Although the

September party conferences revealed serious disagreement on defence policy between the rank and file of Social Democrats and Liberals, the leadership of both parties are in substantial accord.

Before the September party conferences, a key aspect of Alliance nuclear defense policy was a commitment to cancel the Trident missile program and, instead, maintain the Polaris fleet to the end of its service life in the mid-1990s. If a breakthrough in arms control has not occurred by then, a replacement for Polaris would probably be adopted.

In the search for such a replacement the Alliance is also exploring the possibility of a European minimum deterrent based on British and French independent forces. Raised in consultations with the French Government in early September, the idea met with an unexpectedly warm reception. Agreement was reached in principle to discuss co-ordinated refitting schedules for British and French submarines in order to maximize on-station rates; on possible joint targeting; and on co-operative hardware purchases which might include British acquisition of the French M-4 or M-5 submarine-launched ballistic missiles (SLBMs). Another idea raised separately by the leaders of the respective Alliance parties over the summer, but which was apparently not discussed in Paris, is the possibility of a European medium-range cruise missile.

In a joint Defense Commission Report released earlier this year the Alliance endorsed a limited freeze on further US cruise missile deployments in Britain and a dual key arrangement for those already in place. In addition, the report called for removal of battlefield nuclear weapons from Europe and a serious investigation of a nuclear freeze and move towards a policy of no-first-use. Concerning the Strategic Defense Initiative, the Alliance wishes to see the research programme reduced to the status it enjoyed prior to President Reagan's March 1983 speech.

The effects on Alliance strategy of a no-first-use policy for NATO or the removal of all battlefield nuclear weapons have been debated extensively elsewhere and are therefore not treated in detail here. It should be noted, however, that these are decisions which would have to be taken up within the Alliance hierarchy and are not matters which would lend themselves to unilateral decisions by any one member state. Efforts to develop a European deterrent, on the other hand, do not require explicit NATO approval, yet they may raise questions about the future of the treaty.

The rationale for a European minimum deterrent has three additional parts: 1) to reduce Europe's dependence on the United States, 2) to provide a nuclear guarantee for European security, and 3) to ensure against a US withdrawal from Europe.

The essential problem for the United States is not what Britain does with her own nuclear deterrent but what effect her actions will have on the future of NATO policy and, more specifically, the future of US nuclear assets in Britain. It is not clear in 1986 that NATO could survive a reenactment of the events of 1966 when France withdrew from the integrated military command. However, if the cruise missiles remain (at least until negotiations make them unnecessary), if US options to nuclear facilities currently in Britain remain, and if support for NATO conventional strength remains, then - it is hoped - so too will the United States.

The policy of the British Labour Party has some similarities to that of the SDP-Liberal Alliance. They agree that the Trident missile program must be cancelled in favour of greater spending on conventional forces. However, Labour's approach is much more radical. The Labour Party has advocated a non-nuclear defence for Britain and would call for the removal of all US nuclear facilities from the United Kingdom. They have also promised to nullify the co-operative agreement on the SDI and, while the Party says it would retain NATO membership, it would make significant changes in Britain's role within the Alliance and actively lobby for fundamental changes in NATO strategy.

Substantive changes would include converting Britain's attack submarines to a coastal defence role, and moving Tornado aircraft from FOFA deep-attack to ground support missions in Central Europe and naval aviation patrols in the Northeast Atlantic. Emphasis would be placed on non-provocative defence concepts. As a Labour statement on defence said, "we will restructure the Army, Navy and Royal Air Force away from offensive and towards defensive military roles." As part of Labour's desire to reduce Britain's commitments outside Europe, British forces would no longer participate in military exercises outside the NATO deployment area.

Labour sees its role within NATO as an advocate of non-provocative defence, no-first-use, and the creation of a European nuclear-free zone. It would stress a NATO commitment to arms control in all areas.

In order to support a non-nuclear defence policy and reductions in other areas of British defence, Labour has said it would review the process through which threat assessments are arrived at. This would result in a reduced reliance on US intelligence data and some restructuring of British intelligence services.

The Labour policy's impact on the United States has already been foreshadowed by official responses around the time of the September party conference. The US Defense Department warned that Labour policies would severely weaken the Alliance and encourage isolationism in the United States. Members of Congress have expressed concern that they will "trigger a dramatic increase in European anti-nuclear sentiment." The United States clearly fears both the loss of its nuclear bases in Britain and the effect a denuclearized Britain would have on those countries which are now deploying US cruise missiles.

Labour's proposals clearly involve a radical departure from NATO policy. Whether they would actually be implemented if Labour gains power is uncertain; but it must be assumed that they would. Whether they would spell the end of the Alliance depends very much on the reaction of other NATO members to events in Britain. It would also depend on the timing of British moves. Institutions of the size and complexity of NATO do not lend themselves to abrupt fundamental changes. If the policies were moderated and implemented gradually, they would be less likely to cause irreparable fractures in the Alliance.

The German Social Democrats met in late August to set their party platform for the coming elections in January 1987. The defence policy which emerged from the conference, like those of opposition parties in Britain, involved a marked departure from existing NATO strategy. After reaffirming their commitment to NATO and their close ally, the United States, they put forward a policy not dissimilar to that of the British Labour Party.

The Social Democrats declared that an SPD Government would terminate co-operation on the SDI and reject similar proposals for a European Defense Initiative (EDI); request that the United States withdraw ground-launched cruise missiles and Pershing IIs based in Germany; and demand the removal of SS-21s and -23s from the GDR and Czechoslovakia and the return of SS-20s aimed at Western Europe to pre-1979 levels. Recommendations also included the creation of a nuclear-free corridor between East and West in Central Europe in accord with Palme Commission guidelines.

Internally, the party is divided on the extent to which nuclear co-operation with France should be developed. Official policy rejects the need for a European deterrent, but information exchanges, including consultation on French nuclear policy, are still seen as highly beneficial.

SPD conventional defence policy stresses a forward strategy matched with capabilities which are unambiguously defensive in nature. It rejects deep-attack concepts like NATO's FOFA and US Air Land Battle and would reduce the share of the West German budget devoted to defence to its 1982 level.

European Socialists and NATO Strategy

The policies outlined above are part of a broader effort taking place within many West European Socialist parties. In an attempt to co-ordinate their policies towards the Atlantic Alliance, Socialist parties from the Netherlands, Denmark, Norway, Flemish-speaking Belgium and Luxembourg formed the Scandilux group in 1981. The French Socialists and the British Labour Party sent observers to the Scandilux meetings, and Egon Bahr, a West German Social Democrat, was an active participant. In 1984 French Socialists, defending their country's, independent nuclear deterrent, felt isolated from the mainstream of the Scandilux group and as a result formed Eurosud with Socialists from Italy, Spain, Portugal and French-speaking Belgium. Beginning in 1985 joint meetings between Scandilux and Eurosud took place. In November 1985, meeting in Bonn, the two groups issued a joint communiqué calling for a stronger West European contribution to defence and declaring that Western Europeans "cannot delegate responsibility for their security to others."

A third meeting of the two groups took place in Oslo in September 1986. In the communiqué which was issued following the two days of discussions, the NATO Socialists declared that there was "a need to move from a strategy based on a preponderant role for nuclear weapons to the concept of minimum nuclear deterrence as long as nuclear weapons exist."

Leading members of the group hope these meetings will help build a consensus on a new strategy for the Alliance, based on a stronger role for Western Europe and independence from nuclear weapons. The vision of a nuclear-free Europe has yet to address directly the conventional imbalance with the Warsaw Pact, and runs counter to French defence of its own nuclear deterrent. However, discussions will continue among the Socialist and Social Democrat parties in the hopes of achieving a common platform in defence.

CONCLUSION: THE WAY AHEAD

The immediate post-Reykjavik public relations campaigns presented sharply differing views as to whether the hastily convened summit meeting of 11-12 October had been a missed opportunity of historic proportions or merely a stumble on the road to eventual superpower agreement.

Whatever the overall judgment, it is quite evident that spectacular progress was made on arms control and that the potential deal was, in the words of Secretary of State George Shultz, "breathtaking". It encompassed the scrapping of all long-range INF systems in Europe with only 100 warheads being retained in Soviet Asia and in the United States; a freeze on shorter-range nuclear systems accompanied by talks on their eventual reduction; a 50% cut in strategic weapons leaving only 1600 delivery vehicles and 6000 warheads on each side; and talks on nuclear testing limitations to run parallel with cuts in offensive forces.

Despite the undoubtable attraction of such a package, the talks foundered on the rock of the SDI, with President Reagan unwilling to agree that the US programme should be limited to laboratory research.

With the benefit of hindsight it is hardly surprising that agreement was not reached. Twenty years of the arms race could hardly be wiped out over one weekend, however powerful the momentum produced by the accelerating series of offers and counter-offers. Indeed, had a deal been struck at Reykjavik the lack of careful and detailed preparation might have caused serious problems once it came to implementation.

It seems clear that both superpowers will wish to continue research into the feasibility of strategic defence systems and, since this was at the root of the Reykjavik failure, efforts must be made to define the level of such research acceptable to both sides within a revised and strengthened ABM treaty.

President Reagan's concept of the SDI may not have been designed as a bargaining chip, but it could be argued that it has produced progress on arms control which would have been inconceivable two years ago. What the Alliance must now determine is whether the continuation of the SDI in its present form is more important than the prospect of historic cuts in nuclear weapons. Mr. Gorbachev may have been asking for too much too quickly at Reykjavik, but for the European Allies the early removal of the most threatening nuclear weapons is likely to be much more attractive than the distant, dubious and costly prospect of a defence against their use. If the US Administration is determined to put the realization of its total SDI programme before everything else, the current tensions within the Alliance over arms control and nuclear strategy are likely to increase rather than diminish.

NOTES

1. For further explanation see "Nuclear Weapons in Europe", North Atlantic Assembly Paper, John Cartwright and Julian Critchley, Rapporteurs, November 1984.

2. Joseph S. Nye, Jr. "Reagan Could Have It Both Ways On Arms Control", International Herald Tribune, 30 September 1986.

3. Washington Post, 17 August 1986

4. Interview on NBC Meet the Press TV Show, 28 September 1986

5. According to a report which appeared in the Christian Science Monitor on 25 September, the German Foreign Ministry let it be known that it "would like to see this particular burden of INF - and especially the burden for Germany - abolished as soon as possible." See Elizabeth Pond, "Europe Endorses Bid to Cut Medium-Range Missiles", Christian Science Monitor, 25 September 1986

6. This position is maintained despite the evaluation of the Scowcroft Commission of April 1983, which concluded that the "window of vulnerability", on which this notion is premised, does not exist.

7. Time magazine conference on the SDI on 3 June. Reported in Time, 23 June 1986

8. Remarks by Senator Joseph R. Biden to the National Press Club, Washington DC, 10 September 1986.

9. Both Henry Kissinger, New York Post, 4 March 1985 and McGeorge Bundy, Arms Control Today, April 1985, appeared to concur on this point.

10. USIS Wireless File No. 228, 27 November 1985.

11. Statement by the Assistant for Advanced Launcher systems (US Air Force Division) Colonel William Zerson. Reported in Washington Post, 27 June 1986.

12. The Pentagon has begun research work on a gigantic new highly advanced rocket, or "space truck", with the goal of slashing the cost of lifting payloads into space. This will itself be enormously expensive since it will need a revolution in the structure and operations of the aerospace industry, reducing reliance on manpower and increasing the roles of computers and robots.

13. "SDI: Progress and Challenges", Staff Report Submitted to Senator William Proxmire, Senator J. Bennett Johnston and Senator Lawson Chiles by Douglas Waller, James Bruce and Douglas Cook.

14. Walter Slocombe, "Arms Control and Strategic Defences", *Survival*, Sept-Oct 1985. See also his comments before the Military Committee of the North Atlantic Assembly, 31st Annual Session, San Francisco, 11 October 1985.

15. See *Strategic Survey*, 1984-1985, International Institute for Strategic Studies, London.

16. OTA Study on *Ballistic Missile Defense Technologies*, September 1985.

17. Stephen M. Meyer, "Soviet Views of SDI", *Survival*, November-December 1985.

18. Meyer, op. cit.

19. *Tass*, 18 August 1986 in Washington Embassy Press Release.

20. Quoted in Bruce D. Marshall, "The Evolving French Strategic Debate", *Strategic Review*, Spring 1980, p. 72.

21. De Gaulle quoted in Wilfrid Kohl, *French Nuclear Diplomacy*, Princeton: Princeton University Press, 1971, p. 319

22. General Jeannou Lacaze, quoted in David S. Yost, "French Nuclear Targetting", in *Strategic Nuclear Targetting*, Desmond Ball and Jeffrey Richelson, Eds., p. 134.

Appendix A

POLICY RECOMMENDATIONS ADOPTED AT THE
THIRTY-SECOND ANNUAL SESSION
OF THE NORTH ATLANTIC ASSEMBLY

RECOMMENDATION 86
on
NATO'S PUBLIC RELATIONS PROBLEMS
Presented by the Civilian Affairs Committee

The Assembly,

Recalling the terms of its Recommendations 83 of 1984 on "A More Effective Information Policy for the Alliance" and 84 of 1985 on "Informing the Public on Defence and Security";

Satisfied that the Spanish people, in the referendum of 12 March 1986, voted positively in favour of Spanish membership of the Alliance, but concerned that in Spain, as in other Alliance countries, underlying trends show signs of misunderstanding and a low level of accurate information about NATO among regional minorities, young people, women and single interest groups;

Disturbed by the increasing evidence that the transatlantic relationship divides European opinion along lines which reflect party-political and voting behaviours, and convinced that this linkage could rapidly cause lasting damage to Alliance solidarity;

Perturbed by the growing influence in some Alliance member-countries of unilateralist thinking and tendencies, and in others of equilateralist thought;

Attributing these factors to the effects of the economic crisis on Alliance solidarity, and to the increasing weight of purely domestic considerations over international commitments;

Noting with concern the attempt by the new Soviet leadership to drive a wedge between the Allies by showing support for arms control and disarmament, and by making spectacular gestures to this effect;

Welcoming the NATO Council's awareness of the extent of the problem, as voiced by the Comments of the Secretary General of NATO on Assembly Recommendation 84;

Satisfied that account was taken of its proposals;

Hoping that bureaucratic delays will not impede their implementation, and conscious that it may be necessary to give the NATO information structure increased flexibility;

Disappointed by the inability of the NATO Council to agree to the Secretary General's proposal that the NATO information budget be raised;

Concerned that the present network of NATO information correspondents in Alliance member countries is uneven and often inefficient;

Repeating that information offices about NATO in Alliance member countries, reflecting the main political and ideological tendencies and interest groups, would contribute significantly to improving the communication between the public and the Alliance.

RECOMMENDS that the North Atlantic Council:

1. encourage the creation of such offices in Alliance member countries;

2. create a network of information correspondents in Alliance member countries which would include representatives of opposition parties and special interest groups;

3. proceed with speed in carrying out the review of the NATO document classification rules requested by the Secretary General of NATO and in implementing its conclusions, in order to improve the quality of NATO information going to the press and public without jeopardizing NATO security;

4. separate the NATO Information Service from the NATO services and attach it directly to the Secretary General's Private Office;

5. give the NATO Information Service increased resources.

RESOLUTION 172
on
HUMAN RIGHTS AND THE ALLIANCE AGENDA
Presented by the Civilian Affairs Committee

The Assembly,

Recalling the terms of its Resolutions 151 of 1984 on "The Role of Parliaments in Combating the Violations of the Humanitarian Provisions of the CSCE", and 162 of 1985 on "The Maintenance of the Helsinki Process";

Disappointed that the Soviet Union and other Eastern European participants in the CSCE have failed to observe the Helsinki Final Act provisions on human rights and human contacts;

Convinced of the continued need for the Alliance to maintain a common position at CSCE meetings;

Noting with interest that the Conference on Confidence and Security Measures and Disarmament in Stockholm (CDE) has agreed on some modest provisions for Confidence and Security Building Measures which may improve the notification, observation and inspection of military manoeuvres;

Satisfied that the multilateral context of the CSCE provides a useful forum for a positive improvement in East-West confidence;

Aware that the current CSCE Review Conference in Vienna could result in significant progress; but

Convinced that progress will only be possible if it relates equally to all the areas discussed at this Conference;

Concerned, therefore, that progress in human rights by the signatory States should be a priority of the member countries of the Alliance at the Vienna Conference and should not be divorced from matters of security or economic co-operation;

Reaffirming that the member countries of the Alliance must be exemplary in the field of human rights in order to have a positive influence on the other participants;

Recalling that the CSCE process can only succeed if the pressure of public opinion is maintained on diplomacies, particularly through elected representatives of the electorates;

URGES member governments of the North Atlantic Alliance:

1. to co-ordinate effectively their positions at CSCE meetings and conferences, so as to avoid disunity and ensure that the specific interests of each member country are taken into account by all its partners;

2. to ensure that discussions on all CSCE issues proceed at the same pace;

3. to make sure that, if the Vienna Review Conference mandates future subordinate meetings, they be restricted to the discussion of the implementation of the relevant provisions of the CSCE documents and their updating, and leave the improvement of texts to the Review Conferences;

4. to include parliamentarians in their delegations to the different CSCE meetings;

5. to set up ministries or agencies with special responsibility for human rights;

URGES the parliaments of the North Atlantic Alliance:

1. to form groups for the follow-up of the Helsinki Agreements with a view to co-ordinating the work of member country Parliaments in this area;

2. to invite their members to take part in CSCE meetings.

RESOLUTION 173
on
THE ECONOMICS OF ATLANTIC SECURITY

Presented by the Economic Committee

The Assembly,

Recalling Resolution 159 on Economic Interdependence and Alliance Security and Resolution 160 on Economic Relations and the Alliance;

Welcoming the trend towards further economic growth and recovery in Alliance member countries; and

Noting that the fall in the price of oil, the depreciation of the US dollar and the further decline of interest rates improve near-term prospects for sustained non-inflationary growth in most Alliance countries;

Alarmed about the high level of unemployment persisting in many Alliance member countries;

Concerned about the persistence of budget deficits in some countries and obstacles to economic growth in others;

Concerned about the deteriorating trade position of developing countries and the high level of indebtedness of many of these countries;

Convinced that growing protectionist tendencies in some Alliance member countries negatively affect the promotion of economic growth, job creation and debt servicing;

Welcoming the new round of multilateral trade negotiations within the framework of GATT as a positive step towards the elimination of trade restrictions and subsidies;

URGES member governments and parliaments of the North Atlantic Alliance:

1. to take advantage of improved macroeconomic preconditions for the stimulation of sustained non-inflationary economic growth and the creation of new jobs;

2. to reduce budget deficits in cases where this is urgently required and eliminate obstacles to economic growth;

3. to create a more favourable economic and financial environment with a view to assisting the developing countries to overcome their most pressing economic problems;

4. to expand free multilateral trade, reject the imposition of trade barriers and work constructively - both bilaterally and multilaterally - towards the elimination of existing trade restrictions and subsidies.

RESOLUTION 174
on
ECONOMIC CO-OPERATION WITHIN THE ALLIANCE
Presented by the Economic Committee

The Assembly,

Recalling Article 2 of the North Atlantic Treaty, which calls on Alliance members to promote conditions of stability and well-being and to encourage economic collaboration between any or all of them;

Stressing the important role NATO's Southern Region countries play in the overall security of the Alliance;

Concerned about the severe economic and financial difficulties still faced by some of the Southern Region countries; and

Aware of the strain that high defence expenditures place on the economies of these countries;

Noting that the strength of democracy and the confidence of the people in democratic institutions depend on economic progress and improved living standards;

Reiterating the need for the Alliance member states to assume greater responsibility in promoting sustained, self-reliant, economic development in the less prosperous member countries;

URGES member governments and parliaments of the North Atlantic Alliance:

1. to strengthen co-operation and to take combined measures which help the less prosperous Alliance countries to promote sustained, self-reliant, economic development;

2. to increase economic and military assistance to these countries;

3. to explore opportunities for increased industrial co-operation with these countries in the field of defence;

4. to focus economic assistance on programmes that create employment opportunities, improve infrastructures, enhance rural development and promote education;

5. to provide as broad an access as possible for the products of these countries to the markets of other NATO countries, in order to enable them to increase their export revenues;

6. to stimulate co-operation both between the Alliance countries and within the framework of international economic and monetary institutions to achieve financial and monetary conditions which will help the developing countries in general, and the less prosperous Alliance countries in particular, to reduce their indebtedness without hindering sound economic and social development.

RESOLUTION 175
on
US TROOPS IN EUROPE

Presented by the Military Committee

The Assembly,

Stressing that the North Atlantic Alliance is an association of pluralistic, democratic countries, which serves the interest of all members and is the basis of the external security of all the countries within it;

Welcoming in this connection the collective defence effort of the Alliance in Europe, where the military threat posed by the Warsaw Pact is greatest;

Stressing the need to deploy strong troop contingents in Europe in peacetime;

Concerned with proposals for the reduction of NATO forces stationed in Europe as long as efforts aimed at bringing about mutual, balanced and verifiable arms limitations have not been successful;

Taking the view that a continued strong presence of United States' forces in Europe is critical to the success of the forward defence strategy;

Recognizing that a more cost effective defence must also be based on a closer partnership of the Allies and a more equitable sharing of the burdens of NATO's mutual defence efforts;

URGES member governments and parliaments of the North Atlantic Alliance:

to renew their commitment to the demonstrably successful Alliance principles with respect to conventional force levels in Europe, and to endorse the proposition that unilateral reduction on the part of individual countries

(a) would run counter to Alliance efforts to strengthen the conventional component in the flexible response strategy;

(b) would increase the dependency of the Alliance on the early use of nuclear weapons; and

(c) would considerably reduce the prospects for a meaningful and equitable agreement at the MBFR talks in Vienna.

RESOLUTION 176
on
A NATO TACTICAL FIGHTER WEAPONS TRAINING CENTRE

Presented by the Military Committee

The Assembly,

Recognizing the necessity for low-level flight training of military aircraft in order to maintain a high standard of operational readiness and combat performance in Alliance air forces;

Aware, at the same time, of the burdens placed on large numbers of people living in the densely populated member countries of the Alliance in Europe as a result of current low-level training practices;

Welcoming the measures taken thus far by Alliance governments in pursuit of the objective of reducing the burdens placed on populations through the imposition of restrictive regulations governing low-level flights in air space above the densely populated European member countries;

Appreciative of the efforts made to transfer some low-flight and weapons training operations to suitably populated regions in member countries of the Alliance, without posing a danger to the fulfilment of the defence task;

Supporting in this connection planning within the Alliance for the establishment of a NATO tactical fighter weapons training centre; and

Taking the view that a training centre of this kind would be consistent with the need for a high standard of training and to meet new threats and constantly changing military and political realities would require appropriate investment in order to cover operational costs, and would fulfil key Alliance tasks;

Recognizing that it is critical to get more military capability from less spending in an era of fiscal restraint;

URGES member governments and parliaments of the North Atlantic Alliance:

to bring planning for a training centre to a positive conclusion within an appropriate period of time in the most responsible fiscal manner possible.

RESOLUTION 177
on
CONVENTIONAL ARMS CONTROL
Presented by the Military Committee

The Assembly,

Noting that in conventional forces the Warsaw Pact possesses a considerable advantage over NATO, particularly in terms of offensive capabilities;

Convinced that a balanced and verifiable conventional arms control agreement, in the zone "Atlantic to the Urals", would be in the security interests of NATO as it could considerably reduce the potential for a Warsaw Pact "standing start" offensive against NATO forces, and that associated compliance measures might significantly increase the potential warning-time of hostilities;

Regretting the absence of tangible results from the Mutual Balanced Force Reductions (MBFR) negotiations after 13 straight years of such talks;

Encouraged by the September 1986 agreement at the Conference on Disarmament in Europe (CDE) which embodies a package of security and confidence building measures designed to reduce the risk of war in Europe;

Aware that radical cuts in the theatre nuclear arsenals of NATO and the Warsaw Pact could have a negative effect on European security if not accompanied by comparable negotiated reductions in the levels of conventional forces, and in particular short-range nuclear weapons;

Noting that for economic and demographic reasons it is unlikely that NATO will be in a position to increase significantly its active duty forces in Central Europe in the near future;

Noting the general NATO position that recent superpower proposals on conventional arms control are positive and might serve as the basis for serious bloc-to-bloc negotiations;

Supporting, therefore, the decision by NATO Foreign Ministers in Halifax, Canada to set up a High Level Task Force to seek "bold new steps" in the field of conventional arms control, building on the CDE and MBFR negotiations, and taking account of recent Warsaw Pact initiatives;

URGES the North Atlantic Council:

to embrace what is proposed by the NATO High-Level Task Force in the expectation that progress in the MBFR negotiations and in the Conference on Security and Co-operation in Europe, particularly the implementation of the results of the CDE meeting in Stockholm will enhance the objective of reducing force levels, fostering transparency and reducing further the perceived dangers of surprise attack;

URGES member governments and parliaments of the North Atlantic Alliance:

1. to reaffirm their continued commitment to the pursuit of balanced and verifiable conventional arms control agreements;

2. to resist strongly proposals for the unilateral withdrawal of Western troops from Europe.

DRAFT RESOLUTION 178
on
ENHANCING ARMAMENTS CO-OPERATION IN THE ALLIANCE
Presented by the Military Committee

The Assembly,

Convinced that significant progress has been made over the last year in the attitude of member countries towards the imperative of enhanced armaments co-operation in the Alliance, but persuaded that additional concrete efforts are required;

Aware that further progress can only be accomplished if there is sustained and reinforced involvement of legislators and senior government officials in each of the member countries of the Alliance, both in the context of the Independent European Programme Group (IEPG) as well as in transatlantic armaments co-operation;

Welcoming, therefore, the renewed commitment by the US Congress to continue financing, during 1987, collaborative research and development projects between the United States and the NATO Allies at the instigation of Senator Nunn; and

Supporting the continued, regular ministerial meetings of the IEPG and the efforts being made under the Spanish chairmanship to translate expressions of political commitment into meaningful European armaments co-operative programmes;

Encouraged by the agreement reached in June at the North Atlantic Council to proceed with the procurement of a common NATO Electronic Warfare Training Aircraft as part of the project of the NATO Multi-Service Electronic Warfare Support Group (MEWSG);

Concerned with all restrictive protectionist measures which would have negative implications for transatlantic armaments co-operation;

Aware that harmonization of the supply side on the defence market as a basis for co-operation in mutual armaments production can best be achieved through harmonization of the demand side and that standardization of the military requirements within the conceptual military framework are essential to that goal;

URGES member governments and parliaments of the North Atlantic Alliance:

1. to respond positively to the new Nunn Amendment, by concluding additional armaments co-operation statements of intent to take advantage of the new opportunities afforded by this initiative, and to accelerate progress in existing development projects set up in the framework of this amendment;

2. to give urgent, concrete and high-level support to the forthcoming recommendations of the IEPG study to improve the competitiveness of the European defence industry;

3. to resist attempts being made in any member countries to introduce restrictive and protectionist measures which would be contrary to the spirit of Allied defence co-operation and damaging to Allied cohesion.

RESOLUTION 179
on
TERRORISM

Presented by the Political Committee

The Assembly,

Deeply concerned by the rise in terrorist attacks in Alliance nations and throughout the world and by the increasingly lethal and indiscriminate nature of these acts of terrorist violence;

Deploring the loss of life and suffering caused by these acts of violence;

Strongly condemning recourse to terrorism to achieve political or other goals, no matter the principles or ideology that motivate it;

Disturbed by growing evidence of State sponsorship of terrorism, of international collaboration among terrorist groups, and of the new, dangerous connection between terrorists and narcotics traffickers;

Convinced that international co-operation among Alliance member countries is essential to the establishment of effective preventive measures against terrorists;

Recognizing that efforts to curb terrorism must fully protect and respect democratic institutions and civil liberties;

Further recognizing that reasonable additional measures may be necessary to combat this growing assault on democracy;

Welcoming the decision of 21 April 1986 by the 12 Foreign Ministers of the European Economic Community (EEC) to impose stiff restrictions against States determined to support terrorism and the agreement reached by the leaders of the Western industrialized nations at the May 1986 Tokyo Summit to limit the size of diplomatic and consular missions of states which support terrorism;

URGES member governments of the North Atlantic Alliance:

1. to commit themselves never to negotiate with the terrorists, their backers or their protectors;

2. to continue to implement the measures agreed upon within the EEC and at the Tokyo Summit and to apply them consistently against all states which are proven sponsors of terrorism;

3. to respect all international conventions in force against terrorism and to work to upgrade such

conventions to reflect recent developments in terrorism;

4. to assess the merits of negotiating an international omnibus anti-terrorism convention, establishing the prosecution or extradition of any perpetrator of an act of terrorist character committed against international travellers and other innocent victims;

5. to establish an International Terrorism Committee within NATO specifically empowered to study all aspects of international terrorism, to make recommendations to member countries and to serve as a forum at both the political and law enforcement levels;

6. to continue to improve intelligence-gathering capabilities, security at airports and other potential terrorist targets, and co-ordination among national police forces and other governmental agencies;

7. to continue to upgrade and modernize extradition treaties already existing between NATO countries, and to encourage such treaties among all members, especially with attention to prosecution and extradition of any perpetrator of an act of terrorist character;

8. to seek diplomatic and political solutions to conflicts in the Middle East.

RESOLUTION 180
on
THE SOUTHERN REGION

Presented by the Political Committee

The Assembly,

Recognizing the vital contribution the Southern Region makes to overall Alliance security;

Welcoming the strong commitment to national defence demonstrated by the Southern Region countries;

Stressing the importance of political cohesion to the Alliance's deterrent capabilities; and

Welcoming therefore the decision of the Spanish people to remain an active participant in the Atlantic Alliance;

Welcoming the process of democratization in Turkey;

Aware that efforts to maintain a credible defence posture in the region places particular strains on the less prosperous Southern Region countries; and

Concerned that budgetary restrictions in the United States, the largest donor to the region, may reduce the level of US military and economic assistance to the Southern Region;

URGES member governments of the North Atlantic Alliance:

1. to increase military and economic assistance to Greece, Portugal, and Turkey in accordance with the numerous recommendations of the Defence Planning Committee;

2. to discuss means of compensating for possible reductions in US aid to the Southern Region resulting from general reductions in US military and foreign assistance programmes;

3. to promote collaborative ventures, particularly within the framework of the Independent European Programme Group (IEPG), with the less prosperous countries in the region in order to assist them in their efforts to strengthen their national defence industries.

RESOLUTION 181
on
ALLIANCE SOLIDARITY

Presented by the Political Committee

The Assembly,

Aware that political cohesion and solidarity are essential to the collective security of the 16 sovereign nations of the North Atlantic Alliance;

Welcoming the genuine consultations within the Alliance, particularly in the North Atlantic Council (NAC), the

Special Consultative Group (SCG) and the Nuclear Planning Group (NPG);

Convinced that such consultations strengthen Alliance unity on the conduct of East-West Relations as evidenced by the 1984 Washington Declaration and by the October 1986 NPG Communiqué endorsing the programme President Reagan presented to General Secretary Gorbachev at their meeting in Reykjavik;

Supporting strongly the demonstrated Allied commitment to improvements in conventional defence capabilities and the political impetus given to increasing co-operative defence ventures, both of which result from intra-Alliance consultations; whilst

Expressing its continued support for the policy of keeping a balance between conventional and nuclear forces and the strategy of a flexible nuclear response;

Concerned by recent strains within the Alliance;

Concerned by the continuing efforts of the Soviet Union to exacerbate differences between the Allies;

URGES member governments of the North Atlantic Alliance:

1. to continue to consult on a regular basis within existing Alliance fora in order to seek consensus on the challenges and opportunities which may emerge from recent negotiations between East and West;

2. to promote actively improvements in the Alliance's conventional defence posture and increases in the number and scope of Allied cooperative ventures whilst continuing the strategy of a flexible nuclear response;

3. to demonstrate as appropriate the same cooperative approach to all issues which may affect the collective security of the 16 Allied nations.

RESOLUTION 182
on
THE ABM TREATY AND THE PARTICIPATION IN THE STRATEGIC DEFENSE INITIATIVE

Presented by the Scientific and Technical Committee

The Assembly,

Recalling its 1985 Resolution 170 on Strategic Defence and the Alliance;

Aware of Soviet and American strategic defence programmes;

Concerned by ambiguities and differing interpretations of the 1972 Anti-Ballistic Missile (ABM) Treaty;

Acknowledging differences of opinion regarding the military, political, technical, economic, and strategic aspects of such programmes;

Noting that, of the Alliance nations, the United Kingdom, the Federal Republic of Germany and Italy have signed memoranda of understanding with the United States, and that organizations in other Alliance nations are able to compete for SDI contracts;

Recognizing that the duration of the contracting process and the recent origin of SDI participation prohibit authoritative estimates of the ultimate value of SDI contracts to be awarded to non-American bodies;

Concerned by suggestions that the Alliance exploitation of SDI-generated technologies might be unduly restricted;

URGES member governments and parliaments of the North Atlantic Alliance:

1. to co-ordinate where such agreements exist government-supported SDI participation proposals so that they are as far as possible complementary rather than duplicative;

2. to ensure that technologies generated by SDI research may be exploited without restriction subject to the terms of the memoranda of understanding;

3. to support American and Soviet efforts to resolve ambiguities and unclear technical definitions in the ABM Treaty.

RESOLUTION 183
on
NUCLEAR SAFETY
Presented by the Scientific and Technical Committee

The Assembly,

Concerned by the accident at the Chernobyl nuclear reactor on 26 April 1986; and

Disturbed by the various effects of the resulting widespread nuclear contamination;

Disapproving of the initial Soviet reluctance to provide details of the accident; but

Welcoming a subsequent improvement in the provision of relevant information;

Aware of differing national standards regarding acceptable levels of exposure to radiation and of differing national responses to the radioactive fallout from the Chernobyl accident;

Concerned by the lack of mandatory international nuclear safety standards;

Disturbed by the absence of an international framework for arranging compensation for the effects of nuclear accidents;

Welcoming the "Convention on Early Notification of a Nuclear Accident" and the "Convention on Assistance in the Case of a Nuclear Accident or Radiological Emergency" signed at the International Atomic Energy Agency on 26 September 1986;

URGES member governments and parliaments of the North Atlantic Alliance:

1. to develop international standards and methods for measuring radioactive contamination, and for defining acceptable levels of exposure to radiation;

2. to establish at an international level the actions to be taken in response to unacceptable radiation levels in the environment and in foodstuffs;

3. to improve civilian defence arrangements and the training and co-ordination of volunteers;

4. to encourage and support through the appropriate international organizations a mandatory reporting procedure for nuclear accidents, and the creation of a legal framework for arranging compensation for the effects of nuclear accidents;

5. to encourage signatory countries to implement the "Convention on Early Notification of a Nuclear Accident" and the "Convention on Assistance in the Case of a Nuclear Accident or Radiological Emergency";

6. to produce a structure for international action to assist any nation to overcome the nuclear problems arising in the event of a nuclear accident;

7. to recommend the adoption of international regulations on safety regarding the construction and operation of nuclear power stations;

8. to report what positive action has been taken to meet the recommendations of this Resolution.

RESOLUTION 184
on
THE REPRESSION OF THE TURKISH MINORITY IN BULGARIA

Presented by the Standing Committee

The Assembly,

Recalling Resolution 168 passed in 1985, urging member Governments and Parliaments of the North Atlantic Alliance to continue to attach importance to the problem of the repression of the Turkish minority in Bulgaria;

Recalling the provisions of the 1971 Constitution of the Peoples' Republic of Bulgaria guaranteeing equal rights and non-discrimination to the Turkish minority in Bulgaria, and in particular Article 35/3 which recognizes that "all is equal before the law, irrespective of religion, race and culture and that these rights cannot be suppressed" and paragraph 4 of the same Article that "no one can be persecuted because of his race, origin or religious beliefs", which was blatantly ignored;

Recalling also Article 45/7 of the Constitution of the Peoples' Republic of Bulgaria which grants that "Bulgarian nationals of non-Bulgarian origin have the right to study their mother tongue" in spite of which all Turkish schools and publications in Bulgaria are closed and that they are denied their constitutional rights and even barred from speaking their mother tongue in public;

Welcoming the important report of Amnesty International on Bulgaria, entitled "Imprisonment of Ethnic Turks; Human Rights Abuses during the Forced Assimilation of the Ethnic Turkish Minority" published in April 1986, which sheds impartial light on this tragic problem;

Deploring in most categorical terms the killing of more than 100 ethnic Turks by security forces in Bulgaria the names of which were received by Amnesty International;

Noting with great concern that Amnesty International has the names of 250 Turks reportedly arrested, imprisoned and released only after accepting Bulgarian names for themselves and for their dependants;

Disturbed that since 1984 foreign observers have been refused access to areas like Kardzhali where ethnic Turks predominate;

Distressed by the fact that only a few journalists have been allowed into these restricted areas and then under official supervision;

Deplores further the decision to expel foreign journalists from Bulgaria in February 1985, according to Amnesty International;

Condemns the Government of the Peoples' Republic of Bulgaria which refuses to permit journalists and foreign diplomats to visit the areas where violence occurred purporting to deny such events;

Condemns the action of Bulgarian authorities to censor strictly the mail of the ethnic Turkish minority in Bulgaria, as the number of such letters become progressively fewer as reported by Amnesty International;

Disturbed that letters to ethnic Turks in Bulgaria addressed to people with Islamic or Turkish names were returned with "unknown" stamped on them, and that this is the case with all such letters;

Disturbed further that telephone calls between ethnic Turks and relatives living abroad are censored, interrupted and disconnected if Turkish is spoken or the name-changing campaign is mentioned;

URGES member Governments and Parliaments of the North Atlantic Alliance:

1. to continue to attach importance to the problem and their international efforts, to exert pressure through every possible means, until the Bulgarian authorities reverse their decision so that the forced "Bulgarization" policy of brutal repression and mass assassination of the Turkish minority in Bulgaria is prevented;

2. to help the international press to visit Bulgaria to obtain first-hand information on the situation of the Turkish minority and report back on their findings to the Assembly at its next Session;

3. to continue to monitor the situation of the Turkish minority in Bulgaria until the question is solved;

4. to convey the contents of this Resolution to the President of the Bulgarian Parliament.

RESOLUTION 185
on
THE ALLIANCE AND EAST-WEST RELATIONS
Presented directly to the Plenary Assembly by the Hon. Steny Hoyer (Democrat, United States)

The Assembly,

Welcoming continued East-West dialogue on vital questions as exemplified by the recent meeting of President Reagan and General Secretary Gorbachev and expressing the hope that this dialogue will take account of the interests of all the members of the Alliance; but

Concerned by the formidable military challenge posed by Warsaw Pact conventional, chemical and nuclear forces;

Encouraged by the agreement on enhanced notification, observation and inspection of military activities in Europe reached in September in Stockholm at the Conference on Security and Confidence Building Measures and Disarmament in Europe (CDE); and

Acknowledging the constructive contribution of the neutral and non-aligned States to this conference:

Convinced of the importance of achieving concrete progress within the framework of the Conference on Security and Co-operation in Europe (CSCE), especially in the areas of human rights, economic co-operation and confidence and security building measures (CSBMS);

Welcoming the progress being made towards the phased reduction and elimination of intermediate-range nuclear missiles (INF) on a global basis; but

Emphasizing that INF reductions must take into account the new threats to Western Europe presented by Soviet shorter range nuclear weapons (SRINF), particularly the SS-21, SS-22 and SS-23 missiles;

Encouraged by the recent declarations made by the United States and the Soviet Union for the substantial reduction of strategic nuclear systems; but

Aware that verifiable strategic arms reductions can only take place in an atmosphere of East-West stability premised upon trust, confidence and respect for human rights and fundamental freedoms;

Underlining the continuing need to defeat Soviet initiatives designed to challenge Alliance solidarity by the early exchange of information and consultation among all the Alliance members and by a strong commitment to a genuine negotiating effort with the opposite side;

Stressing the continued validity of the Alliance strategy of flexible response and forward defence, and the enduring principles of deterrence, defence and dialogue as defined in the 1967 Harmel Report and reaffirmed in the 1984 Washington Declaration;

Convinced that the deployment of North American forces in Western Europe is an important component of the credibility of the Alliance's deterrent;

URGES member governments of the North Atlantic Alliance:

1. to continue to implement the strategies and principles established by the Harmel Report and the Washington Declaration;

2. to insist that the Soviet Union cease its violations of the 1972 Anti-Ballistic Missile (ABM) Treaty and the Helsinki Final Act;

3. to promote and secure implementation of all the provisions of the Helsinki Final Act and the Concluding Document of the Madrid Follow-up Meeting, in particular with respect to human rights;

4. to encourage the Soviet Union and the United States to:

   A. work towards strategic stability through significant reductions in the numbers of all categories of nuclear weapons;

   B. ensure that any INF agreement be accompanied by measures to rectify existing imbalances in shorter range nuclear forces and conventional forces, to avoid a decrease in Alliance security;
   C. resolve to the extent possible questions of compliance with the ABM Treaty and the SALT II

Accord within the Standing Consultative Commission as established by Article XIII and Article XVII of these respective agreements;

5. to monitor closely the results of the Stockholm CDE Agreement with a view to pursuing within the framework of the CSCE Vienna Review Conference - linked to substantially improved Soviet and Warsaw Pact compliance with their Helsinki human rights obligations - a broader regime of confidence-building measures designed to enhance crisis stability, reduce suspicion, foster transparency, and provide reassurance about intentions on both sides; and

6. to reaffirm their continued support for the North American presence in Western Europe.

Appendix B

COMMITTEE OFFICERS FOR 1986

CIVILIAN AFFAIRS COMMITTEE

Hon. Robert GARCIA (Democrat, United States) Chairman
Dr. Herbert HUPKA (CDU/CSU, Federal Republic of Germany) Vice-Chairman
Mr. Klaas de VRIES (CDA, Netherlands) Vice-Chairman
Dr. David CLARK (Labour, United Kingdom) Rapporteur

ECONOMIC COMMITTEE

Hon. Charles ROSE (Democrat, United States) Chairman
Mr. Keven McNAMARA (Labour, United Kingdom) Vice-Chairman
Dr. Ludolf-Georg von WARTENBERG (CDU, Federal Republic of Germany) Rapporteur

MILITARY COMMITTEE

Sir Geoffrey JOHNSON SMITH (Conservative, United Kingdom) Chairman
Sen. Severino FALLUCCHI (Christian Democrat, Italy) Vice-Chairman
Sen. William V. ROTH (Republican, United States) Vice-Chairman
Mr. Jules de WAART (Labour, Netherlands) Rapporteur

POLITICAL COMMITTEE

Mr. Claude-Gérard MARCUS (RPR, France) Chairman
Sir Julian RIDSDALE (Conservative, United Kingdom) Vice-Chairman
Hon Sala BURTON (Democrat, United States) Vice-Chairman
Mr. Bruce GEORGE (Labour, United Kingdom) Rapporteur

SCIENTIFIC AND TECHNICAL COMMITTEE

Sir Peter EMERY (Conservative, United Kingdom) Chairman
Hon Earl HASTINGS (Liberal, Canada) Vice-Chairman
Mr. Lother IBRÜGGER (SPD, Federal Republic of Germany) General Rapporteur
Mr. Robert BANKS (Conservative, United Kingdom) Special Rapporteur

SPECIAL COMMITTEE ON NUCLEAR STRATEGY AND ARMS CONTROL

Sen. Joseph R. BIDEN (Democrat, United States) Chairman
Mr. Klaus FRANKE (CDU/CSU, Federal Republic of Germany) Vice-Chairman
Mr. John CARTWRIGHT (SDP, United Kingdom) Rapporteur

Abbreviations

ABM - Anti-Ballistic Missile
ABMT - Anti-Ballistic Missile Treaty
ACA - Arms Control Association
ACDA - Arms Control and Disarmament Agency (US)
ACE - Allied Command, Europe
ALCM - Air-launched Cruise Missile
ASALM - Advanced Strategic Air-launched Missile
ASAT - Anti-Satellite
ASW - Anti-submarine Warfare
ATBM - Anti-tactical Ballistic Missile
ATM - Anti-Tactical Missile
AWACS - Airborne Warning and Control System
BMD - Ballistic Missile Defense
BSTS - Boost Surveillance and Tracking System
C^2 - Command and Control
C^3 - Command, Control and Communications
C^3I - Command, Control, Communications and Intelligence
CBO - Congresional Budget Office (US)
CD - Conference on Disarmament (formerly UN Committee on Disarmament)
CDE - Conference on Confidence and Security Building Measures and Disarmament in Europe
CDI - Conventional Defence Initiative
CIA - Central Intelligence Agency
COCOM - Co-ordinating Committee for Multi-lateral Export Controls
CRS - Congressional Research Service
CSCE - Conference on Security & Co-operation in Europe
CTBT - Comprehensive Test Ban Treaty
CVP - Flemish Christian Social Party
CW - Chemical Weapons
D-Mark - German currency unit
DEW - Directed Energy Weapons
DPC - Defence Planning Committee
DoD - Department of Defence
EADS - Extended Air Defence System
ECCM - Electronic Counter-countermeasures
ECM - Electronic Countermeasures
EDC - European Defence Community
EDI - European Defence Initiative
EEC - European Economic Community
ERIS - Exoatmospheric Re-entry Vehicle Interceptor Sub-system
EW - Electronic Warfare

FEL - Free Electron Laser
FLAGE - Flexible Lightweight Agile Guided Experiment
FOFA - Follow-On Forces Attack
FROG - Free Rocket Over Ground
GATT - General Agreement on Tariffs and Trade
GDP - Gross Domestic Product
GLCM - Ground-launched Cruise Missile
GNP - Gross National Product
HEDI - High Endoatmospheric Defence Interceptor
HOE - Homing Overlay Experiment
IAEA - International Atomic Energy Agency
ICBM - Intercontinental Ballistic Missile
ICTO - Dutch Interchurch Committee for Bilateral Disarmament
IEPG - Independent European Programme Group
IISS - International Institute for Strategic Studies
IKV - Dutch Interchurch Peace Council
IMF - International Monetary Fund
INF - Intermediate-range Nuclear Forces
IOC - Initial Operational Capability
JSTPS - Joint Strategic Target Planning Staff (US)
KEW - Kinetic Energy Weapon
KGB - Soviet Committee for State Security
KHAD - Afghan Security Service
KKN - Committee Against Cruise Missiles
LRINF - Longer-range Intermediate-range Nuclear Forces
MBFR - Mutual and Balanced Force Reductions
MEWSG - Multi-service Electronic Warfare Support Group
MI5 - British Military Intelligence
MIRACL - Mid-Infrared Advanced Chemical Laser
MIRV - Multiple Independently Targettable Re-entry Vehicle
MIT - Massachusetts Institute of Technology
MLRS - Multiple-Launch Rocket System
MX - Missile Experimental
MoD - Ministry of Defence (UK)
MoU - Memorandum of Understanding
NADC - NATO Air Defence Committee
NADGE - NATO Air Defence Ground Environment
NATO - North Atlantic treaty Organization
NDRC - National Defense Research Council
NPG - Nuclear Planning Group
NST - Nuclear and Space Talks
OCA - Offensive Counter-Air
OECD - Organization for Economic Co-operation and Development
OPEC - Organization of Petroleum Exporting Countries

OTAN - Organisation du Traité de l'Atlantique Nord
PADP - Panel on Air Defence Philosophy
PADW - Panel on Air Defence Weapons
PCM - Physical Countermeasures
PNE - Peaceful Nuclear Explosions
PSOE - Spanish Socialist Party
SACEUR - Supreme Allied Commander Europe
SALT - Strategic Arms Limitation Treaty
SAM - Surfact-to-Air Missile
SATKA - Surveillance, Acquisition, Tracking and Kill Assessment
SCC - Standing Consultative Commission
SCG - Special Consultative Group
SDI - Strategic Defense Initiative
SDIO - Strategic defense Initiative Organization
SLBM - Submarine-launched Ballistic Missile
SLCM - Sea-launched Cruise Missile
SNDV - Strategic Nuclear Delivery Vehicle
SPD - German Social Democratic Party
SR-HII - Small Radar-homing Intercept Technology
SRF - Short-range Nuclear Forces
SSBN - Sub-surface Ballistic Nuclear
SSTS - Space Surveillance and Tracking System
START - Strategic Arms Reduction Talks
STRIDA - Système de Traitement des Informations de Défense Aerienne (Aerial Defence Information Processing System)
TASM - Tomahawk Anti-ship Missile
TLAM-C - Tomahawk Land Attack Missile - Conventional
TLAM-N - Tomahawk Land Attack Missile - Nuclear
TNF - Theatre Nuclear Forces
TTBT - Threshold Test Ban Treaty
U.K. - United Kingdom
U.N. - United Nations
U.S. - United States
U.S.S.R. - Union of Soviet Socialist Republics
UGT - Spanish General Workers' Union
V/STOL - Vertical/Short Takeoff and Landing
VAKA - Flemish Action Committee Against Nuclear Weapons
WTO - Warsaw Treaty Organization

About the Authors

Dr. David Clark (United Kingdom) is a member of the Labour Party and currently the member of the Labour Shadow Cabinet responsible for the Environment. Born on 19 October 1939, Dr. Clark studied at Manchester and Sheffield Universities where he received his B.A., M.Sc. and Ph.D. From 1965 to 1970 he was a lecturer in Public Administration at Salford University. Elected to the House of Commons in 1970, Mr. Clark was the Front-bench Spokesman on Agriculture, Fisheries and Food from 1972 to 1974, the Opposition Front-bench Spokesman on Defence from 1980 to 1981, and since 1981 he has been the Opposition Front-bench Spokesman on the Environment.

Dr. Ludolf-Georg von Wartenberg (Federal Republic of Germany) is a member of the Christian Democrat Union (CDU) Party from Lower Saxony. He was born on 22 September 1941 and studied Economics and History at the Universities of Belfast and Göttingen. From 1970 to 1976 he was a member of the Lower Saxony State Parliament. Elected to the Bundestag in 1976, Dr. von Wartenberg is currently a member of the Committee on Finance.

Dr. Jules de Waart (Netherlands) is a member of the Dutch Labour Party (PvdA). Born on 13 February 1942 he received his Ph.D. in Physical Geography from the University of Amsterdam. Prior to being elected to the Second Chamber of the States-General in 1981, Dr. de Waart worked as a geologist in Zaire, and was a civil servant in the Ministries of Environmental Protection and Housing. He was formerly a member of the Committees on Foreign Affairs, Defence, and Development Assistance.

Mr. Bruce George (United Kingdom) is a member of the Labour Party from Walsall South. Born 1 June 1942, Mr. George received a B.A. from the University of Wales and an M.A. from Warwick University. He has extensive academic experience having been Assistant Lecturer in Politics at Glamorgan College from 1964 to 1966, Lecturer in Politics at Manchester Polytechnic from 1968 to 1970 and Senior Lecturer in Politics at Birmingham Polytechnic from 1970 to 1974. Mr. George was elected to the House of Commons in 1974 and is a member of the Select Committee on Defence and the Select Committee on Violence in the Family.

Mr. Lothar Ibrügger (Federal Republic of Germany) is a member of the Social Democratic Party (SPD) from North-Rhine-Westphalia. Born on 24 December 1944, Mr. Ibrügger studied Architecture and Town Planning at the University of Berlin. He was first elected to the Bundestag in 1976 and serves as a member of the Committee on Transport. Mr. Ibrügger was also a member of the European Parliament from 1978 to 1979.

Mr. John Cartwright (United Kingdom) is a member of the Social Democratic Party (SDP) from Woolwich. He was born on 29 November 1933 and began his career in 1952 as a civil servant in the War Department and then the Board of Trade. He became active in politics in 1955 as Labour Party Agent, a position he kept until 1967. From 1971 to 1978 he was a member of the Labour Party National Executive Committee. Elected to the House of Commons in 1974, Mr. Cartwright served as the Parliamentary Private Secretary to the Secretary of State for Education and Science from 1976 to 1978 and from 1979 to 1981 he was Chairman of the Labour Party Defence Group. In 1981 he left the Labour Party and has since been the SPD Chief Whip and the Spokesman on Foreign Affairs, Defence, Housing, and Local Government.

Index

For Product Safety Concerns and Information please contact our EU representative GPSR@taylorandfrancis.com Taylor & Francis Verlag GmbH, Kaufingerstraße 24, 80331 München, Germany

Batch number: 10725903

Printed by Printforce, the Netherlands